# HAVE WE OVERCOME?

# Have We Overcome?
# Race Relations Since *Brown*

*Essays by:*

C. ERIC LINCOLN

VINCENT HARDING

HENRY M. LEVIN

WILLIAM E. LEUCHTENBURG

ROBERT H. WIEBE

MORTON J. HORWITZ

LERONE BENNETT, JR.

*Edited by:*

MICHAEL V. NAMORATO

UNIVERSITY PRESS OF MISSISSIPPI

JACKSON 1979

This volume is sponsored by the
*University of Mississippi*

*Library of Congress Cataloging in Publication Data*
Main entry under title:

Have we overcome?

    "Volume is sponsored by the University of
Mississippi."
    Bibliography: p.
    1. United States—Race relations—Addresses,
essays, lectures.  2. Afro–Americans—Civil rights—
Addresses, essays, lectures.  I. Lincoln, Charles
Eric.  II. Namorato, Michael V.  III. Mississippi.
University.
E185.61.H38       301.45'1'0973       78–31357
ISBN 0–87805–099–X
ISBN 0–87805–100–7 pbk.

*Dedicated To*
MICHAEL  JOHN
MY 5-YEAR-OLD SON
*In the Hope That*
*He and His Generation*
*Will Have Overcome*

# Preface

On May 17, 1954, the United States Supreme Court rendered its historic decision in the *Brown* v. *Board of Education of Topeka* case, declaring that the doctrine of "separate but equal" was unconstitutional. Approximately one year later, the Court went one step further in the "second" *Brown* decision by insisting that the integration of American schools be effected "with all deliberate speed." Some people at the time believed that the Court's decisions would be implemented so quickly that segregated schools in the South would disappear by the end of the decade. Others, not so optimistic, thought it might take somewhat longer to desegregate. And still others believed that the Court's decisions would never be carried out. What few people realized, however, was that the *Brown* decision went well beyond the question of schools and their racial make-up. *Brown* in fact was only the beginning of a movement which would affect every aspect of American life and society. Today, on the twenty-fifth anniversary of this historic decision, we can now see how all-encompassing that case was. Twenty-five years later, we can now see that the civil rights movement of the 1950s and 1960s had a tremendous effect on how each and every one of us perceives and relates to each other. Yet, twenty-five years later, can we honestly say that we have overcome? Has racial prejudice been obliterated from our thinking— in terms of education, employment, housing, and all other areas of political and social existence? In the essays that follow, seven of the most prominent scholars in the United States have tried to answer this question. Indeed, their answers are not by any means definitive nor conclusive. But they are at least a beginning, a beginning for all of us because all of us must confront the question of race relations today.

It is appropriate and symbolic that the papers in this volume were presented at the fourth Chancellor's Symposium on Southern History, held on October 2, 3, and 4, 1978, at the University of Mississippi in Oxford. Approximately sixteen years ago, the university was a different place, a different cultural environment. It was in many ways symbolic of the South generally, and it is not surprising that the Meredith incident did take place here. Times have changed, however. Much progress has been made and more will follow. The simple fact that this conference was held on the Oxford campus is indicative of what is and will occur. For that reason, what was said and done at the university during this symposium is important for all Americans and why it is appropriate that we publish these papers.

Planning, organizing, and implementing the myriad of details that a conference like this entails is a time-consuming and absorbing task. As symposium director, I relied on and was assisted by many people within and outside of the university. I would like to take this opportunity to thank all of them for their help. On behalf of the University of Mississippi and the Department of History, I would like to gratefully acknowledge the partial financial assistance provided by the S and H Foundation, sponsored by the Sperry and Hutchinson Company (Professor Richard Schlatter, executive director of the lectureship program) and the Mississippi Committee for the Humanities (Dr. Cora Norman, executive director, and Dr. Dennis Mitchell, assistant director). A special note of thanks is extended to the scholars who served as the presiding chairpersons at each session of the symposium, including Dr. John Marszalek, Dr. Derrick Bell, Dr. Stanley Engerman, Dr. Margaret

Walker Alexander, Dr. Martha Bigelow, Aaron Henry, and Dr. Arthur DeRosier. Also, a special note of thanks is extended to the University of Mississippi Black Student Union Choir, directed by Ezelle Wade, for their participation in the conference and to Dr. Cleveland Donald, director of the Black Studies program at the University of Mississippi, for his help on a number of details.

Before and during the symposium, the university administration consistently offered its help. I would like to thank Dr. Porter L. Fortune, Jr., chancellor of the University of Mississippi, for his continued support for the symposium as well as Dr. Harvey S. Lewis, vice-chancellor for academic affairs, Dean Joseph Sam, Graduate School, H. Dale Abadie, associate dean of the Graduate School, and Dean Gerald Walton, College of Liberal Arts, for their assistance and advice.

The actual administration of the conference was carried on jointly by the Department of History and the Division of Continuing Education. I would like to thank Maurice Inman, director of the Division of Continuing Education, for his and his staff's support; Dr. Ann Abadie and Pamela Tims for their patience, understanding, and efficiency in helping me meet deadlines; and Otis Tims, director of news service, for assisting me in publicizing the conference. Within the Department of History, I am grateful to all of my colleagues for their support. I am particularly indebted to Dr. Robert Haws, Dr. David Sansing, Dr. James Cooke, and Dr. Jackson Taylor for going "above and beyond the call of duty" in assisting me. A special note of thanks is extended to my chairman, Dr. Frederick Laurenzo. As a colleague and as a friend, he advised, assisted, argued with, and supported me throughout the last eighteen months that I have worked on this conference. While I am certain that I'll never find a way to completely express my gratitude, I am also certain that he will make every effort to do so. Finally, as with all of my undertakings, I could not have completed this one without the loving assistance and understanding of my wife, Karen. As always, she made a potentially difficult task a highly enjoyable experience.

MICHAEL V. NAMORATO
*University of Mississippi*

# Contents

# Introduction

For the last four years, the Department of History of the University of Mississippi has sponsored the Chancellor's Symposium on Southern History dealing with the problem of race relations in the American South. For each symposium, prominent scholars from across the United States have been invited to present their latest research and findings on issues related to the race relations question. In 1975, the symposium dealt with the question of slavery in the American South. Carl Degler, Eugene Genovese, David Brion Davis, Stanley Engerman, William Scarborough, John Blassingame, and Kenneth Stampp each confronted and analyzed one specific aspect of slavery and offered his interpretations of it. Under the editorship of Professor Harry P. Owens, the proceedings of that conference were published as *Perspectives and Irony in American Slavery* (Jackson, Miss.: University Press of Mississippi, 1976).

With the success of the slavery conference, the following year's symposium continued the race relations topic by dealing with the issue of race relations during the Reconstruction period. Willie Lee Rose, Joel Williamson, Richard Sutch and Roger Ransom, George Fredrickson, and C. Vann Woodward each approached the question from his own individual perspective. Under the editorship of Professor David Sansing, the papers from this conference were published as *What Was Freedom's Price?* (Jackson, Miss.: University Press of Mississippi, 1978).

In 1977, with the success of two symposia as a basis, a third conference was held on race relations in the United States from 1890 through World War II. Derrick Bell, Mary Francēs Berry, Dan Carter, Al-Tony Gilmore, Robert Higgs, and George Tindall all analyzed the race relations problem during this period. Under the editorship of Professor Robert Haws, the papers from this conference were published as *The Age of Segregation: Race Relations in the American South, 1890–1945* (Jackson, Miss.: University Press of Mississippi, 1978).

Having brought together an impressive array of leading scholars for three consecutive conferences, the Department of History approached the 1978 conference with a firm resolve and purpose. Since it was the logical topic given the preceding three years and since the symbolism of the issue and the place was so forceful, it was decided that the 1978 symposium would deal with the problem of race relations since the historic *Brown* decision. However, an added dimension to this conference also seemed natural. Not only would this symposium take place at the beginning of the twenty-fifth anniversary of *Brown*, but it also would coincide reasonably well with another important case which the Supreme Court was hearing—*Bakke*. In light of these coincidences, we all realized that this conference would be especially significant and, for that reason, we were very careful in selecting our participants. Each speaker was given a broad topic to deal with, thereby giving each scholar as much leeway as possible. Also, each speaker was asked to deal with the question of race relations today, to offer his own scholarly appraisal of where we as Americans are and where we as a people are going. While the papers in this volume are the answers provided by the participants and while the answers themselves may not be definitive or conclusive, they are still very important because they offer each and everyone of us something to think about. More importantly, whether people agree or disagree with them, no one can deny that these scholars have and are challenging us each individually to consider our own opinions on the race question.

Professor C. Eric Lincoln, in his essay "The New Black Estate: The Coming of Age of Blackamerica," analyzes the effects that the *Brown* decision had on the black community. Defining the black estate as a culture within a culture or a black culture within American culture, he argues that blacks have survived in America without developing a genuine sense of belonging—"a sense of *included identity*." Still, America is home to Blackamerica because black culture developed here. The significance of the *Brown* decision in this situation is that it changed the rules in such a way as to permit Blackamerica to identify and define itself. It was "the official recognition that the black estate had changed and was changing" and its effects were far-reaching. Limiting himself to those effects that he considers most important, Lincoln critically studies *Brown*'s effect on education, employment, black political involvement, and the strain on black ethnicity. His conclusion, moreover, while startling, is quite profound. To Lincoln, the black estate is dividing with the black middle class exploiting its social and economic mobility and, thereby, moving further away from the black masses. What effect this upward movement will have on black culture is difficult to assess. But, as far as Lincoln is concerned, the effect(s) will be far-reaching for all involved.

While Lincoln assesses *Brown* vis-à-vis black culture, Professor Vincent Harding approaches it from a more individualistic viewpoint. In his essay "So Much History, So Much Future: Martin Luther King, Jr. and the Second Coming of America," Harding tries to sustain the emotional rapport he had developed with his audience during the symposium. Freely admitting that he is "an engaged participant" in the black movement for freedom and "a committed historian and critical analyst of its development," he offers a personal yet scholarly perspective of Dr. King. In Harding's thinking, King was "at once created by the [black] movement and a creator of some of its major thrusts." While King made history, he was also helped and affected by it. He was an interpreter, inspirer, a prophet, a man who saw the larger, global meaning of what blacks in America were fighting for in the 1950s and 1960s. He sought to lead his people—whether at Montgomery, Albany, Birmingham, Washington, D.C., Riverside Church in New York, or Memphis—to goals and objectives he believed they needed to strive for. Yet sometimes, as in the 1960s when black militancy appeared, he was affected too and adjusted accordingly. In the end, King too became more militant in his attacks on American involvement in Vietnam and in his commitment to forming a nonviolent revolutionary army, but by then it was too late. An assassin's bullet ended whatever plans and hopes he had. Nevertheless, Harding believes that King left his legacy. He helped all of us to see a new vision, to hope for a second coming of America.

In assessing the importance of *Brown*, both Lincoln and Harding concentrate on the black community's response to the Court's decision. Professor Henry Levin, in "Education and Earnings of Blacks and the *Brown* decision," on the other hand, perceives *Brown* in terms of its effects on the American educational system and the resultant economic status of blacks. In Levin's opinion, *Brown* set the stage "for the ensuing rise of black political activism, for legal challenges to racial discrimination in voting, employment, and education, as well as for creating a favorable climate for the passage of the subsequent civil rights legislation and the initiation of the War on Poverty." *Brown*, in short, legitimatized the black cause. To prove his point, Levin presents a detailed statistical analysis of racial differences in education from 1954 to 1978, of earning differentials of blacks and whites, and a critique of alternative explanations for black-white trends in education and employment. He specifically argues against the human capital theory in explaining these developments and concludes his paper by analyzing the impact of *Brown* on the American people's sense of fairness and justice. Although his study shows rather convincingly that progress for blacks has been made, Levin also believes that much more needs to be done to help the black people achieve an equitable level of educational and economic status when compared with whites.

Whereas Levin argues that the civil rights legislation of the 1960s did much to provide more economic opportunities for blacks, Professor Leuchtenburg goes one step further in specifying the role the federal government has played in the race relations issue since 1954. In his essay "The White House and Black America: From Eisenhower to Carter," Leuchtenburg critically analyzes the contributions of each of the presidents since *Brown*. In his thinking, Eisenhower was not sympathetic to the black cause nor to the Supreme Court's decision and, as a result, he did little to foster black equality. President Kennedy, while cautious and circumspect at first, did respond to the problems of blacks and, after the Meredith incident, he took a more active and strong position. However, it was Lyndon Baines Johnson who not only promoted the civil rights movement with congressional legislation but who also represented the highpoint of presidential cooperation with civil rights objectives. After Johnson, though, the presidential record was not so impressive. Neither Nixon nor Ford was as committed to black goals and neither personally was willing to utilize their authority to promote the black struggle for freedom. Today, Leuchtenburg believes that Carter's record on civil rights leaves much to be desired, but he is hopeful that, if Carter revitalizes the civil rights momentum, much will be accomplished for whites and blacks alike.

Legislating prejudice away is a difficult means of overcoming the racial issue. As Robert Wiebe in "White Attitudes and Black Rights From *Brown* to *Bakke*" demonstrates, white America has undergone changes regarding the civil rights movement. In Wiebe's opinion, there were several reasons why the black movement gained momentum in the 1950s and 1960s. American economic prosperity and the role of the federal government in sustaining it, the average American's belief in justice and equality, the homogenization of American life, changes in the South, and the Cold War—all helped in promoting the blacks' struggle for equality after 1954. But, in 1966, a turning point occurred as far as white acceptance of black demands. After 1966, many whites wanted the civil rights movement to slow down because the demands it was making involved intimacy and closer relations with blacks; black militancy was aversely affecting white opinion; many whites started thinking that blacks wanted more than they (the white blue-collar worker) had; and, most of all, opposition to the federal government's intervention in American life coincided with the growing opposition to blacks' demands for their rights. White attitudes, in short, had been transformed; the civil rights movement was no longer so readily accepted.

While white attitudes were undergoing these changes, another significant consequence of *Brown* appeared. In his essay "The Jurisprudence of *Brown* and the Dilemmas of Liberalism," Professor Morton Horwitz studies the legal implications and meaning of the Court's decision. In Horwitz's thinking, *Brown* "represented the beginning of the disintegration of a progressive consensus on the nature and function of law and of the role of courts and legislatures in our constitutional system." The "progressive consensus" calling for judicial restraint was seriously challenged by *Brown* and, in so doing, it created serious problems for American liberals. Liberals have been and are caught in a conflict between their "opposition to racial discrimination and [their] equally strong conviction that the courts ought not to be involved with the problems of social and economic inequality." The resolution of these fundamental problems is of the utmost importance and, for Horwitz, the answers lie principally in the way we view the court's role in American society and the tenets of our Constitution.

If the legal questions raised by *Brown* and *Bakke* are difficult to answer, then, what of the more fundamental question of "Have We Overcome?" Lerone Bennett, senior editor of *Ebony*, offers at least one way of looking at it. A native Mississippian, Bennett couches his response in a metaphor—"We crossed a river, and now we've got to cross a sea." Practically speaking, Bennett argues that we as Americans have not yet overcome nor have black Americans defined what they must now do to overcome. While the outward signs of racism are dead, institutional racism still exists. It can be destroyed; but racial prejudice will disappear only if, as Bennett forcefully points out, both black and white Americans learn from history.

A careful reading of the papers in this volume will show that all the authors agree in principle with Bennett's conclusions. While each author approaches the issue of race relations since *Brown* from his own perspective, they all ultimately agree that progress has been made since 1954, but that more must also be done if we as Americans are to achieve full equality. How, who, where, and when all this is to be done is now the subject of the debate. But, the answers to the questions raised by *Brown* and *Bakke* may rest with those who know the least about race relations. Perhaps, as the dedication to this volume indicates, it may be that our children will provide the answers, that our children will face the problems, and that our children will, on the fiftieth anniversary of *Brown,* say that, indeed, we have overcome.

HAVE WE OVERCOME?

# The New Black Estate: The Coming of Age of Blackamerica

C. ERIC LINCOLN

*. . . indolence and sloth . . . improvidence and carelessness mark the independent savage . . . .*

> PROFESSOR THOMAS R. DEW
> William and Mary ( 1832)

*If we support ourselves and our masters while we are slaves, we can surely take care of ourselves when we are free.*

> ILLITERATE BLACK PREACHER,
> Washington, D. C.
> Response to Dew

*It is time that the Spirit of Christ should be manifested in the making and execution of laws.*

> "Why We March" (leaflet).
> The Negro Silent Parade of
> July 28, 1917 ( New York)

Perhaps as many as 25–30 million people identifiable as "black" live in the United States. A significant minority of them manage to avoid the census rolls for a variety of reasons, which added together suggest that merely to be black is to have certain impair-

3

ments that make official anonymity a practical way of life. There are many others who are genetically or legally "black" who are statistical transfers rather than dropouts. Their motivations are essentially the same, but their techniques for survival have the advantage of visual anonymity. Since being identified as black can be a distinct liability in America, those who can pass, often do. Those who cannot, or will not, belong to and participate in one of the most distinctive subcultures in the world.

The black estate is the *elan vital,* the vital principle of the black subculture expressing itself as its own quiddity. It is black interests and black affairs, black accomplishments and black dreams, black people in pursuit of their own destiny as they perceive it, in their own way. It is the sum total of the meaning of being black in the midst of an overculture that is white. It is participating in two worlds, but belonging to one.

*Brown* v. *Board of Education* shook the foundations of both worlds when it struck down the legal bases which dictated the structure and the conditions of the black estate. But the implications of *Brown* are not immediately apparent, and we must turn back the pages of history if we are to provide a perspective from which evaluation may proceed. The black subculture did not spring full-blown from the head of Zeus, nor was *Brown* v. *Board of Education* produced in some kind of a social and legal vacuum. America is often misunderstood and misinterpreted, and Americans often misunderstand themselves and their own motivations and behavior because the temptation to deal with the apparent— so often referred to as "the obvious"—precludes the real understanding that can come only when the antecedent facts have been examined. The answers are not always neatly summed up in the bottom line. They are as often distributed in bits and pieces all over the page. Hence, to talk about the black estate, we must first talk about how and why it was created. Only then will it make sense in relation to a Supreme Court decision handed down nearly a quarter of a century ago.

*On Being "American"*

It has been a scant thirty years ago that the most destructive war machine in the history of mankind clanked finally to a halt. All over the world people came out of their holes in the ground, their caves in the rocks, their jungle retreats to assess the holocaust, and to see what could be done to get on with the business of living. The Great War was officially over, but the end was not yet, and the spasms of response and readjustment continue even to this day to haunt the bastard peace we declared three decades ago. In Southeast Asia, in Africa, in the Middle East, in South America, in Eastern and Western Europe, between factions and between nations the conflict continues, and we live with the uncomfortable realization that any recent yesterday could have been the last day of general peace in the world, and that any given tomorrow could be the first day of a new world cataclysm. The continuing hostilities that illustrate the felt grievances of people in Zimbabwe or Eritrea, in Cambodia or on whatever bank of the Jordan, in Eastern Europe or South Africa are not merely the isolated interests of the parties who confront each other in the pit. Far more than that, they are the brush fires which spotlight the ominous political bastions of the major fiefdoms that now divide the world, and they shift and shimmer with the prevailing winds that blow from their respective sources of support.

The point is, that having come out of World War II with an imperfect peace, we are left with a legacy of sporadic conflict that is a continuous threat to the peace we do have. For us in the United States, our sensitivities to this state of affairs have been honed by two miniwars in Southeast Asia, and by two decades of social turmoil at home. Unlike the situation in other parts of the world, when the Great War was over, Americans had no need to come out of hiding. They had no holes in the ground, no caves in the rocks, no jungle retreats to abandon. We were the winners. Our homes were unscathed, our factories undemolished; our government was intact and our political and social perceptions unaffected. There had been a world-wide holocaust, and we had played a major role in its determination. But our own determination seems to have been that whatever happened "over there" was over and done with, and that here at home we would go on as we had gone on: the status quo ante would prevail. Looking back, such social and political naïveté on the part of one of the most advanced nations of the world seems incredible—incredible, that is, unless one understands the peculiar American mindset that contributed both to our greatness and to our vulnerability. For to be "American," prior to the late war, still meant among other things to be right, to be invincible, to be innately superior to most of the peoples of the world, and to own an inviolable destiny appropriate to those signal, national attributes.[1] It is not that the typical American spent his waking hours contemplating his favored condition: that was taken for granted, an obvious condition of the fact of his existence. Buried deep in the American self-consciousness there lay the seminal convention that the American heritage was a uniquely valuable parquetry that drew its religious values from the Protestant Reformation, its political understanding from the French Revolution, its intrepidity from the traditions of the English yeomanry, and its peculiar proficiency from its own developing technological genius. This was what "American" meant. The conviction was self-affirming, collateral to the fact of being; it required neither explanation nor apology. To be "American" was to be a privileged participant in a most notable human enterprise to which not all were called, and fewer still were chosen.

Every society has some kind of idealized notion of itself, and to the degree that the national self-image is reasonably consonant with reality, it can be a remarkable instrument for the realization of the unity-potential inherent in participating in a common identity. Nevertheless, an idealized construction of the national "we" is not without its hazards. In our own times madmen obsessed with the pursuit of power through the contrivance of a national "Herrenvolk" succeeded in the tragic manipulation of an otherwise sane and rational people to the end that a thousand years of civilization were eclipsed in a single spasm of self-exaltation, and *six million* human beings were sacrificed on the altar of national chauvinism.

Here in the United States we have managed more restraint, and, in consequence, history has been more benign; for while we have been called "Ugly Americans" for our behavior abroad, and while our national history must be charged with the attenuation of the lives and fortunes of countless millions we found here or brought here for the national convenience, genocide has never been an official expression of our national will. Nevertheless, by the decimation of the indigenous Indians for the sake of territorial aggrandizement, and by the importation and enslavement of Africans from the other side of the world in the interest of psychological and economic aggrandizement, one must assume that the American self-image was magnified, for such derring-do was conventional to the national estimate of most contemporary Western civilizations. In fact, the conquest of the American West (which tripled the size of the country) and the forcible importation of a servile caste to release the creative energies of the privileged classes for more properly patrician pursuits were accomplishments which from the very beginning were suggested as self-justifying as well as *de facto* evidence of a superior culture. And since neither the conquered Indians nor the chattelized Africans were white, it seemed no less evident that race no less than culture must be a factor of more than passing moment. At that point American identity took on an expanded definition. There were, of course, Americans who were embarrassed by such claims as were being argued, for they seemed to be in patent contradiction to the prevailing ideologies with which our emergent nation had first identified itself. In consequence, a war was fought, but the issues were not resolved. Instead, a consent without consensus was arranged in the interest of the preservation of the Union. It was in effect a *modus vivendi pro tempore*, a purchase of time, in the hope that with the physical integrity of the nation restored, it might yet, in time, fulfill the true destiny to which it has been called. We pause now for an assessment of history—to offer some opinions as to how far we have come, and to make some determinations about how far we shall have to go. We note with satisfaction and encouragement that the empirical evidence of movement in the American odyssey is everywhere apparent. The physical signs and symbols of segregation are long since gone. Men and women of whatever race find congress at will without the demeaning objection of the law. The institutions that were the citadels of segregation are now, with the notable exception of the church and the private clubs, in apparently serious effort at reassessment. The willingness to reflect on the living body of experiences that blacks and whites have shared and have fashioned for each other during 370 years of cotenancy in America, is surely a sign of movement, and if movement is not of itself synonymous with progress, it is at least change—in the absence of which progress cannot occur.

## The Problem of Identity

I have devoted my initial commentary to the American self-perception because critical to any sensible assessment of where we are today is the recognition that "Americans" are what black people who live in the United States are not. "Americans" are what they may become when they "overcome," but that is a speculation about a future which has not arrived.

Probably the most painful feature of the black experience has not been the empirical problem of overt discrimination and its attendant annoyances and inconveniences. Overt discrimination is a palpable thing: it can be avoided, resisted, retaliated, or simply endured. This is a salient teaching of the art of survival learned early under the peculiar exigencies of a peculiar institution. Survival meant the development of that uncertain spectrum of responses which enabled the slave (and his successors) to protect his persona with the least risk to his life. Survival meant being alive and being sane, but with some small private clutch of dignity in the bargain.

Black people have been able to manage survival; considerably more elusive has been a genuine sense of belonging—a sense of *included identity*. The fact that this problem is a recurrent theme in the literature of the black experience from Phyllis Wheatley and William Wells Brown to such contemporary writers as W. E. B. Du Bois and Ralph Ellison illustrates the continuing difficulty black people experience in rationalizing their arbitrary exclusion from the American mainstream.[2] None of the nineteenth-century resettlement schemes had any significant impact on the black population in this country because blacks were never able to accept the notion that "home" was somewhere other than where they had suffered, toiled, and died for generations on end. They saw themselves and they see themselves as "Americans," but not, to be sure, in the chauvinistic meaning of the term. They wanted recognition as legitimate cosharers of responsibility and privilege as well as physical cotenants in a country which has at one time or another preempted their labor, exploited their allegiance, manipulated their political rights, but never forfeited their trust. For all its failings, America is home to Blackamericans, because America is not only the prevailing source of their cultural nurture, it is also the canvas on which the black experience took its shape and marked its distinctive development.

But home is more than a place to be; home is a place to be recognized as belonging. Home implies the close association of identity with investiture, and the absence of the one inevitably qualifies the other. Hence, the fortunes of the black estate have been seriously compromised by the lack of an identity that properly relates Blackamericans to the only home they have ever known, or are likely to know this side of Jordan.

The problem of black identity is the bitter legacy of the ego-stripping which was a part of the success of enslavement. The slave was summarily bereft of his name, status, roles, affiliation—

everything that contributed to the sense of who he was. Once he realized that his African identity was irretrievable, the African in America began the painful, frustrating search for a new one— an identity that recommended him as a person, a man among men, despite the awesome array of social and legal contrivances designed to dehumanize him and make him a thing. What he got was not identity, but identification. Identification was a gratuity of the system, a designation of convenience that called him a Negro, or a nigger, or a darky, or simply "colored," and set him apart. This identification made it clear that his physical visibility was the primary prism through which his persona was to be refracted. Identification is initiated in the perception of others, but identity balances external perception with self-estimate and self-definition. It is a negotiable construct in which the individual and significant others in his world find reasonable accord, to the end that the language of social relations is mutually understood, and the intercourse of social relations is not inhibited by mutual misperception. But if black people yearned simply to be "Americans," and insisted on being known as such, that yearning blew apart in the face of experience. They could not do what Americans could do, and their claims were rejected with hostility and derision. That is the essential relevance of *Brown.*

### *Brown v. Board of Education: The Cumulative Fruit*

*Brown* v. *Board of Education* signaled the beginning of a process which in the course of time has changed—and will change significantly—the character and the fortunes of the black estate; because in changing the rules for exclusion, it changed the identity of the Blackamerican. "A rose is a rose is a rose." True. But a rose is also a flower. And it never smells so sweet or forms so perfectly as when it blooms in a garden of roses. Despite the accusations of "treason" hurled at the Supreme Court, there was nothing precipitous in the ruling that declared racial segregation to be an inherent violation of the civil rights of those locked beyond the

pale. *Brown* could be treasonable only to the conventional understanding that black people were *never* to be American. More than
that, *Brown* was the cumulative fruit of a long history of litigation—the logical fulfillment of the promise inherent in the Constitution of the United States as well as in an impressive series of
rulings which had been chipping away at the exclusive white prerogative for a generation.[3]

Decisive action was overdue. We were foundering in the aftermath of a long war that was all the more frightening for the problems it left unresolved. As we looked for familiar structures and
conventional landmarks in our efforts at personal and social and
political reconstruction, it was clear to those willing to see that
the world had changed. And we had changed with it. We would
never again be the way we were. Too many new truths had been
discovered; too many old myths had been decoded; too many
sacred taboos had been violated, and God struck nobody dead.
Too many icons had been smashed; too many hole-cards had been
peeped at; too many brass idols had been toppled, and alas! . . .
when the dust had settled, they all had feet of clay! *Pedes terra
cotta!*

## A *Vegetative Undercaste?*

There is no romance and there is no glory in modern war, for wars
are no longer fought in isolation from the people. Whatever the
business of war uncovers, the people see and react to it. So it
turns out that in a rather unexpected way war may indeed be a
great liberator, but the liberation is not necessarily from the desig-
nated enemy. It may well be from the constraints of political and
social convention at home that have been strained by the exigencies of the struggle. Nothing did more to destroy the racial mystique which had been so assiduously cultivated in this country for
three and a half centuries than the autistic savagery of the "civi-
lized" Germans, unless it was the official American refutation of
the Nazi theories of a "master race." For if the allegations of a

master race in Germany were spurious, why not in America? And if the Jews deserved liberation, why not the Asians? Why not the Africans? Indeed, why not the black people of America?[4]

But it was more than a war and its implications for new ways of seeing things that marked the timeliness of *Brown* v. *Board of Education.* Nobody seemed to realize that the black community had changed, and that that change would inevitably seek its logical expression in some modification of the existing structure of American social relations. The prevailing social patterns which defined the society (or at least the South) were given definition when the South recovered its regional hegemony hard on the heels of the Reconstruction. But the South had its own notions about the nature and character of the African diaspora, and these notions reflected not so much the African character and personality as they did the psychological needs of a people burdened by ideological disappointment and military defeat.[5] Their views were not necessarily consonant with objective reality, or even with the cumulative learnings derived from three centuries of contact with black people. The world of the post-Reconstruction chose rather to continue the denial of the obvious, which was that the Africans among them, however presently reduced in circumstances by the exigencies of recent history, were quite as human as themselves, with all the potentials for glory or for disgrace with which the species is everywhere endowed. Had America been sober enough, or clairvoyant enough, at the crisis of its rebirth to have entertained this notion, we would have been spared the agonies, the tragedies, and the tremendous waste in human energy and human lives *Brown* v. *Board of Education* finally declared to be *passe.* However, it is apparent that history, once it has been wound and set, has to run its course, toppling all reason in its wake. And so it turned out that when the Civil War was ended and when the national order had been restored, the blacks were "free," but there was no room in the new order for black initiative, pride, sensitivity, cultural invention or mobility. The apparent expectation was that the "free" black undercaste would simply vegetate in a kind of cultural isolation while the rest of America rejuvenated itself and got on with the business of its destiny. In the light of the southern experience, this would seem to be a curious reading of history, for it was in the South that black ingenuity in agriculture, construction, mechanical arts, animal husbandry, and the like had been translated into white economic advantage for generations; and it was in the South that black initiative was legendary in the countless instances where black slaves voluntarily doubled the extraordinary requirements of the slave workday for years on end in the effort to purchase themselves and their loved ones. If the desire for freedom was a powerful incentive for initiative, why should not the realization of that dream fan the fires of initiative rather than damp them out? Further, the expectation that the black undercaste would be culturally stagnant apparently gave no consideration to the institutionalized systems of legal and conventional proscription which had fixed the limits of personal and cultural expression when blacks were slaves, and which fully intended to replicate that arrangement for their "freedom." Why was such an elaborate panoply of constraint necessary to control a people who were "naturally" indolent, vegetative, satisfied, and unaspiring?

Whatever the conventional expectations may have been, in the nine short decades between the emancipation from absolute slavery and the removal of some of the more crippling of the residual civil restraints by the Supreme Court decision of 1954, the Black-american undercaste managed some remarkable accomplishments for a "stagnant" subculture. They sharecropped for subsistence; but they also bought land and farmed for themselves. They continued to work as servants and menials; but they also opened their own small businesses—occasionally providing employment for their families and others. They homesteaded and gained local reputations for honesty and industry; but they also traveled the country and learned new ideas and ways of doing things and relating to people. In most instances they were effectively excluded from meaningful political participation in the larger society, but they learned and practiced the political arts in their religious, fraternal, and social organizations. They developed such major institutions as the black church, the black press, the black college. They founded banks, insurance companies, and a network of voluntary social organizations for the expression of their cultural interests. They produced great scientists and men of letters, actors, artists, humanists, musicians, politicians, educators, exceptional notables in sports and entertainment. They went to war for their country whenever their country went to war, and they won their fair share of recognition for exceeding the requirements of duty. They saw the world and its peoples and learned from them; but above all, they struggled to be educated, for from the beginning they were committed to the notion (however arguable it may be) that in America, education is the key to adequacy, to acceptance, to access. From almost total illiteracy to near total literacy in ninety years, and with signal achievements far beyond—that is the record. Of all the liberated peoples in recent history, few have come so far so fast. And yet the black odyssey has always been a struggle with a liberation that was imperfect from the start. *Brown* v. *Board of Education* is a belated acknowledgment of that fact.

## Time to Change

But *Brown* v. *Board of Education* was also the official recognition that the black estate had changed and was changing. In 1954 there were more Blackamericans in college than there were students in a majority of the nations of the world. The blacks in the armed forces of the United States numbered more than the men under arms in many sovereign states. Blackamericans earned and spent more money than was represented by the gross national product of half the countries the U.S. was courting politically in order to protect its market relationships with them. Clearly the black undercaste, while still severely restricted by the racial policies of the United States, had been somewhat more than vegetative and culturally quiescent. It was time for a change.

Change came, and the rest is history. But it is history in the making, not a *fait accompli*. Social change is always in the nature of process. It is seldom cataclysmic or episodic. The problem is that people are seldom alert to the signs, the signals, the indices of change, and even when the signs are self-evident and everywhere apparent, we tend to resist recognition, as if the refusal to see is somehow an effective negation of the reality we abhor. We need not document here the extraordinary evidences of social frustration and disruption occasioned by the requirements of *Brown* v. *Board of Education*. What we shall do instead is to examine some of its consequences in terms of what appears to have been the basic intent of the ruling: *i.e.*, to extend more fully the blessings of liberty, responsibility, and participation in the common ventures of the American commonwealth to the black estate and to its posterity.

All major interests of the black estate are inevitably intertwined because the ultimate subject of our discourse is the survival and projection of the black subculture as a recognized and respected entity in the American social and political cosmos. Hence, a proper examination of the effects of the *Brown* decision on the black community would cover all the major areas of social intercourse in which the ramifications of desegregation distribute themselves. But this, of course, would be a task far beyond the scope of our present enterprise, and though the need to know and to review constantly what we think we know demands that such an effort be made eventually, our present attempt to address that challenge is considerably more modest, and in part. I shall therefore limit myself to but four of the more obvious areas in which the black estate has been affected by that momentous decision of the United States Supreme Court twenty-five years ago. They are education, employment, political involvement, and internal cohesion or ethnicity. Left for some other occasion or for some other observer/ commentator are such critical interests as housing, family relations, military involvement, business enterprise, demography, racial etiquette, African/Blackamerican relations and so on.[6] It is not that I consider the areas I have chosen either more or less important, but they are at least typical, and one may as well begin with the obvious.

## Education

Perhaps the first place to look for the effects of the *Brown* case on the black community is in education, for that was the salient issue of the suit. The consequent issue is whether the education of black children has been significantly improved by classroom desegregation. But the issue is far more complex than that question admits, and it cannot effectively be resolved in a simple statement of yes or no. In the first place, the intent of the decision has undoubtedly been frustrated to an important degree by the politics of delay and erosion, by the necessity of extensive busing to achieve racial balance, by the elimination of large numbers of black teachers and administrators from effective role assignments, by the hostility and indifference directed by some teachers to black students, by the crisis atmosphere pervasive in some schools, by the racial clanishness which envelops the academic enterprise, and by the implication often read into the thrust for desegregation that there is some intellectual mana to be derived by some magical osmosis from the mere physical presence of white children. As a result, expert opinion on the basis of the accumulated research is predictably divided, and the issue of superior academic benefits for black children in integrated classrooms is inconclusive.

Considerably more concrete is the fact that the per capita amount spent to educate the black child is for the first time in history near the amount spent to educate his white counterpart, and that professional preparation of black teachers must now approximate that of white teachers. Inadequate physical plants for black children suddenly improve or disappear under threat of integration, and the "differential school year" of seven or eight months for black children is no longer a feature of southern education. On the other hand, while the integration of classrooms is desirable as a *de facto* evidence of racial parity and as a critical learning experience in social relations for both races, these are not the principal concerns of the black estate. To put it another way, the reasonable proximity of blacks and whites in the classroom situation is considered the normative mode for the educational process in a society seriously committed to the democratic ideal, for in such normative situations, peer relationships and understandings find their own denominators, and the influence of external, stereotyped determinations are minimized. However, the private notion that racial proximity functions, or is intended to function as an academic *modus vivendi* for the osmotic transfer of intelligence is universally resented and categorically rejected by black people everywhere.

Beyond the secondary level well over a million black youth, or at least 25 percent of the 18–21 age group, are pursuing some form of higher education. About 60 percent of these are in two-year community colleges or in trade or technical schools, but fully 20 percent are enrolled in the 144 traditional black colleges whose critical usefulness to the black estate has not been diminished by *Brown* v. *Board of Education*. Certain critical conclusions must be drawn from these informal statistics. First of all, there is a sharply improved perception of the value and the need of higher education among blacks. When the high dropout rate at the high school level, the concomitant low level of encouragement or preparation for college most black students experience in integrated high school settings, the high cost of college matriculation, and the dwindling base of support opportunities for black college youth are considered, then a black college population of 25 percent would seem to compare reasonably well with the 34 percent of white youths now in college.

Second, access to technical and paraprofessional training is helping to modify the traditional patterns of black employment. Except during national emergencies such as World War II, black employment has always been heavily concentrated in unskilled, menial occupations relieved only by a relatively small number of professionals—doctors, teachers, clergymen, and the like—whose services were almost exclusive to the black community trapped behind the walls of segregation. There was no substantial tradition for skilled, technical, or paraprofessional training, because neither the training nor the positions it envisioned was generally available to black people. The accessibility of such training has increased substantially since *Brown*, and more than a half-million blacks—many of them one-time dropouts or working adults—now attend these middleground institutions. They will be a factor in changing the traditions and the configurations of black employment, for they are already a significant leavening in the "lump" of the black lumpen proletariat.

The third conclusion to be drawn from our statistics is that the traditional black colleges remain the critical components in black higher education, despite the fact that in terms of aggregate enrollments more blacks now attend white colleges than black ones. However, the distorted implications of the *Bakke* case notwithstanding, the impact of black enrollment on the white campuses of America is quite miniscule—a mere 5 percent of the total distributed among an aggregate of more than a thousand white institutions of higher learning. American education has generally proceeded on the assumption that the relevant education is one which reflects the interests and values of the white middle class, duly modified in some instances to account for local tradition and convention. Since blacks and their interests were by common consensus excluded from the official American universe of significant values, public education, by design and by default, has always been a major source of the devaluation of black people. In consequence, the low self-estimate of black people dictated by their peculiar "place" in the society was reinforced and encouraged by the educational system itself, thus all but insuring the self-fulfillment of an alleged train of pejorative stereotypes.

Since black people lacked the resources for an extensive network of private or parochial schools, their principal protection from the deadly cancer of self-denigration lay in the black church and the black college. The black church sought generally to resolve the problem by reference to the common fatherhood of God, and to a final judgment in some world of the future where once and for all the equality of all men would be irrefutably established. The black college elected to meet the opposition on its own terms in this world. In the first place, the black college considered its own existence to be a *de facto* refutation of inferiority. Beyond that, while none of the black colleges in the relatively short span of their existence has been able to develop the graduate and research facilities of the long-established white institutions from which emanate the "official" appraisals of the black estate, these same black colleges have produced a rather creditable number of scholars, scientists, statesmen, and the like whose contributions belie the tenuousness of their existence and are the most eloquent arguments for their relief.

Most critical has been the success of the black college in providing visible role models for black youth and in confounding the incredible myth that black people somehow arrived in the twentieth century without any trace of a projective culture. More than any other institution, the black college has provided a solid affirmation for black identity, thus freeing the black ego from the nagging doubts that are the inevitable corollaries of a total life experience in a minority perspective. Nonetheless, it is probably in the area of higher education that the blessings of *Brown* are most mixed. The saw cuts two ways, and even as the decision opened up a whole new world of opportunity for technical, graduate, and professional training, it also threatened the survival of one of the institutions most crucial to the interests of the black estate. In the wake of *Brown* the black college is endangered, for desegregation has brought a number of problems to the black campus. The most persistent one stems from the curious notion that "integration" ought to mean the abandonment of practically all black colleges, because black students may now attend white institutions. Only the most impatient consideration is given to the individual merit of these schools, or to the enormous cultural investment they represent, or to the fact that they are still the first choices of some 200,000 students. The problem is compounded by the fact that few white colleges make any substantial provisions for a community of black students which is capable of continuing the role of the black college as a conduit of black culture and a wellspring of black pride and self-affirmation. Even more threatening is the substantial loss of identity some state-supported black colleges have experienced with increasing white enrollment and the concomitant arrival of increasing numbers of white faculty.

In the early years of the *Brown* implementation, the private black colleges lost most of their best students and faculty to prestigious white institutions, and their support from private sources and philanthropic institutions was seriously affected by the popular notion that they were superfluous. Moreover, when it became clear that the continued maintenance of state-supported segregated black colleges was not an effective protection against the admission of blacks to state-supported white institutions, many southern states developed strategies for submerging their black colleges in nearby white universities, or else phasing them out altogether. Additional pressures from the federal government (which spends only 5 percent of its budget for higher education on black colleges) to drastically increase the enrollment of white students and the employment of white faculty on black campuses continues to contribute to the uncertainty surrounding the future of the black college. In all probability, it will survive as an academic institution, but there is no dearth of "academic institutions" in America. The critical question is whether it will survive as the principal curator of the black experience, leavening the black sub-culture with a sense of its own accomplishment and an affirmation of its own identity.

## Employment

It is difficult if not impossible to separate education from employment as critical interests that ramify each other as major determinants of the quality of life in America. The *Brown* impact on black employment has been far-reaching and its ultimate influence is still a matter of conjecture. In theory, however, *Brown* and its successors did away with conventional understandings which openly or tacitly defined "Negro work," or which reserved certain categories of employment for whites. Traditionally, blacks were expected to perform whatever labor was hot, heavy, dirty, menial, low-paid, and devoid of any satisfaction deriving from a sense of creativity or from the possibility of advancement. In the twenty-five years since 1954, the employment base of the black community has been considerably broadened and diversified, and blacks who are well prepared in their areas of interest are less frequently rejected by racial selection when they apply for the jobs for which they have been trained.[7]

Discrimination remains a formidable factor in employment, of course. Blacks still have only token representation in some unions, and there is still a very large number of skilled jobs and professional positions in industry, communications, and management which are considered racially sacrosanct. There are signs that these preserves will be breached in time under pressure of affirmative action requirements and the performance record of black workers in collateral fields. More troubling is the growing conviction that while *Brown* and its aftercrop have brought increased expectations to the black masses, the realization of many of these expectations is frustrated by reality. For example, advanced technology has practically eliminated the need for the kind of labor the unlettered and the unskilled are equipped to do, thus threat-

ening them with obsolescence as workers and as persons at precisely the time that a newly appreciated sense of self-worth clouds
the attraction of low-paid, dead-end jobs. But machines are
cheaper and more efficient than people. Machines require no
fringe benefits; they may be amortized for tax credits; they have
practically no absenteeism and require no humanitarian consideration. Hence, the numbing fear that there is a real possibility that
substantial numbers of the massive reservoir of unemployed black
workers will ever again have sustained employment grows more
persuasive. Even more depressing is the picture for unskilled black
youth, many of whom will never have the experience of a regular
job. The available alternatives point to a national junkyard of
human potential: all black, all American, and all around us.

*Political Involvement*
Except for the brief interlude of the Reconstruction, the black involvement in the American political process has been largely
ceremonial until the last decade. In the South, blacks were effectively disfranchised by the poll tax and other strategies. In the
North, the patterns of residential segregation combined with the
exigencies of the two-party system to neutralize the black vote in
most cases. Hence, the sense of powerlessness, of near-absolute
contingency was pervasive in the black community and deeply
etched on the black psyche. There were no black senators, or governors, or mayors, or state representatives, or commissioners, or
heads of school boards. The tedium of exclusion was relieved only
occasionally by the rare election of a black congressman, such as
Oscar DePriest or Adam Clayton Powell, who was made to function as the symbolic representative for the whole black community.

But the typical black citizen, whether in Birmingham or Buf-
falo, Memphis or Minneapolis, arose to face each day with the
comfortless knowledge that in the world beyond his door he was
a cipher, and that whatever transpired in the day-to-day order of

human events would not reflect any input he would have. Whether there was war or peace, whether there would be a bus line near his neighborhood, when, where, or if his children would go to school, or his garbage would be collected, or in what cemetery he could be buried were all decisions to be made by others. For a hundred years he had been a citizen bearing all the burdens that citizens bear, but for that hundred years he had shared none of the responsibilities that citizens share in a democratic society. He was a nonentity and he resented it. When at last his cup of anguish would hold no more and he screamed out for a share of power, America was alarmed, aggrieved, annoyed, and unforgiving. *Black Power?* Incredible. Whatever for?[8]

But times change with the votes, and the successful registration of over a million additional blacks following passage of the new voting rights legislation that followed *Brown* opened the door for meaningful black participation in the political process. With the help of federal registrars, and despite the most determined opposition, by the early seventies voter registration campaigns had broken the back of black disfranchisement in the South. The breakthrough was timely, for in the North (which had become the new battleground for civil rights) the ardor of protest confrontation had been considerably dampened by the defection of the more visible white liberals, the internal problems of the protest organizations, the ferity of the opposition, the uncertain interests of the Federal Bureau of Investigation, and the mounting competition of the mushrooming "liberation" groups spawned in the furrows of the civil rights movement. In the South where there was an established tradition of political replevin, none of the gains imposed by such "outside agencies" as the Supreme Court or the various civil rights organizations could be considered "final" unless and until they had received local ratification. In consequence, the breakthrough in registration and voting was in the long run the indispensable corollary for the implementation of *Brown*, for in the absence of the diligent exercise of the black franchise at the state and local level, experience has shown that there is no effective way to protect the interests of the black estate, no matter how well intentioned the federal establishment or how carefully drawn its decrees.

As black voters, South and North, began to recognize the potency of a unified black electorate, some remarkable things began to happen. Suddenly there were black mayors in the big cities of the North and West, and in the small towns of the South. Blacks were appearing in the state legislatures and there were more than a dozen black United States congressmen. There were black faces in the state highway patrols, in an occasional sheriff's uniform, even on the judge's bench. In the 1976 presidential election, 90 percent of the blacks who voted cast their ballots for Jimmy Carter, thereby insuring his election as president of the United States.

Altogether this adds up to power. But how much? It depends on how you look at it. Certainly there is not a formidable amount of power inherent in being mayor of a city like Gary, Indiana, or Newark, New Jersey, or Detroit. While such an office is certainly not ceremonial, the economic and political realities are such as to rule out an extravagant exercise of personal whim or racial prerogative. At the state level, in only one or two states, if any, are there enough blacks in the legislature to make their presence felt as a black caucus, and in such instances white voters are usually needed for their election or reelection. All things considered, including the size of the black population, the number of black elected officials is still miniscule—considerably less than 1 percent of the total. Moreover, despite one or two showcase appointments, or an occasional "summit meeting" of the president with selected black leaders at the White House, black political influence does not begin to approximate that of an ethnic group like the Jews, for example, who have perhaps one-fifth the potential numerical voting strength of the national black community, but who manage a much greater impact on domestic and foreign policy.

How much power? Not much if power is translated to mean
"clout," or if it means the control over critical decisions that affect the integrity and interests of the black estate. Certainly, it is
not the feared and calumniated Black Power visualized by whites
in the late 1960s. Rather, it is the curious phenomenon of *blacks
in power positions* from which the essence of power has been
largely extracted by a multiplicity of factors. In the big cities the
erosion of the tax base, the control by or the opposition of party
machinery, the effective veto power of white commissioners and
of entrenched, inherited white subordinates, the dependence upon
the cooperation of various federal agencies, and the necessity of
white backing at the polls leave the black mayor essentially neu-
tralized as far as the promotion of substantial racial interests is
concerned. This situation is replicated in the state legislatures
where the program interests of one or two blacks may safely be
ignored unless they make effective alliances across racial lines.
The same is true when a lone black (as is often the case) wins a
slot on the local city council. Indeed, in some instances the political realities black elected officials must face render them less
able to address directly the needs of their black constituencies
than whites would if holding the same office. Too many black
appointments to positions previously held by whites or any prone-
ness to tamper with "settled" policy in such sensitive areas as
housing, education, welfare, or law enforcement are likely to raise
questions and evoke controversy that can further reduce political
effectiveness of the black officeholder, or insure his defeat at the
next election.

It is clear then that "black power" is not yet a reality, but the
picture is not so dismal as it first appears, for there are significant
gains which are not immediately apparent. First of all, the dis-
ability regarding the franchise has been substantially removed
and black citizens everywhere have an increased option to participate in the political process. There are still pockets of intimidation, and there are still islands of apathy; but the official barriers
are down and the option is being tested. Second, black office-

seekers *are* being elected, as are whites who are sensitive to the interests of the black estate; so the black citizen is no longer a cipher. If his vote counts, *he* counts, and the recognition that he is a force to be reckoned with is at least a kind of protopower. Despite the limitations on the power of black mayors and others who hold high elective offices, for the first time in history significant numbers of Blackamericans all over the country represent the administrative leadership for local governments. They are elected by blacks and whites; they are highly visible; and considering the fact that they are generally returned to office after a first term, if their performance is not impressive, it must at least be acceptable. To be voluntarily governed by blacks is something new for Americans, wherever they are. That black political aspirants continue to win elections on a margin of white votes may well be a signal that America has finally matured enough to be fair, and that it feels secure enough to share some of the power some of the time. Voluntarily. That is an auspicious sign for the country and for the black estate. We have come a long way, and we have a long way to go down the road together. Sharing the power and sharing the responsibility is the best way to get where we all want to go—with expedition and with grace.

### The Strain on Black Ethnicity

It is fair to say that the quality of life for the black contingent has changed dramatically, and in many ways since the *Brown* case was argued in 1954. There are young adult blacks in Mississippi and North Carolina who have never seen the back of the bus from the inside, and who have never had to go to the alley entrance of a restaurant to buy a sandwich. There is a generation of black youth who do not find it strange or awkward to compete with whites on the gridiron or in the classroom or in the job market, or to have white friends. They have no special animosities, or epithets, or strategies reserved for the whites with whom they are in contact day by day. If through their survival mechanisms they know intuitively or instinctively that they themselves are somehow perceived as "different," and that to most white people their difference makes a difference, that is dismissed as the white man's problem. Only he can solve it. These black youth have no identity problems, no strong racially based anxieties. Although they are vaguely aware that America is still a "racist society," most of them have had no direct, personal racial confrontation of any consequence.

Who is this generation of Blackamericans? They are the sons and daughters of the newly emergent black middle class. Their fathers and mothers are black professionals who struggled against the odds of segregation and discrimination to educate themselves for what was at best an uncertain future. The odds paid off far better than expected, for the ramifications of *Brown* first required thousands of instant blacks in highly visible positions in industry and government and academe. This was followed by affirmative action programs that gave an element of solidity to what was initially a superficial put-on. In the meantime, as the older blacks, who were mostly educated in the black colleges of the South, dug in to preserve and maximize their new opportunities, their children, with greatly extended expectations, prepared themselves for a considerably broadened spectrum of opportunities. They have not been disappointed. They are the self-confident young men and women who are today finding their way into a thousand job categories not even known to their parents when *Brown* was in its infancy. What is even more significant, they are not only finding well-paid, challenging positions, but they are increasingly finding genuine acceptance as people. Perhaps the two go together in the American understanding of practice, property, and personhood.

In any event, the emergence of a substantial black middle class with indications of both vertical and lateral mobility is a signal achievement, for it means that the bonds of caste are finally broken. It also implies a reconstruction of the model on which

American society has heretofore depended, for the notion of class implies a particularized structure of relationships to other identifiable groups within the same social cosmos. The two groups of greatest importance to the black middle class are upper-class whites and lower-class blacks. The white middle class (except perhaps the uppermost tier) is potentially bypassed because of its own sense of vulnerability, and because the blacks who now seem to have it made needed much more of everything to make it with. In addition, the job entry level of well-prepared blacks is relatively high, although the jobs are relatively few in number. This translates into a situation in which middle-class black professionals are often more likely to have peer relationships with high status whites than with middle- and lower-middle-class whites. This should not be startling, for the Old Line white liberals with black middle-class friends were themselves, in most cases, middle class only by courtesy. Since the "great middle class" is considered the democratic norm in America, it is simply not good taste to admit to any other claim. In consequence, the middle class is both utopian and euphemistic, accommodating in turn the requirements of dignity of those who have a little too much to feel poor, those who have a lot too much to feel respectable, and all those who range in between. But even with so many ports of entry, the black masses are a class below and a caste apart. They do not belong.

Thereon hangs a tale, the prognosis of which is grave, for the black masses appear to be in steady decline even as the black elite search for their niche in the American dream. The gulf widens; the old bonds are raveling under the tension of new opportunities, new privileges, new interests, and new horizons—*for some*. But there is nothing new for the black masses except the reality of their own dereliction. In the old days, the black undercaste was absolute, and in an absolute caste everybody is equal and fraternity is a condition of existence. There may be pretensions of differential status, but the ceiling on upward mobility is an absolute barrier common to all, and the pretensions of differential status evaporate in the acid of reality. Hence, the class structure within the black caste never amounted to much, as the black bourgeoisie and the black bootblack were alike subject to the embarrassments of external evaluation that recognized no distinctions.[9] Now the integrity of the black estate is at stake because the rules have been changed. The lines of division have been laid between the few and the many, and the challenge to the few is to prove themselves worthy to be a people apart from their roots. In short, there are signs that America is prepared to write off the black masses in exchange for accepting the black elite.

It is a sad tale, a pernicious proposition. To divide the black community is, of course, to destroy the black estate. The black elite is the flower, the creative exponent of the black masses, and there is nothing in past experience to suggest that the aerobics of the situation are transferable. Or, to put it another way, there has always been a certain security for the black estate in the tacit understanding that the inevitable marginality of those blacks who somehow surmounted the barriers of caste and color always pushed them back to their origins for nurture. Not only was it inconceivable that the distinctiveness of the black subculture could be maintained in some other ether in some other cosmos external to itself, but the exigencies of personal survival have usually made living beyond the barrio an unattractive adventure in the conventional mind.

There is an in-group anecdote to the effect that so long as the black expatriate comes home to the ghetto three days a week—on Friday evening to get his hair cut, on Saturday night to party, and on Sunday morning to go to church—then, "ain't nothing moved away but his clothes, and even they try to make it back on Monday in time for washing!" While the pattern of maintenance of close social and cultural ties with the black community is still the prevailing mode for the overwhelming majority of blacks who now live in suburbia or other traditionally white enclaves, for at least some of them the need for frequent trips "home" for whatever reasons seems less compelling. Personal services such as grooming, laundry, tailoring, etc. can often be managed satisfactorily where they are. Indeed, more and more blacks seem willing to make personal adjustments wherever possible in the effort to reduce any teratological impact their distinctive cultural or physical requirements may require, if such adjustments seem likely to increase their acceptability. In consequence, more blacks find themselves "exceptions," and as such they turn up with increasing frequency at parties in their new neighborhoods on Saturday night and (considerably less often) at white churches on Sunday morning. In short, the conventional wisdom about black marginality, while still intact, is no longer reliable or conclusive. And while it is still undoubtedly true that the distinctiveness of the black subculture cannot—and will not—be maintained by its expatriates, it is also true that the inconveniences of expatriation constitute a declining factor in maintaining the integrality of the black community.

Where does that leave the black estate? If the white establishment has written off the black masses as unproductive, unsalvageable, and undesirable, and if the black elite in full pursuit of the normative "American" rewards for individual diligence, education, and effort accept the long overdue fruits of their exertion, what is the future of the black subculture as a distinctive experience in the American ontogeny? The distribution of the accumulating evidence is not yet decisive, but one thing *is* clear: the coming of age of America is bringing with it some very strange fruit, so delightfully different, and yet so hauntingly familiar.

# So Much History, So Much Future: Martin Luther King, Jr., and the Second Coming of America

VINCENT HARDING

We can not be impartial,
  only intellectually honest.
Impartiality is a dream,
  honesty a duty.

  GAETANO SALVEMINI[1]

We have hung our heads and cried
  for all those like Lee who died,
Died for you and died for me,
  died for the cause of equality.
We've been 'buked and we've been scorned,
We've been talked about, sure as you're born.
But we'll never turn back, no,
  we'll never turn back,
Until we've all been freed and
  we have equality.

  BERTHA GOBER[2]

*Introduction*

"Have We Overcome?" The committee responsible for organizing this important symposium has set each participant a formidable and unenviable task. For it has placed us in the lively context of that large, provocative, and crucial question, and at the same time has asked us to speak primarily to certain other subthemes, leaving the largest question and its tentative answers to the closing session and Lerone Bennett's presentation there.

Now I must confess at the outset that I am not disciplined enough, especially not on these grounds, to contain myself until the last session, and I want to open my remarks on Martin Luther King, Jr., by unashamedly dabbling into Lerone Bennett's territory. Since Lerone and I have been friends and comrades for many years, and since I am certain that he will address the issue with his usual wisdom and eloquence, I am emboldened to leap foolhardily into his arena and offer a few introductory thoughts of my own on this overarching question.

To do that I would begin where all such answers must begin—where we are. Thus our own present search for answers to the question "Have We Overcome?" fittingly begins here at the University of Mississippi, and my comments are set against the background of a special, paradigmatic moment of history on this campus. Let me read an account of the too familiar/too easily forgotten event, as reported in what I consider to be the best high school/college text on the history of this state, *Mississippi: Conflict and Change*. There we are told,

On January 26, 1961, James Meredith had applied for admission to the University of Mississippi. In his letter Meredith, an Air Force veteran, let the registrar know that he was a student at Jackson State University. Three times the registrar refused to answer letters sent by Meredith. Finally he returned Meredith's room-reservation fee.

By now Meredith was convinced that he would have to force Ole Miss to admit him. After many legal battles and delays, the Fifth Circuit Court of Appeals ordered Ole Miss to admit Meredith. The court found that "from the moment the defendants [Ole Miss] discovered that Meredith was a Negro, they engaged in a carefully calculated campaign of delay, harassment, and masterly inactivity."

The idea that a black man might enter Ole Miss aroused many white Mississippians. On a state-wide telecast, Governor Barnett placed his own authority as state governor between Mississippi citizens and the federal government. He demanded resistance: "We must either submit to the unlawful dictates of the federal government, or stand up like men and tell them 'Never.' . . . Every public official, including myself, should be prepared to make the choice tonight whether he is willing to go to jail, if necessary to keep faith with the people who have placed their welfare in his hands."

Events at Ole Miss moved swiftly. The first federal marshals arrived on Sunday afternoon, September 30, 1962, and moved to the Lyceum building. A crowd gathered. It grew larger as students returned from the football weekend in Jackson. Chants such as "Go to hell, JFK" filled the air. Few in the crowd realized that Meredith had been flown in from Memphis and was already in a dormitory room on the edge of the campus.

As night approached, students began throwing gravel and lighted cigarettes at the marshals. Soon the crowd was pelting the marshals with rocks, bottles, and lengths of pipe. Nearby cars and trucks were overturned, smashed, and set on fire. Bullets began to whiz out of the night. At 8 P.M. the marshals fired tear gas to hold off the mob. By now it was clear that Ole Miss students no longer dominated the crowd. Armed groups of outsiders, some of whom were die-hard segregationists from neighboring states, were firing rifles at the federal marshals. Before the night was over, a local jukebox repairman and a French newsman lay dead —both victims of shots from the crowd.

As dawn broke on Oxford, burned-out cars still smoldered. Smashed glass, rocks, and pipes lay everywhere. One hundred and sixty marshals were hurt, of whom 28 had been shot. It had taken the use of National Guard troops, mostly native Mississippians, to halt the violence. Finally President Kennedy sent in more than 20,000 federal troops.[3]

Have we overcome? Have we overcome at Ole Miss? Whenever, wherever we ask such a question we realize that "overcoming" has meant different things at different times in our struggle for justice in this land. In 1962, we overcame when one black native son, under federal protection, was able to force his way onto the violently defiant campus of his own state university—a signal victory, won at great human cost. Now, in 1978, we have some eight hundred black students moving with apparent ease across these grounds, doing a variety of things, including forgetting at times the costs that were paid for them to be here.

Have we overcome? Yes, we have overcome. So far as our right to attend one of our own state universities, we may say unequivocally that we have overcome. We now have the right to be here as students, to do as much or as little work as anyone else. We have the right to go to as many football games as anyone else. We apparently have the right to be present on major varsity teams in disproportionately larger numbers than anyone else. We certainly have the right to be as fraternity-oriented as everyone else. But is that sufficient for 1978? Was that the purpose, the real purpose of all the sound and fury, of all the blood and dying of 1962? Have we overcome?

What are the new questions, the new issues for this moment of history? Does this university ever intend that its black student body should approach the percentage of blacks in the state? Whatever our numbers, should we be asking what is taught at this university? What is the content, the spirit of the education we are receiving here? Is it preparing us to receive the ideas and beliefs of this society as they are handed to us, or is it instilling in us a spirit of creative questioning, a desire to create a new future, a vision of a better America, not simply a richer America? Why are we here?

Have we overcome at Ole Miss? Where are the black administrators on this campus, the black decisionmakers at the highest levels? Where is the black faculty on this campus? Does the university ever think of the money earned for it by its outstanding black varsity athletes when it considers funds for Black Studies and similar programs on campus? Have we overcome? What are the real relationships between black and white students, between black students and white faculty on this campus? Of even deeper importance, what is the relationship between the black students at Ole Miss, fighting our way into a middle-class world, and that other world of the hundreds of thousands of our people who are locked into the structures of poverty and feelings of powerlessness that are built into this society? Are we here for our people, for those who have sacrificed so much to establish this right, or are we here selfishly, individualistically, for ourselves? Are we rising with our people or from our people?

At every stage of our struggle, each set of victories presses us forward to new directions and demands that the objectives be enlarged, opened, pushed forward. Thus at each moment of history a new set of goals must be formulated—involving a serious encounter between those who have lived and known the past and those who must forge forward into the future. These new goals then become the standards, the touchstones for our answers to the question "Have we overcome?" The answers for 1962—or 1972—will not do for 1978. (Again we are driven back to the wisdom of Frantz Fanon: "Each generation must, out of relative obscurity, discover its mission, fulfill it, or betray it."[4])

We certainly know what that means for the overall question of this symposium. Yes, in some things we have overcome. In others we have not, have not even begun to understand the meaning of the term. Beyond that, as Eric Lincoln reminded us, there are certain crucial matters which can never be answered in any categorical sense, but must be seen in part as an on-going, developing process. In many cases, then, the question might better be "Are We Overcoming?" Even there, no adequate response can be found before we define the "we" and demand of ourselves that we define the goals for our own time.[5]

But enough of that. I must still remember that my task is not to continue the fascinating encounter with the overall topic, but to try to provide an assessment of Martin Luther King, Jr.'s role in the freedom movement, along with some sense of his effect on the movement after his death. These are critical questions for us as a nation, and it was the challenge of the subject matter that played a major role in my decision to participate in this symposium. (Allow me to add parenthetically that as I prepared this presentation I focused my mind and my hopes on two groups of persons in the audience: those of you who are students and who must help shape the future for us all, and those of you who are veterans of the long struggle to transform this state and this nation into a more humane place, you who made it possible for us to be here now. I speak to you, I question you, I celebrate you, and I invite all others to listen in as well.)

Before entering into the heart of the topic, though, it is important to me that I make clear how I come to such a task. After having been in Mississippi many times, this is my first visit to the university, and in such a setting I want it known that I do not approach King's life and work as a cool, detached, objective scholar-observer—whatever that is. Rather, three personal and political realities are critical to my angle of vision as I approach this assignment, as I meditate and reflect on this man and this movement, and I want you to understand those central elements that deeply affect what I see, what I say, and how I feel.

First, I met Martin King in 1958, twenty years ago this month, and for the ten years of his life that we knew each other he was for me, to me, a brother, comrade, neighbor, and friend. From 1961 to the time of his death he regularly encouraged me to carry out the role I had chosen for myself as one who was both an engaged participant in the movement, and at the same time a committed historian and critical analyst of its development, as one who worked at the vortex of the struggle and yet remained outside of the official structures of the main civil rights organizations. Thus I could be relatively free to speak the truth about their strengths and weaknesses—about his strengths and weaknesses. I

respected Martin King for encouraging me to march *and* to analyze, to join him in jail *and* to critique his positions, to be more
comrade than follower. So, Martin King is very real to me, continues to be very real, and I do not consider it my scholarly duty
to place a distance between that personal/political reality and
the obligations of my role as a historian of the struggle. I come
then as Martin's friend, his brother, as one who is crazy enough
still to find myself talking to him on occasion, sometimes shouting
his name—along with Malcolm's, along with Fannie Lou's, along
with Clarence Jordan's and Tom Merton's and Ruby Doris
Smith's.[6] (Many of these names you don't know, and if you are
to get an education at this university—or any other—you must demand to know them.)

The second thing I need to indicate is probably already im-
plicit in my first comment. In 1961, three years after first having
met King, I came south from Chicago with Rosemarie Harding,
my wife and comrade, to work full-time in the freedom struggle. I
do not hesitate to proclaim that I am biased towards that struggle
and its participants. Indeed, at the same time I seek to understand and record its past, I am totally committed to work actively
towards the creation of its next, still unclear stages of development. And I expect always to maintain that partisan bias in favor
of a new, more humane American society, in favor of freedom for
all the men, women, and children who seek new beginnings, new
opportunities to break the shackles of the many external and internal oppressive realities that still bind so many of us down to
lives that are less than our best, most human selves.

Finally, to identify my angle of vision, I want to say that it is
also twenty years since I first set foot in Mississippi, and it has
clearly had a strange and special attraction for me. Having
walked and ridden its roads and known its people from Holly
Springs to Biloxi, having fought the fear that was so easy to overcome us in Greenwood and Leland and Meridian and Ruleville,
having met and loved so many of the women and the men who

risked and sometimes lost their lives to transform this state, having been here last for the funeral of Fannie Lou Hamer, that magnificent freedom-fighter, I do not, cannot walk lightly on this ground. Indeed, it is hard to stand here and not want to cry. It is hard to stand here and not want simply to read a list of names, to call a roll of courage and honor of the fifties and sixties—and the seventies. Herbert Lee and Medgar Evers, Hartman Turnbow and James Meredith, Amzie Moore and Brenda Travis, Bob Moses and Hollis Watkins, Willie Peacock and Sam Block, Mickey Schwerner and Jimmy Chaney, Diane Nash and Bob Zellner, Aaron Henry and Jim Forman, Unita Blackwell and June Johnson, Vernon Dahmer and Jimmy Travis, Lawrence Guyot and Herbert Steptoe, Jane Stembridge and Charlie Cobb, Bill Mahoney and Stokely Carmichael, Ed King and Fanny Lou Hamer, Owen Brooks and Skip Robinson. And the list could go on, interminably on, tracing a path of blood and tears and struggle from Hernando to Gulfport, reminding us, reminding us, of all the rivers and their terrible bloated secrets, of all the trees and their strange human fruit, of all the buried bodies—but reminding us even more of all the courageous men and women and children who refused to turn back, who said, with Bertha Gober, "no we'll never turn back."[7]

In other words, Mississippi is special, was special. We all knew it all the time. Reflecting, intensifying the evils that we saw everywhere in this country, somehow Mississippi was the heart of darkness where if a light could be set ablaze, then we knew our light could shine anywhere, everywhere. Mississippi was the hard rock at the center of America's national racism and we knew if we could begin to crack this rock, then there was hope for us all, black and white. Thus in the post-1954 period of our centuries-old struggle for freedom, justice, and equality, Mississippi was the quintessential local battleground, symbol of all our pain, all our fear, and all our hope.

I

It is perfectly fitting then that we should stand on this ground today to assess Martin Luther King, Jr., and his role. For he would have had no role were it not for men like George Lee and Gus Courts, those courageous NAACP leaders who gave their lives back in 1955 in Belzoni. There could be no movement for King to represent were it not for a Herbert Lee, willing to go to his death in an attempt simply to register to vote.[8] There could be no movement without a James Meredith walking the gauntlet of hatred and fear on this campus. There could be no movement without a Fannie Lou Hamer praying for the men who beat her unmercifully in the Winona jail. There could be no movement without Annelle Ponder coming out of the same jail with her battered face swollen, so swollen that speech was an agony, and yet insisting on saying one word, just one word: Freedom. Freedom.[9]

There could be no movement without the thousands of men and women and children of Mississippi who risked their lives in the toughest state of them all. There could be no movement without the older folks, like 60-year-old Cleveland Jordan in Leflore County, who declared, "I'm fighting for my grandchildren's freedom." There could be no movement without the small band of courageous older preachers like Reverend E. D. White of Greenwood, who repeatedly risked his life to walk through fire with the children, holding their hands as they entered the Carroll County school, persisting even after his church at Mitchell Springs was burned down, even after a threatening visit from the Klan, because he was "determined to have whatsoever is rightfully mine and to see that the children got what was rightfully theirs." There could be no movement without the many other older folk like the woman in Greenwood's jail in 1964 who prayed out one of those musical prayers that we know how to pray so well, seeking for reconciliation—with justice—in Greenwood:

"Please," she cried, "[Lord,] go into the hospital, hold the church of God, you told us to love one another, there does not seem to be any love in this, look this town over, Jesus, and do something about the condition. Whatsoever a man soweth, that also shall he reap, that we might have our equal rights."[10]

In spite of, because of every beating, every prayer, every death, every refusal to yield, the struggle for freedom in Mississippi was the hardest in the South; and yet we overcame, again and again and again. At the same time, of course, all we need is a glance at Tupelo to know that the struggle still continues and that we must continue enduring, keeping on, overcoming, again and again.[11]

But before we let the power of the present overtake us, let us remember the focus of our time now, and say that it is good to be in this place, to talk about Martin Luther King here; for it is from this angle of vision that we can see that there was, is, indeed a freedom *movement*, a *movement* towards inner and outer freedom in the lives of millions of men and women, and Martin King was both child of that movement and its greatest symbolic representative, its internationally recognized spokesman, its leader, but in a very special sense of that word; and it was only for a limited time that he served that role before sharp challenges rose to his leadership.

In other words, King and Mississippi and the larger movement they represent remind us of the words that C. L. R. James, that great revolutionary scholar, constantly paraphrases from Karl Marx: "Men and women do make history, but only so much history as they are able to make." Within that context, it is clear that we shall understand the role Martin King played in the movement only as we understand that he was at once created by the movement and a creator of some of its major thrusts. He made much history, but in doing so he was aided, limited, and defined by the struggle that was mounting all around him, making him.[12]

This dialectic, the dynamic, ecstatic, often agonized interplay between Martin and the movement may be illustrated in many ways, at many points, but we shall choose five developments to illustrate briefly the relationship between the man and the movement and to comment on its nature and its strengths and weaknesses. Those reference points are Montgomery, Alabama, in 1955–1956; Albany, Georgia, in 1961–1962; Birmingham, Alabama, and Washington, D.C., in 1963; Mississippi and Chicago in 1966, and the fateful, desperate road from Riverside Church, New York, on April 4, 1967, to Memphis, Tennessee, on April 4, 1968.

Let us begin at Montgomery, where black folks took the U.S. Supreme Court more seriously than the court took itself, firmly grasped the *Brown* decision, intuitively recognized its many broader implications, and began immediately to press it far beyond the limited arena of the segregated school systems. Even before he arrived in Montgomery as the new pastor of the prestigious, black middle-class-dominated Dexter Avenue Baptist Church, Martin King had entered the dialectic. He was a child of one of those comfortable Atlanta black bourgeoisie, church-dominating families; but nothing could insulate him against the reality of his people's existence in the South, in America. Nothing could blind him to the fact that ever since World War II a new phase of our freedom struggle had been mounted against rugged, often savage opposition, and he knew that what we were doing, largely through the courts at first, and through early, dangerous attempts at voter registration, was somehow tied to the anticolonial struggles being waged across the world.[13]

Then, just a bit more than a year after he had been in Montgomery, not long after he had completed his doctoral dissertation for Boston University, while thoughts of a relatively easy life as part-pastor and part-academic danced in his head, a strong, gentle woman named Rosa Parks refused to do the usual, agonized black dance on a segregated Montgomery bus. As a result, she was arrested, and a new time was opened in the struggle. But it was not out of synchronization with the past. Indeed, Rosa Parks had been an NAACP officer, as was E. D. Nixon, the Pullman car union official and local leader who bailed her out. Rosa Parks had not been the first to act in such a way on the Montgomery bus, but she had a wide and highly respected reputation in the black community. Moreover, the news about and the indignation over what had happened spread quickly, because a group of black women in the city had set up a telephone tree to help in their earlier voter registration campaign work. And now they put that system to work in this new cause. So the new time was building on the efforts and the people of the time before, and King was initially pressed into the role by a small group of genuine local leaders who had proven themselves in the past, and in a real sense he was later anointed by the larger masses of the Montgomery black people to be the public representative of their struggle. Even then no one fully realized that the new time had really begun to come, that it was possible now to make more history than they had ever made before in Montgomery, Alabama.[14]

At the urging of Nixon and others, King agreed to become president of the Montgomery Improvement Association. What did that mean? What was his role? Initially it was to be a spokesman, to articulate the hopes and aspirations of his people in ways, in words that they were not able to formulate. But his role was also to help reshape and reformulate these goals in the light of his own special developing vision.

Before examining that particular vision and role, it will probably be helpful to remind ourselves that at the outset of the Montgomery struggle the black folk of the city established their boycott of the segregated buses for very simple goals. They did not initially demand an end to bus segregation. Indeed, as late as April, 1956, four months after the beginning of the boycott, King was articulating three objectives which assured continued segregation. The three goals were:

1. More courteous treatment of black passengers.
2. Seating on a first-come, first-served basis, but with blacks

continuing the current practice of filling up from the rear of the bus forward, while whites filled in from the front towards the back,

3. Hiring of black bus drivers on predominantly black lines.[15]

That was all. That was all they asked at first, and they did not march, sit-in, or fill up the jails—they just refused to ride the buses. That was all. It seems so simple now, but it was a great step then, and it was the local context in which King began.

In the weekly mass meetings that developed as a series of increasingly politicized, religious revival sessions, King set out to put forward his evolving philosophy of Christian nonviolence.[16] At first, it was defined primarily as a refusal to react violently to the violence of whites, as a willingness to return love for hatred, and a conviction that their action was not only constitutional but within the will of God—therefore also within the onward, righteous flow of history. So, at the first mass meeting on December 5, 1955, in his exhortation to the fearful, courageous, wondering, determined people, King said, "We are not wrong in what we are doing. If we are wrong, the Supreme Court of this nation is wrong. If we are wrong, the Constitution of the United States is wrong. If we are wrong, God Almighty is wrong. If we are wrong, Jesus of Nazareth was merely a Utopian dreamer who never came down to earth." Then he closed with one of his typically rousing and inspiring perorations: "When the history books are written in the future, somebody will have to say, 'There lived a race of people, a black people, fleecy locks and black complexion, but a people who had the marvelous courage to stand up for their rights and thereby they injected a new meaning into the being of history and of civilization.' And we are going to do that."[17]

From that auspicious beginning, one of King's major roles was interpreter, inspirer, the prophet who saw the significance, the larger meaning of what was happening in the immediate movement. He learned that role, grew into it, made important errors in it, but it was his. As he developed this sense of vocation, King tried constantly to interpret the black struggle as one that was ultimately of benefit to the entire society. He insisted that as blacks fought for their own human rights they were indeed working for the common good, for the good of their white neighbors and fellow citizens, for the building of the good society in America. In addition, King urged his people to believe that their struggle was also part of the world-wide movement of nonwhite men and women breaking the bonds of colonial oppression, creating a new world order.

So the young pastor, moving into his twenty-seventh year, had found a black community ready to take certain initial risks on behalf of a limited vision of its rights and a new determination to establish its dignity. Beginning where they were, he took the people's courage and lifted it to the highest possible level, called upon them to see themselves as far more than black men and women of Montgomery Alabama, striving for decent treatment on a bus. Instead he pressed them forward, urging them to claim their roles as actors in a great cosmic drama, one in which they were at once in unity with the best teachings of American democracy, with the winds of universal social change, and at the same time walking faithfully within the unchanging will of God.

It was a heady mix, but when the going got hard, when the bombs began to explode, when the white employers threatened to fire women and men who needed the work so badly, such a leader/teacher and his teachings were critical factors in helping an essentially Christian people remain faithful to their own best visions. Meanwhile, King was deeply inspired by their courage and determination, by their willingness to take great risks for freedom. In playing this role, King, of course, was totally within a great black tradition himself, following the pathway of the giants who had taught him, the preacher-educator-political leaders who had affected his life, men like Benjamin Mays, Mordecai Johnson, Howard Thurman, and Vernon Johns.[18]

Moreover, King brought to the people his own clearly developing courage in the face of harsh danger—and this was critical to
the creation and legitimizing of his role. For instance, early in the
struggle his house was bombed, nearly destroying his family, but
he neither retreated nor encouraged retaliation by an angry black
populace. He was faced repeatedly with threats on his life,
threats that the history of Montgomery, Alabama, made very easy
to believe, and yet he overcame the very natural fear that welled
up within him, fear for himself and for the life of his young family. On one of many such occasions in Montgomery, King insisted
on using the "white" side of the segregated railroad ticket office.
The first time he did it a police officer insisted that King "use the
entrance for niggers." Martin refused, then after an exchange in
which Martin King kept his cool—one of his great gifts—the officer said, "All right, King, I'm going to let you through this time,
but if you ever dare to use this door again, I . . . will kill you with
my own hands." Martin picked up his bag and said, "Sir, I am
sorry you feel this way about me, and I bear you no ill will, but
every time I leave Montgomery by train, I shall be compelled by
conscience to use this door."[19]

Knowing the grapevine of the black community as we do, it
was obvious that word of such encounters, embellished many
times in the telling, ran like fire through their lives. Inspired by
the courage of his people, King repeatedly set his own example
of courage, and they in turn were enabled to hold out for week
after difficult week, for 381 days of boycott. So, by the time the
boycott had successfully ended in December, 1956, by the time
blacks were free to sit wherever they chose on the city buses, the
possibility of an entire community of black men and women in
the South taking large risks on the basis of conscience, justice,
and a belief in the will of God had begun to be established.
Those men and women and children of Montgomery, with their
leader-spokesman, had made it possible for others to go beyond
them and make even more history, create an even greater future.

## II

By this time, King had become nationally and internationally known, not yet on the scale of the mid-sixties, but clearly he was the coming new spokesman for the movements towards freedom in the black South at least. And yet, once the Montgomery bus boycott had ended, King was without the base of direct mass action that he needed for the fullest, continuing development of his own role. Of course, action was taking place all over the South, largely focused on the issue of token desegregation of the schools. Very often it was hard, explosive, sensational action, with young black children and their families taking fantastic risks, symbolically culminating in the experience of Little Rock, Arkansas, in the fall of 1957, when federal troops were called in to desegregate a high school. Though he was not personally involved in many of these activities, King was still the leading interpreter of their meaning, and by the time of Little Rock's agony it had been suggested to King that he try to develop a major regional action organization based on the rising black momentum and on the tremendous power of the black religious leaders of the South. So in 1958, Ella Baker, one of the key architects of the idea, a former NAACP field worker in the region—and one of the greatest heroes of our struggle—returned South to become the first executive secretary of what was to become known as the Southern Christian Leadership Conference, based in Atlanta. Though he was still in Montgomery at the time, King naturally became its first president.[20]

But the establishment of an organization of black, mostly Baptist ministers did not create a movement. The giving of 200 speeches a year by King did not create a movement. Besides, as whites continued their resistance to change, both in the courts and through the uses of fierce, extralegal means of intimidation and violence, King's philosophy of nonviolence in the cause of a largely undefined integrated society was being seriously challenged. In the North the deepest, broadest questions seemed to be coming from the revived forces of black nationalism, most clearly seen in the growing Nation of Islam and in its increasingly popular national representative, Malcolm X. In the South, the message of nonviolent resistance was challenged by the action of Robert Williams and his armed self-defense group in Monroe, North Carolina, in 1959.[21]

Nevertheless, in spite of, because of all these things, beyond all these specific developments, a movement was mounting in its own sporadic, unpredictable way, as mass movements always do, as they always will. And King recognized both the presence and the potential power of the movement. In November, 1959, the leader of Montgomery's movement resigned his pastorate in that city and turned towards his organizational and family base in Atlanta. Before he left the city and the people who had played so critical a role in the creation of the rising southern movement, King held a press conference in which he made clear both his own sense of the critical moment of history and his determination to find, to shape a new, even more decisive and active role for himself. On the last day of November, 1959, Martin King announced his decision to move to Atlanta by February 1, 1960. Then he said, "The time has come for a bold, broad advance of the Southern campaign for equality . . . a full scale assault will be made upon discrimination and segregation in all forms. We must train our youth and adult leaders in the techniques of social change through nonviolent resistance. We must employ new methods of struggle involving the masses of the people."[22]

Clearly, King was speaking to himself, to the moving black community, and to the white and nonwhite world all around. Then, only two months after the announcement, on the very day of the planned move, almost as if by orchestrated agreement, an explosive response to King's vision came from the very "youth" he had hoped to train. They were not waiting for that training, and when the student sit-in movement erupted, beginning in February, 1960, in Greensboro, North Carolina, it drove immediately towards the center of King's life, transforming it in ways that he had likely not quite anticipated. That was, of course, appropriate. For these neatly dressed, amazingly disciplined black young men and women, who with a few white allies began the new phase of the movement, were not only the products of the on-going school desegregation struggles of the South, they were really the children of Martin Luther King. In spite of many mixed feelings about him, they saw him as hero and model. But as is so often the case in such situations, they also went beyond him, creating what he could not create on his own, establishing the basis for the South-wide movement of massive, direct nonviolent confrontation with the segregated public facilities of the section which King had just announced. They were, of course, also the first generation of blacks to grow up in a world where the power and legitimacy of the white West was being challenged across the globe.

By the time they held their organizing conference at Shaw University in April, 1960—under the urging of Ella Baker, and with some financial support from SCLC—the student movement had reached into dozens of cities and enlisted the active engagement of thousands of young people and their older supporters. Indeed, through the power of mass media they had already cast their image and their reality across the earth. Not long after the Raleigh, North Carolina, organizing conference they had decided to call themselves the Student Non-Violent Coordinating Committee, better known, sometimes lovingly known as SNCC—"SNICK." Picking up much of the nonviolent rhetoric of King and SCLC, SNCC literally became the shock troops of the massive movement for direct nonviolent confrontation with the white keepers of southern law, order, and power. And for many of them it was, at first, much more than rhetoric. They truly believed that through the power of their organized, disciplined, confrontative, nonviolent struggle, they were to be the builders of "the beloved community" in America, the harbingers of the new society Martin King had so continually evoked. Black and white together, they believed and they struggled, taking into their own flesh and spirit many of the hardest blows of white hatred and fear.[23]

In 1961, this rapidly spreading movement was given dramatic and explosive emphasis with the coming of the "freedom rides," originally organized by the Congress for Racial Equality. The meeting of these two elements, freedom riders and sit-in students —sometimes involving the same persons—their mutual, harrowing, radicalizing experiences at the hands of southern white mobs and in southern jails, provided the vanguard force that was needed to break open and give new shape to the struggle which had been developing since Montgomery. Added to these human elements was the startling power of the mass media—especially television—to help create (as well as destroy) a sense of mass movement. Surely by 1961, the new time had really come. These young people pouring out into the streets and into the jails of hundreds of southern towns and cities, these high school and college students being beaten on national television, these youths shaking a nation, drawing the attention of a world to their demand for rights, dignity, justice, and human recognition, these were the children of Martin King, of Rosa Parks, of all the singing, praying mothers and fathers of Montgomery.[24]

### III

But because we often create more history than we realize, because we often give birth to children that we do not understand and cannot control, it was not until the development of the Albany movement that Martin King was really able to catch up with the newest, rapid, explosive expansion of his people's struggle. What happened in this southwestern Georgia community from the fall of 1961 through the summer of 1962 was critical to the development of his role in the movement. Having moved from Montgomery to Atlanta in 1959, having developed no similar nonviolent mass action base in Atlanta, but sensing the new moment of history and its needs, King now became a kind of roving leader, responding to calls from the local movements that were springing up in hundreds of communities all over the South. In Albany, the black community had had some earlier sporadic, largely unsuccessful experiences of attempting to negotiate with their all-white city administration for change. But there was no concrete, responsive action until the fall of 1961 when, as part of their voter registration campaign—a story in itself—SNCC sent two of its young field secretaries, Charles Sherrod and Cordell Reagon, into this tough and dangerous community. They became the "outside agitators" who quickly developed themselves into inside organizers, and their courageous defiance of the city's white leadership and the arrest of a mini–freedom rider expedition at the train station helped to stimulate the local black community to form the Albany movement. Soon, Albany went beyond the sit-in stage and became the first deep southern community to engage in the kind of focused mass civil disobedience, through marches and prayer vigils as well as sit-ins, that Martin King had seen coming and had hoped to stimulate through SCLC. When in December, 1961, the Albany movement invited King to come and help them, new patterns in his role began to be clear.[25]

One of his major functions was admittedly to help inspire the local populace to greater efforts, for by now King had begun to be idolized by large sections of the black community, a development fraught with great pitfalls, of course, both for the idol and his idolizers. Nevertheless, King was their national leader, the acknowledged symbol of their struggle. And he was a great exhorter in every sense of the word. In addition, his presence was now considered a guarantee of national and even international media attention. Moreover, because Martin had begun since Montgomery to establish certain ambivalent contacts and significant influence with "liberal" white forces, especially in the religious, educational, and labor union communities, he began to be seen as the one person who could mobilize the "people of good will" (as he called them) from across the nation to come help in the struggle of local southern communities. Even more important in the minds of some persons was the fact that King seemed to have access to the Kennedy White House and its great potential power. Of course, it also came to be understood that Martin would lead marches and go to jail, and that his own organization, SCLC, with its rapidly growing staff, would provide experienced aid to those who might be new in the ways of nonviolent struggle. Albany actually was the first real testing ground for this developing role of King, the visiting leader/symbol, and SCLC, the black church-based organization, in the new phase of the southern movement.

In many ways, as one might have expected, the first experiment was an ambivalent one. In Albany, King was able with the local movement leaders to test what was essentially a new strategy, one forced upon them by the powerful thrust of the freedom movement. Rather than focusing on a single issue, such as bus desegregation, they decided to make multiple demands for changes toward racial and economic justice in their city. The internal force of the people's rush towards justice, their sense that the new time was indeed upon them, their growing understanding of the wider significance of their movement and the stubborn recalcitrance and evasiveness of the white leadership—all these pushed the black freedom fighters out of the churches, out of the train and bus stations, out of the dime stores, out into the streets.

In this motion, King was a crucial element, constantly in dynamic interaction with the force of its thrust. Through his words, his actions, and the very fact of his presence, Martin served as a great inspiration to the movement of the local black community, especially in the early weeks of their activity. Hundreds of persons for the first time in southern freedom movement history volunteered for acts of direct action civil disobedience right out on the streets—which meant certain jailing in some of the most notorious and dangerous jails of Georgia. Out from the church mass meetings they marched, singing *We Shall Overcome, Ain't Gonna*

*Let Nobody Turn Me 'Round,* and *This Little Light of Mine.*
They went to jail, singing, "I'm gonna let it shine." They sang and
prayed in jail, "Paul and Silas locked in jail had nobody to go
their bail, keep your eye on the prize, hold on." In the dirty jails
where the memories of blood from older times were still present,
they were threatened for singing and praying, and they kept on
singing and praying, "Oh, Kelly; Oh, Pritchett; Oh, Kelly; Open
them jails." They were beaten and kicked for singing and praying,
and they kept on singing and praying, scores and hundreds,
young and old. "Over my head I see freedom in the air. There
must be a God somewhere." Indeed out of the Albany jails came
one of the most dynamic cultural forces of the southern movement, the SNCC freedom singers, carrying the songs of the movement across the nation and over the world, songs which were
bought at a great price. *Woke up this morning with my mind
stayed on Freedom.*

In these transformed, transforming jails, many other important
developments were also taking place. Not only were some men,
women, and children being tested, honed, and readied for the
years of struggle ahead, but the invidious class distinctions that
had plagued Albany and so many other similar black communities were momentarily forgotten as people from every level of life
and experience were jammed into cells. One woman, Norma Anderson, the wife of the osteopath who led the movement, told me
that she had never known an experience of communion in a
church which equalled the deep unity that she felt one night as
she and eight other tired, thirsty, frightened, but courageous
women in a cell built for two persons, passed around an old can-
ning jar of water, sharing so much more than the lukewarm liquid
that they drank. Moreover, scores of white and black sympathizers and comrades from the North were drawn to the struggle,
and some were arrested and briefly jailed, thus sharing pieces of
the deepest joys and agonies of the experience (providing, too,
both cocktail-hour stories and life-changing momentum for years

to come). All the while, at least for a while, the mass media certainly came on the scene, according to plan. So much that was new to the' larger southern movement and to King's role became sharply focused in Albany. Here on the banks of the Flint River, Martin King was again being shaped and developed by the movement of a creative, courageous black community. He was making history, but only so much history as he was able to make in the context of his people's thrust towards justice.

But there were major problems as well. The Albany movement had not really jelled as an organization before they called on King. Thus, there were both understandable confusions in its goals and in his role. On the one hand, their sense of the need for nonviolent struggle was constantly being strained by the rush of their own motion and the violence they were meeting. On the other hand there was a temptation to see King, to encourage him to see himself, as a savior—too often a peripatetic savior, one who had to leave town at various points to keep speaking and fund-raising engagements elsewhere. This created real difficulties, especially for a leader who was not essentially a day-to-day strategist in the first place. In addition, there were understandable hard feelings among the SNCC forces—who were often brilliant, brave, and sometimes foolhardy strategists. These young people were often resentful when, after their initial, lonely, and often dangerous weeks of local organizing, Martin King would arrive on the scene, trailing a coterie of supporters and a crowd of media persons behind him, and the hard, dangerous spade-work of these young freedom soldiers would tend largely to be forgotten in the aura of *Martin Luther King*. Moreover, King's leadership style, which was also SCLC's style, derived largely from the semiautocratic world of the black Baptist church, and it simply grated against the spirits of the young people from SNCC. For they were working out their own forms of sometimes anarchistic-appearing participatory democracy.[26]

Unfortunately, as time went on, more than style and attention were at stake, for attention was tied to fund-raising, and competition over fund-raising began to sour what should have been healthy, necessary debates over the essential goals and strategies of the movement. Those debates did take place, but from the outset—just as later on Mississippi's Highway 51 in 1966—they were too often mixed with too many other elements of personality, media attention, and finances. Then, too, what must also be said about Albany and King's role is that he was not really able to enlist the federal government as an ally. Indeed, it was a federal court that later struck a harsh blow against the Albany movement, its organization, and its leaders, opening their eyes to crucial realities regarding the federal government's essential ambivalence—at best—towards the struggle for black freedom.

Nevertheless, two final words must be spoken about Albany. First it is to King's credit that he recognized many of the problems that were built into his own new role and tried to deal with some of them, but the role of a roving leader in the midst of a mass movement spread over such a massive area, often under the glare of television cameras, was fraught with deep and intrinsic difficulties. These were especially dangerous when added to the tendency to sycophancy and adulation that was building in some of the people around him, and the tendency to psychic murder that was built into the media of mass television. Secondly, in spite of the mistakes of King, SCLC, SNCC, the NAACP, CORE, and the Albany movement itself, Albany and its black and white people were changed and have been changed in profound, significant ways. There is no way that the black community will ever be pushed back to 1961; there is no way that white Albany will ever be the same again. But the question blacks now ask, as we must all ask, as Martin asked, is, where do we go from here?[27]

IV

In 1963, for King and SCLC, the geographic answer to that question was Birmingham, Alabama. But as we all knew, Birmingham, like Mississippi, was much more than a physical place. It had a bloody reputation, it was a frightening name. It was pronounced by some as "Bombingham" because of the violence whites had consistently brought against any black movements towards justice and equal rights there. And every black person in this country likely knew someone who had been run out of, beaten or killed in Birmingham, Alabama. But the Reverend Fred Shuttlesworth had not been run out, though he had been beaten more than once and almost killed, at one point with national television cameras running. It was largely at Shuttlesworth's insistence that King and SCLC came to Birmingham in the spring of 1963.

Because the story of Birmingham is somewhat better known than Albany's, I will not go into as great detail, but the developments in that city in April and May, 1963, are most important for our sense of the developing role of Martin Luther King, Jr., in the exploding mass freedom movement of his people. Shuttlesworth's organization, the Alabama Christian Movement for Human Rights, had been active longer than the Albany movement, so King had a somewhat sounder base. In addition, attempting to learn from the Albany experience, SCLC spent several months sporadically exploring and analyzing the Birmingham situation before they moved in to initiate mass demonstrations.[28]

When the demonstrations began on April 3, it was clear that King's new role which had been clearly marked in Albany would see some important reshaping and refining in Birmingham. With the Birmingham black leadership, he decided again to put forward a broad array of demands; so not only the desegregation of all public facilities, but the hiring of black policemen and the employment of blacks in all parts of the public and private sectors were now new, key items on the agenda.

But by the time that King himself began to lead demonstrations—a week after they began—he was faced with the reality that a very volatile situation was at hand, the most difficult he had ever faced. Birmingham was "bigger and badder" than either

Albany or Montgomery, and whites were not the only bad dudes in that town. So certain powerful contradictions began to surface. On the one hand, the "Commandments" handed out to demonstrators began, "Meditate daily on the teachings and life of Jesus," and included such additional admonitions as "walk and talk in the manner of love for God is love . . . . Refrain from violence of fist, tongue or heart." But at the same time, Jim Bevel and other staff members were confiscating a good number of knives and other weapons from some of the brothers who had come prepared for other ways of walking and talking. Obviously, then, the tensions were there, felt more sharply, drawn more clearly than ever before. In many ways the black community of Birmingham in 1963 was a long way from the praying and singing folks of Montgomery in 1955. Still the leaders moved from a religious base. On Good Friday, when King and Ralph Abernathy led their first march, Martin quoted from Jesus: "Peace I leave with you, my peace I give unto you, not as the world giveth . . . . let not your heart be troubled, neither let it be afraid." Ralph said, "You may call it city jail, but I call it Calvary . . . where he leads I'll follow." And Reverend Lindsey, one of the many courageous local leaders, perhaps caught the dilemma of the situation best of all, when just before marching out to meet Bull Connor's police and dogs and high-powered firehoses, he said, "We are going to set this city on fire with the Holy Ghost." [29]

The internal tensions were real, for there were many young people and older ones as well who were indeed on fire, caught up in all the anger and defiance that were building in the sixties in the black community, North and South, as we met white resistance, defiance, and violence everywhere. These were young men and women who now had heard the powerful voice and seen the piercing eyes of Malcolm X on their television screens, and they had to understand how they might at once be faithful to his calls for black pride, resistance, defiance, and even retaliation, while at the same time heeding the call of their traditional, respected leaders, above all, Martin Luther King, who spoke the language of the deep places of the black southern experience. So the young people went out into the streets with even more explosive potential than Albany had known. They taunted the police, they broke out of the marching lines when faced with barricades of police and firemen; they did their own speedy end runs downtown; they poured into the department stores and spread out, sitting on the floors, singing freedom songs until the police caught up with them, threw them into vans, and took them away, trailing behind them the sound of their songs—"I ain't afraid of your jails, 'cause I want my freedom. I want my freedom now."

These young people of Birmingham and others like them had a powerful effect on Martin King, on the shaping of his role, on the history he was making. He saw the great forces of energy and power, black power, stored up within them, and he knew where it could lead. He realized that now they were at least potentially the children of Malcolm X as well, and he was not unmoved by that recognition. He saw them take on the dogs and the firehoses with courageous anger, and he knew that anger was not easily controlled.[30]

So his rationale for nonviolence began to expand to account for such young men and women in Birmingham and everywhere, began to account for Malcolm and the Nation of Islam and other, even more radical and revolutionary voices abroad in the land. Now it was not simply a weapon of love. As he explained it to an increasingly perplexed white world, nonviolence was also a defense against black retaliatory violence. More explicitly than ever before, King was forced to face the stormy potential of the black young people around him, and what they meant for his own sense of the future. When forcibly given a time to rest and think in the Birmingham jail, these children, spawned out of his own body, were clearly on his mind as he wrote his famous letter. Speaking of the American blacks he said,

Consciously and unconsciously, [the Negro] has been swept in by what the Germans call the Zeitgeist, and with his black brothers of Africa, and his brown and yellow brothers of Asia, South America, and the Caribbean, he is moving with a sense of cosmic urgency toward the promised land of racial justice. Recognizing this vital urge that has engulfed the Negro community, one should readily understand public demonstrations. The Negro has many pent-up resentments and latent frustrations. He has to get them out. So let him march some times; let him have his prayer pilgrimages to the city hall; understand why he must have sit-ins and freedom rides. If his repressed emotions do not come out in these nonviolent ways, they will come out in ominous expressions of violence. This is not a threat; it is a fact of history.[31]

From that point onward, King increasingly found himself caught between the rising rage, nationalistic fervor, and questioning of nonviolence in the black community, and the fear of the white community that would seek to hold down all those black energies, to break them up, at worst to destroy them. So while Birmingham represented the largest number of blacks ever engaged in massive direct civil disobedient action up to then, and while the agreement worked out with the city was considered a victory of sorts, King's role was clearly undergoing transition again. Forces were now at work that had long been kept in check; new people had been born, older ones—like Malcolm Little—had been reborn, and their presence demanded gradual changes in King's vision of the movement and of himself. Indeed, the night after the formal agreement was announced in Birmingham, bombings of the black motel where King had stayed and of his brother's home goaded an enraged group of blacks into a burning, car-smashing, police-battling response. In a sense, this was the first of the period's urban rebellions.[32]

Meanwhile, the television screens had carried pictures of Bull Connor's hounds and heavily armed police across the country and throughout the world. Black men and women everywhere never forgot the snarling dog charging at the young boy demonstrator, never forgot the black woman on the ground with a white policeman's knee on her neck. They watched through tears of outrage and pride as teen-aged girls held hands and stood fast in the face of pounding streams from high-powered firehoses. Thus the very victories of Birmingham had unleashed new forces of anger, commitment, and temporary unity, as well as many doubts about nonviolence across the black nation. At the same time, all through that spring and summer the streets and roads were simply streaked with the tears and blood of demonstrators in some eight hundred communities throughout the South, challenging the old ways, the old times, calling for a new America to be born.[33]

V

In a sense, Montgomery was a long, long time ago. Seen from the late spring of 1963, the bus boycott was now a time of quiet, gentle protest compared with the massive action sweeping across the South, challenging the old regime, eliciting some of its most brutal responses. This new massive direction-action pressed King more fully into another role—that of chief movement emissary to the White House. John Kennedy, who had said in January, 1963, that civil rights action was not among his highest priorities, was forced to change his priorities by the whirlwind of the black movement. So White House conferences with King and others, by phone and in person, became almost *de rigueur*. But some persons soon learned—King later than some, earlier than others— that conferences with presidents may do more to divert the force of a movement than to fuel and inspire it, especially if that is one of the intentions of the president. So, while Kennedy began to face the issue of the rights of black people more fully than ever before, instead of using his vast executive powers to make the first move, he threw the weight on Congress, calling for civil rights legislation. He then asked King and other civil rights leaders to help create the climate to bring about the passage of this legislation (including much that blacks in the South had already seized with their own courageous lives). Essentially, that meant trying to cool out the rising force of the southern movement. As a result, King became, partly unwarily, a tool for defusing a powerful current in a critical struggle for the future of the movement.[34]

This is what I mean: for more than two years before Birmingham, Martin and others had talked about the development of a trained, disciplined nonviolent army that would become the spearhead for a national movement of powerful, disruptive nonviolent civil disobedience, from coast to coast. Some persons took the idea more seriously than others, among them James and Diane Nash Bevel, James Lawson and Rosemarie Harding and me. This group, and others with them, believed that 1963 was the logical year for the development of such a cadre, clearly a potentially revolutionary force for a uniquely American revolution. At the 1963 SCLC convention, Wyatt T. Walker, King's executive director, declared, "The question is . . . whether we want to continue local guerilla battles, against discrimination and segregation or go to all out war." He went on, seeming to suggest an answer to his own query, all the while continuing to expand the question, the possibility:

[H]as the moment come in the . . . nonviolent revolution when we are forced . . . on some appointed day . . . literally to immobilize the nation until she acts on our pleas for justice and morality . . . is the day far off that major transportation centers would be deluged with mass acts of civil disobedience; airports, train stations, bus terminals, the traffic of large cities, interstate commerce, would be halted by the bodies of witnesses nonviolently insisting on "Freedom Now." I suppose a nationwide work stoppage might attract enough attention to persuade someone to do something to get this monkey of segregation and discrimination off our backs, once, now and forever. Will it take one or all of these?[35]

During the Birmingham demonstrations the group pressing for the development of such a nonviolent army proposed that its first action be aimed at Washington, D.C., to shut down the activities of the city until adequate civil rights legislation of many kinds was passed. Without going into the details of the transformation, it is enough to say that King allowed himself to be convinced by other more moderate black and white leaders of the civil rights coalition that such a move would be exceedingly unwise. They were convinced and were probably right that it would lose friends and anger many "neutrals" in the white community. It would certainly lose the president's supposed support for civil rights legislation specifically and racial justice generally. So, instead of a disciplined, nonviolent force—largely from the southern testing grounds—descending on Washington for an extended campaign of disruptive civil disobedience, the summer of 1963 produced the one-day, unthreatening March on Washington for Jobs and Freedom. As a result, King passed up an opportunity possibly to transform his role in the struggle, to transform the struggle itself, losing perhaps more than we can ever know. And it was not until the fiery, bloody summers of 1964–1967 had passed that he was eventually forced by the movement of his people and the larger forces of history back to the idea of an organized, national nonviolent revolutionary force. By then it would be too late—at least for *that* time.[36]

Now, it should be noted that in spite of what the March on Washington was not, it definitely was another advance in King's public recognition as a spokesperson for the black freedom movement, and together with Birmingham it was probably the major single factor in his justly deserved nomination for the Nobel Peace Prize. At the same time, within the movement, the level of diversity and disagreement over goals, strategy, tactics, allies, and spirit had increased so much that there was no way in which any one man could any longer represent that spread of ideas and directions. So the public-directed role of spokesperson was increasingly at war with the actual role King played within the movement, for the movement itself was increasingly unsure of its direction and many voices needed to be heard and tested. Meanwhile, the mainline civil rights leaders gave their major energies to work on the passage of the Civil Rights Bill, and SNCC and CORE prepared for the Mississippi Freedom Summer of 1964.[37]

All the while, King was under many pressures, making more than five hundred speeches a year in 1963–1964, traveling over 300,000 miles in that year, constantly voicing to his close friends his need for time, time, time to reflect on where we were as a people and a movement and where he was as a man, a leader, and a symbol. The deaths and sufferings in Birmingham's Sixteenth Street Church and then later in Mississippi, and the explosions that began in the northern cities in the summer of 1964 added their pressures. He had to deal increasingly with the clashing forces of white resistance and rising black militance. Regardless of what he said publicly, King had likely heard the many voices of Malcolm from the black cities of the North, understood and felt much of their relentless logic in his very sensitive soul, and so by the end of 1964 he told an interviewer from *Playboy* magazine that he himself was "militantly nonviolent" now. Accordingly, he began to try to speak more forcefully on behalf of the urban black community and all the nation's poor, calling for an alliance between blacks and poor whites to "exert massive pressure on the government to get jobs for all." Together, he said, they "could form a grand alliance." This was the end of 1964. King was being transformed, gradually attempting to transform himself at once into a spokesperson for the explosive urban black North and for all the poor people of the society. The movement was clearly enlarging itself, becoming more complex in his mind, and in America. He in turn was attempting to open and enlarge his own vision of himself to accompany that internal and external development, making as much history as he could, seeking new visions of the future to be created.[38]

The Nobel Peace Prize added another pressure and heightened another element of his vision. Almost from the outset an opponent of the American war against Vietnam, he had begun speaking out more clearly, more publicly about the need for negotiation. With the Nobel Prize, King clearly saw himself newly commissioned as a spokesperson for world peace and justice for the oppressed— especially the people of Vietnam—and he increasingly took that stand, much to the dismay of some members of his own family, his organization, some of his fellow civil rights leaders, and the president of the United States—to say nothing of J. Edgar Hoover and his minions. Still King went forward, sometimes hesitantly, but moving forward, recognizing that there was again a new time coming, perhaps already present, for the movement, for the nation, for himself, perhaps a more dangerous time than any before.[39]

So, when the march on Selma came in 1965, it was really anti-climactic. In a sense, it was the last of the traditional southern movement spectaculars. It was marked by a serious mistake in judgment and what was likely a temporary failure of nerve by King at Pettus Bridge, but that is not our point now. It was the last of its kind, the triumphal entry into Montgomery with hosts of liberal friends and supporters locking arms—with the young people yelling out:

> Oh Wallace, you never can jail us all,
> Oh Wallace, segregation's bound to fall.

They were right (as blacks in struggle have been right about so much of the reality of American life), and a new time in the movement had already begun.[40]

## VI

Fittingly enough, that new moment was symbolized right here in your tough, old, bad, violent, beautiful, new, overcoming home state of Mississippi, right on Highway 51 on the Meredith March. The issues which had been simmering, roiling the waters of the movement for a long time—sometimes pressed audaciously to the surface in the recent speeches of Adam Clayton Powell, Jr., the issues of power, the issues of racial pride, solidarity, and nationalism that had poured out anew in the North after the assassination of Malcolm X, El Hajj Malik El Shabazz; the issue of black control over the organizations of our struggle; the issue of the role of whites in the struggle; the issue of the need for black "liberation" as opposed to "integration," raised to a new level by the introduction of Frantz Fanon's *Wretched of the Earth* into the reading experience of many of the SNCC members; the concomitant rising discussion of black "revolution" as opposed to finding a place in the American status quo; the issue of the relationship between the black middle class and the masses of poor blacks, South and North; the issue of the need for the development of black leadership; the issue of sexual relations between white women and black men—all these exciting, frightening, dangerously explosive matters and many more leaped out in a compressed code from the lips of Willie Ricks of SNCC and they found their national identity in Stokely Carmichael, 24-year-old veteran of the freedom rides, of the Black Panther party in Lowndes County, Alabama, of Greenwood, Mississippi. (Always remember that Stokely at his best was no dilettante. But, like the rest of us, he was not always at his best.) *Black Power! Black Power!* Black Power had officially begun its time: June, 1966, on the road from Memphis to Jackson, cities of our music and our martyrs.[41]

Now, Martin King had been, in more ways than they ever dreamed, the best friend that white folks ever had. He was smart enough to know that and sensitive enough soon to realize that the cry for Black Power had touched deep nerves in the black and white communities. White allies had been crucial to King's vision of the movement, and some of his earliest responses to Black Power as a slogan reflected his fears about the loss of many such allies. Nevertheless, such fears did not mesmerize him (nor did they press him to join with Roy Wilkins of the NAACP and other mainstream black leaders in such public condemnations of Black Power in large *New York Times* advertisements). For King had already been changing, struggling to understand all the new movements streaking through our lives. Because he truly felt the pulse and the heartbeat of his people and was trying by then also to deal with the cold, cold heart of white power, Chicago style, Martin King knew that he had to deal with Black Power, knew that it would deal with him. He had already shifted from the strategy of nonviolence as a way to white consciences and was describing it much more as a militant, disruptive strategy and as an alternative to the urban rebellions. So during the heated public and private debates in the course of the Meredith March, King was likely much more responsive to the fervent arguments of Carmichael, Floyd McKissick, and their comrades than any of the participants immediately recognized.[42] Then, when the SCLC convention met down in Jackson later in the summer of 1966, it was clear that Martin had been listening and was trying to be on time when in his annual report he stated, "The continuing struggle for civil rights now shifts into a new phase: a struggle for power." Indeed, he attempted to equate his hero Gandhi's description of nonviolence as "an experiment with truth" with his own new sense that militant, radical nonviolence could also be "an experiment with power." That was one of his great roles, trying to stay on time, trying to be on time, trying to understand what was happening with and to his people, with and to the oppressed of this nation and the world and then trying to move on time.[43]

It was no easy task. Indeed, at many points in the fall and winter of 1966–1967, after another summer of urban rebellions, as the fierce debate over Black Power raged, as he recognized the essential failure of his heroic/quixotic foray into Chicago, as the war in Vietnam continued to expand, as white anger mounted and black criticism of his positions grew more strident, King seemed at times like a great, courageous, but deeply perplexed

captain, trying desperately to control a ship that was being rocked
by mutinies from within and raging storms from without.

Yet, the truth of that perilous time was even more difficult. For
by then there was no longer any one entity—even symbolically
speaking—which could be called the Black Freedom movement
and which Martin could really lead. Indeed, the very internal
power of the movement that he had done so much to create and
focus, that had shaped and molded him, had now broken out in
many new directions, reviving, inspiring a plethora of older
black—and white—traditions. Now, for instance, a militant, sometimes militaristic nationalism was sweeping the northern cities, at
once a revival of earlier black American movements, and at the
same time linking itself to the liberation struggles of nonwhite
men and women across the globe. Talk of "urban rebellions" had
now replaced the idea of "riots," and there was active, serious
discussion in various quarters concerning the coming "black revolution," concerning the struggle for "black liberation" in America.[44]

Meanwhile, in spite of presidential declarations of a "war on
poverty," and hastily organized, often ill-conceived "anti-poverty"
programs, it was clear to King and many other black people that
this was not really the quintessential American response to black
needs and demands. Rather, it seemed more likely that the federal
troops and their armored equipment sweeping through the black
communities, the helicopters with their floodlights, the national
military alerts, and the intelligence agencies' infiltration of black
organizations were at least as descriptive of the federal government's real responses towards black aspirations as any other programs coming out of Washington.

It was impossible for King—or any other single individual—to
understand, much less command all the tendencies now set loose
in the black communities of the land. (Of course, he knew that he
was being falsely identified as an "Uncle Tom" by many northern
black rhetoreticians of revolution who had never once risked their
lives as King had done so many times in the cause of his people's

freedom.) At the same time, Martin was trying to understand where the real, critical centers of power lay in American society, trying to understand how he could tackle the powerful forces that supported war, racism, poverty, and the internal subversion of the freedom movement's many parts.

VII

No easy task. Still King seemed convinced that he would be unfaithful to the history he had already made with others, untrue to his forebears and his children in the struggle for justice, unless he followed what appeared to be the logic of the movement. For him, that logic, that history, that sense of integrity pressed him toward a more radical challenge than he had ever mounted before, one that would leave him more naked to his enemies than ever before. Very little that he had learned in all the dangerous campaigns of the South had prepared him for the task of striking toward the heart of America's real political, economic, and social structures of oppression, exploitation, and greed. Not even the bitter Chicago experience had been lived with long enough to help him build the kind of analysis, organization, and strategy that were needed. Yet, moving as much as anything else on the power of his deep sense of compassion and courage, he determined to go in that direction, tried to fashion a two-pronged attack on the center of America's foreign and domestic policies of repression, cooptation, and dehumanization. He had concluded that there could be no black freedom, no true freedom for anyone without such a challenge being raised, and he knew that he could no longer assume that the federal government would even be a reluctant ally. No, that government and its policies were now the prime target.[45]

First, King decided to try to respond fully to the unspeakable agony, the terrible crime of Vietnam, defying all his critics and many of his friends, from the White House to members of his own organization and his own family. On April 4, 1967, at Riverside Church in New York City, the struggling leader-searcher addressed a major meeting sponsored by Clergy and Laymen Concerned About Vietnam. Near the beginning of his vibrant presentation, King admitted that he had not spoken clearly and early enough, but vowed that he would never make that mistake again. Justifying the connection he saw among the struggles for equal rights and economic justice in America and the demand for an end to American military involvement in Vietnam, King placed them all within the context of his commission as a minister of Jesus Christ and a Nobel Peace Prize laureate. Unflinchingly, he identified America as the essential aggressor in the war and called his nation "the greatest purveyor of violence in the world."

Attempting to give voice to the many millions of the voiceless of the world whose "movement" towards freedom he now felt he was representing, Martin called to the American nation, to President Lyndon Johnson, to men and women everywhere and said,

Somehow this madness must cease. We must stop now. I speak as a child of God and brother to the suffering poor of Vietnam. I speak for those whose land is being laid waste, whose homes are being destroyed, whose culture is being subverted. I speak for the poor of America who are paying the double price of smashed hopes at home and death and corruption in Vietnam. I speak as a citizen of the world, for the world as it stands aghast at the path we have taken. I speak as an American to the leaders of my own nation. The great initiative in this war is ours. The initiative to stop it must be ours.[46]

The black struggle for freedom had served to inspirit and inspire the rapidly mounting American antiwar movement. Now King was urgently placing himself into the center of this force that he had helped to create, calling for conscientious objection, even draft resistance, following the earlier examples of such SNCC leaders as Bob Moses, Jim Forman, and Stokely Carmichael, as well as James and Diane Bevel of his own staff. But King was still ahead of most of SCLC, its board and its staff, and some persons within his organization were seriously opposed to so forceful a move into the anti–Vietnam war arena. Indeed, this was one of Martin's major difficulties through much of the post-1965 period: the vision that he was trying to fashion, the history he was trying to make, was often beyond the capacities, the aspirations, the politics, and the imagination of most of the men and women who made up SCLC, his only real organizational base.[47]

At the same time, of course, as head of the organization, he had to accept at least some of the blame for its political backwardness. Still, King drove forward, was driven forward by all the explosive forces around him, by all the history he had helped to make, and soon he turned from Riverside Church to forge the second prong of his militant challenge to white American power. In the summer of 1967, after two of the decade's most deadly urban uprisings—in Newark and Detroit—had stunned the nation, after a national Black Power convention had done much to stamp that variously defined slogan in the minds of black folk everywhere, King announced his plans for a major attack on America's internal structures of inequality and injustice.

On August 16, 1967, the *New York Times* carried a story from SCLC's tenth annual convention in Atlanta, a story that began, "The Rev. Martin Luther King, Jr. said today that he planned to 'dislocate' Northern cities with massive but nonviolent demonstrations of civil disobedience before Congress adjourns its current session." According to the reporter, Martin had said that "he had decided on the step to provide an alternative to rioting and to gain large federal spending for impoverished Negroes."

It was a version of the nonviolent army again, now surfacing at a far more volatile, confused, and dangerous moment in the nation's history and in King's own career. There was much unclarity and disagreement within the ranks of SCLC and among the many-faceted freedom movement organizations, but by the end of 1967, King and his staff had again decided to focus this potentially revolutionary challenge in Washington, D.C., fully aware of the ugly, angry, and unreceptive mood at work in the White House and elsewhere.[48]

At his radical best, King was determined to press the logic of his position, the movement of his people's history. Having attacked the nation's antiliberationist overseas actions, he now intended to move on the heart of the government, demanding a response to the suffering of its own semicolonized peoples. (Nor was King paving a way of welcome for his move by saying late in 1967: "I am not sad that black Americans are rebelling; this was not only inevitable but eminently desirable. Without this magnificent ferment among Negroes, the old evasions and procrastinations would have continued indefinitely." He was not paving a way, but he was indicating his own way, his own movement in the vortex of "this magnificent ferment."[49])

Martin was trying to be on time, trying to be faithful, trying to go forward, to create whatever openings towards the future that he could. Jamming his life against the advice of many of his black and white movement supporters, defying the angry warnings of Lyndon Johnson, King searched for his new role, for the new role of his people. In an America that seemed at times on the edge of armed racial warfare, an America increasingly torn over the Vietnam war, an America unresponsive to the deepest needs of its own people, especially its poor—in the midst of this history King was desperately searching for the connections with his past, for the openings to his and our future.

By December, 1967, Martin had at least temporarily taken his new powerful and dangerous position. In a series of broadcasts for Canadian public radio, he said, "Negroes . . . must not only formulate a program; they must fashion new tactics which do not count on government goodwill." Instead he said the new tactics must be those which are forceful enough *to compel unwilling authorities to yield to the mandates of justice.* But here at the end, at the beginning of the end, in his last major published document, King was not talking about blacks alone. The movement had grown; there was no way to "overcome" without taking on much more than we had ever taken on before. Thus he said,

The dispossessed of this nation—the poor, both white and Negro —live in a cruelly unjust society. *They must organize a revolution against that injustice,* not against the lives of the persons who are their fellow citizens, but against the structures through which the society is refusing to take means which have been called for, and which are at hand, to lift the load of poverty.[50]

Martin King was talking about a nonviolent revolution in America, to transform the entire society on behalf of its poorest people, for the sake of us all. Martin King was moving towards an experiment with truth *and* power, and he was calling for three thousand persons to join him for three months of intensive training to begin that revolution at the seat of America's political power, Washington, D.C. Martin King was shaping a new role for himself, leader of a nonviolent revolutionary army/movement, one which he also saw connecting with the oppressed peoples of other nations.

For some time he had been talking about the need for "a revolution of values" within America which would deal with the needs of our own exploited and dehumanized peoples and place us at the side of all men and women struggling for justice and liberation throughout the world. Now, at the end, at the beginning, the words were clearer, sharper, harsher, no longer the vague "revolution of values." Martin King, who had begun twelve years before as the spokesman for a people who wanted to be treated with dignity on a segregated city bus, was now calling for nonviolent revolution against all the "structures" of injustice in America. He had declared nonviolent war against all the political, economic, and social structures that denied dignity, hope, and the opportunities for the fullest self-development to all the black, white, red, and brown brothers and sisters of those early pilgrims towards freedom in Montgomery. Although the seed for such a development was present in every fundamental black challenge to the racist powers of the society, surely no one in Montgomery—including Martin Luther King, Jr.—ever imagined that a dozen years later the history they and others had made, the future which their opponents had fought to deny, would now lead King to call for nonviolent revolution in America.[51]

In 1967, no one, including King, really knew what such a revolution would mean, how it would really be organized and mounted, what its concrete, programmatic goals might be; but he was determined to move forward. At Riverside Church, precisely one year before his assassination, Martin had proclaimed the fullness of time, declaring, "Now let us begin. Now let us re-dedicate ourselves to the long and bitter—but beautiful—struggle for a new world. . . . The choice is ours, and though we might prefer it otherwise, we *must* choose in this crucial moment of human history."[52]

For him, the nonviolent army of revolution was his own choice, his own contribution to the worldwide struggle of the oppressed. Here, again, almost no one on his staff was ready for this, ready to move directly against the ruthless, brutal power of white America's most deeply vested military, political, economic, and racial self-interests. Unclear, often afraid, everyone, including Martin, tended to drag their feet through the winter of 1967–1968, the winter of preparation. All the while, they were taking harsh criticisms on every hand, palpably sensing the dangers of this new more radical direction mounting all around them, dangers from within and without.

Perhaps Martin King had seen and felt more than he was able to accomplish. Perhaps he could not ever be ready for this new role. Perhaps in the violent climate of America, it was impossible to be ready for such a campaign of revolutionary, nonviolent civil disobedience without an organization that was fully prepared for all the dangers, all the opportunities, and all the long, hard, preparatory work. SCLC was not that organization. Nevertheless, ready or not, King appeared to be trying to get ready—facing toward Washington, D.C.[53]

But first there were garbage collectors to help in Memphis, and there were powerful forces at every level of American society who were determined that Martin Luther King would never be ready for the kind of revolution he had now announced. As a result, Martin never made it to Washington, never found out if he was ready or not.

VIII

When the word of his death was flashed to the black communities of America, they sent up their requiem screams of anguish and rage. When they heard that the King was dead they lighted great fires everywhere, especially in Washington. Were these simply continuations of the long, hot summers, the burning of the dream? Were they no more than angry, flaming protestations? Were they funeral pyres for the King, for the hope, for the dream? Or were they, possibly, just possibly, torches, torches of continuing hope, searching for a way to the future, a way to that future that Martin King did not have a chance to make?[54]

If they were flaming searchlights, then after the fires, after the screams, the search seemed to be dramatically intensified. All the tendencies towards inner and outer rebellion, towards black questioning of America's very nature, towards the search for black identity, all the outrage and the passion were poured into a thousand projects, conferences, caucuses, organizations, in countless strident demands upon existing institutions. (And all the attempts at official subversion were also intensified, of course.) Black students, black welfare mothers, black preachers, black lawyers, black policemen, black congressmen, black psychologists, black priests and nuns, black elected officials—all these and many more were driven toward each other, at least temporarily, seeking to touch, to hold and to organize and make demands as never before. For a while, a powerful thrust of solidarity seemed to pull together many who had been fragmented, seemed to energize others who had been apathetic.[55]

At the same time, over the years immediately following King's death, many other diverse persons and groups had taken up the torches, searching for their own new way. The revived force of the black movement helped stimulate new groupings and revitalize older ones in the women's movement, among Native Americans, Chicanos, Latinos, and white ethnics. The various splintered Marxist movements in America gained new courage and new converts. The homosexuals formed a "liberation" movement. The prisoners across the country (mostly black, of course) fought for rights long denied them, fought and died, with Attica, 1971, as the symbol of all these struggles for new levels of freedom, justice, and dignity behind prison bars. Meanwhile, the antiwar movement grew in force and breadth; draft resistance became almost respectable. Then after terrible final crimes of destruction, American forces were finally pushed and pulled out of Vietnam, ending at an embassy wall, with one last mad, American-like scramble of each man and woman for themselves, seeking to escape the judgment of history. Later, across the globe in South Africa, the children of Soweto, inspired by the children of Malcolm and Martin, raised their fists in defiance and hope, were beaten and shot down, but will rise again, with the judgment of history.[56]

Martin King was part of it all. He had helped to create this history, in his life and in his death. Indeed, it is likely fair to say that this man who grew from a spokesperson for his people's search for simple dignity in a medium-sized southern city to become a giant symbol of the search for justice across the globe— this man, with all his weaknesses, all his flaws, all his blindspots and all of his creative, courageous greatness, made all the history he could make. Perhaps of even more importance to us here and now, we are able to see that he helped force open the way to the possibility of a new vision, a second coming of America, an America in which justice, compassion, and humanity prevail.

Now, largely as a result of the movement King represented, as a result of the significant developments since his death, the old

America has been cracked, wedged open, cannot be the same again. Now, the forces which were absent from the first official beginning of America, in the days following July 4, 1776—the blacks, the women, the Native Americans, the Chicanos, the students, and many more—all who were then pressed aside are now present, are all more aware of themselves, of ourselves, than ever before. King helped create the possibility that all of us might break beyond our own individual and group interests and catch a vision of a new America, create a vision of a new common good in a new future which will serve us all. He saw that our needs were economic *and* spiritual, political *and* moral, social *and* personal, and as the end, the beginning approached, he was groping his way towards a new integration—one that had very little to do with the legalities of *Brown* v. *The Board of Education.*

But in the midst of this struggle, this groping, this searching, King learned some things, and the message he left was the message he had learned, the message he had been given by the earlier generations of our freedom-striving people: Freedom is a constant struggle. The message he left was that a new America cannot be created without an even more difficult, radical, and dangerous struggle than we have known up to now. The message he left is that black people can no longer make any separate peace with America, that our needs are the needs of other millions of Americans, that the entire society must be challenged with the force of revolutionary change in all its political, economic, social, and psychic structures.

The message he left for those who would create a new future was that we cannot find the jobs we need, we cannot find the education we need, we cannot find the health care we need, we cannot find the physical and psychic security and development we need, we cannot find the creative male-female relationships we need, we cannot build the mutually nurturing relationships to our environment that we need, we cannot create the nonexploitative relationships to the raw-producers of the world we need, we cannot develop the fraternity with the freedom-lovers everywhere we need—we cannot find/create these things in an America as it is presently structured, in an America that makes financial profits and personal prestige "the bottom line."

Thus, like King, we must be driven, we must press forward towards revolutionary transformation of ourselves and of our nation, for the good of all its people. The bottom line must become compassion and the attention to human needs, which has no bottom, no end. The message he left, then, was that for all who would create a future which is at once worthy of our past struggles and capable of moving us far beyond those struggles, we must be prepared to move forward as never before. And this time, I am sure he would urge us to know that we cannot wait for a messiah, not even a black one. No, only many groupings of serious, disciplined, organized, and self-confident men, women, and children can bring about the transformation that we now need.

At Riverside Church he called us: "Now let us rededicate ourselves to the long and bitter—but beautiful—struggle for a new world." Closely examined, we realize that King's Riverside statement is no different than the last testament of Frantz Fanon, especially if we substitute King's America for Fanon's Europe:

Humanity is waiting for something other from us than . . . imitation. . . . if we want humanity to advance a step further, if we want to bring it up to a different level than that which [America] has shown it, then we must invent and we must make discoveries. . . . For [America], for ourselves and for humanity, comrades, we must turn over a new leaf, we must work out new concepts, and try to set afoot a new [being].[57]

Yes, that is essentially the message King left as he made all the history he could, as he opened the future for us to make, to remake. Serve the people. Serve humanity. Let the oppressed go free. Let America be born again. A wild and visionary set of ideas, of course; but our struggle for freedom, like all struggles for freedom, has been wild and visionary from the very beginning. (Remember, once it was wild and visionary to believe that such words as these would ever be spoken at the University of Mississippi and published by its press!)

So I am not afraid to be wild and visionary, with Martin, brother, comrade, and friend. And I dare with him to believe, to hope, to risk the charge of madness and supersubjectivity. Indeed, I dare to believe that somewhere, perhaps everywhere, Martin and Chairman Mao, Martin and Malcolm, Martin and Fanon, Martin and Fannie Lou, Martin and Medgar, Martin and A. J. Muste, Martin and Tom Merton, Martin and Emma Goldman, Martin and Clarence Jordan, Martin and Ida B. Wells-Barnett, Martin and Slater King, Martin and Ralph Featherstone, Martin and Ruby Doris Smith, Martin and Bertha Gober, Martin and all those folks and many more, indeed Martin and Jesus of Nazareth—all of them, I believe all of them, somewhere, perhaps everywhere, are having a grand time discovering, rediscovering themselves, each other, moving ever more deeply into that ultimate, overwhelming light of freedom out of which we all came. And I dare to believe that they are hoping for us, hoping that we will find again, within ourselves, that we will dredge out from all its dark and hidden places, that infinite capacity to hope and struggle which is stored up like a great light within us all.

I dare to believe that they are hoping that *we* will dare to believe that we can do the impossible, that we will, that we can make America a new society for all its people. I dare to believe that they are hoping for us, believing that we can, that we shall continue overcoming—overcoming today, overcoming tomorrow, overcoming the fears, overcoming the complacency, overcoming the desire for nothing more than security and safety. I dare to believe that Martin is hoping, knowing that the power to continue overcoming is within us as it was within him, within all of them, wherever they are. And I dare to believe that Bertha is still singing her song, somewhere, everywhere, still singing our song, our

special Mississippi song, our American song, our worldwide song,
for us, for them, for everyone:

> We've been 'buked and we've been scorned,
> We've been talked about, sure as you're born.
> But we'll never turn back, no,
>   we'll never turn back,
> Until we've all been freed and
>   we have equality.

# Education and Earnings of Blacks and the *Brown* Decision

HENRY M. LEVIN

## Introduction

In May, 1954, the U.S. Supreme Court handed down its well-known decision in the case of *Brown* v. *Board of Education*.[1] That decision declared that segregated schools are inherently unequal and that when racial segregation results from state laws, those laws are unconstitutional and must be struck down. Since that date, scholars have taken a great interest in the consequences and meaning of *Brown*. In particular, *Brown* has stimulated numerous studies of the extent and process of desegregation,[2] of the impact of desegregation on scholastic achievement and attitudes and on migration,[3] of the role of social science evidence in the judicial process,[4] and of the limits or potential of the courts to serve as an agent of social change.[5]

In contrast there has been much less attention devoted to the impact of *Brown* on improving more generally the educational and economic attainments of black Americans. This is somewhat surprising because the Court argued:

Today, education is perhaps the most important function of state and local governments. Compulsory school attendance laws and the great expenditures for education both demonstrate our recognition of the importance of education in our democratic society. It is required in the performance of our most basic public responsibilities, even service in the armed forces. It is the very foundation of good citizenship. Today it is the principal instrument in awakening the child to cultural values, in preparing him for later professional training, and in helping him to adjust normally to his environment. In these days, it is doubtful that any child may reasonably be expected to succeed in life if he is denied the opportunity of an education. Such an opportunity, where the state has undertaken to provide it, is a right which must be made available to all on equal terms.

Presumably the Court was assuming that a movement toward greater equality in the educational setting between blacks and whites would initiate a process of equalization in life chances for success between the two groups. Certainly, if *Brown* improved the quality of schooling for blacks relative to whites, it might reasonably be expected that the relative occupational achievements and earnings of blacks would also improve.

But *Brown* did much more than this. *Brown* set the stage for the ensuing rise in black political activism, for legal challenges to racial discrimination in voting, employment, and education, as well as for the creation of a favorable climate for the passage of the subsequent civil rights legislation and the initiation of the War on Poverty. Perhaps even more noteworthy was the role that *Brown* played in creating the overall legitimacy of the black cause, with major changes occurring in the attitudes of both black and white Americans and in the racial conduct of our institutional life. While the narrower effects of *Brown* on economic equity might be addressed through an analysis of the extent and effects of school desegregation on the earnings of the races, such a picture would be very incomplete. Rather, it is necessary to explore the broader impact of *Brown* on the very climate of race relations and its impetus in setting in motion a wider range of social and political movements in behalf of black Americans. To the degree that these broader effects have shaped both the provision of education and the translation of education and other factors into economic results, it is likely that they had had an effect considerably broader than school desegregation.

In the following pages we will examine the possible impact of *Brown* on the relative educational and economic status of black Americans. First, we will examine racial differences in education from the pre-*Brown* period to the present. Second, we will inspect the changes in earnings differentials between whites and blacks. Third, we will attempt to evaluate alternative explanations for the black-white trends in education and earnings. In the final sections we will examine the impact of *Brown* from a more general perspective in order to speculate on its possible effects beyond those associated only with alterations of the racial composition of schools. In general, it will be argued that the role of *Brown* in improving the educational, economic, and political status of black Americans can only be understood within this larger framework.

## Racial Differences in Educational Attainments

Before it is possible to speculate on the impact of *Brown* on changes in the relative educational patterns and earnings of blacks and whites, it is necessary to establish the nature of those patterns. The purpose of this section is to provide a brief historical picture of changes in educational attainments according to race. The next section will provide a parallel presentation for earnings. Many of the data that will be presented will refer only to males of each race. The reason for this restriction is due to the regularity of male labor market behavior over the life cycle in contrast with that of females. Differences in behavior between the races among females with respect to their labor force participation tend to inhibit a useful comparison of relative earnings. However, it should be noted that the restriction of the analysis to males is attributible only to this criterion of practicality. Applying a similar analysis to females would encounter a number of obstacles that would require the establishment of controversial and highly arbitrary assumptions to provide comparability.

YEARS OF SCHOOLING COMPLETED.[6] One of the most important measures of educational attainment is the number of years of schooling completed. It is useful to examine the patterns for this measure of educational attainment at different points in history. Table 1 shows the estimated years of schooling for U.S.

TABLE 1   Estimated Years of Schooling of U.S. Males by Year of Birth, 1973

| Year of Birth | Age in 1973 | Black | Other (excluding hispanics) | Difference |
|---|---|---|---|---|
| 1947–1951 | 22–26 | 11.9 | 13.0 | 1.1 |
| 1937–1946 | 27–36 | 11.4 | 12.9 | 1.5 |
| 1927–1936 | 37–46 | 10.1 | 12.2 | 2.1 |
| 1917–1926 | 47–56 | 8.6 | 11.6 | 3.0 |
| 1907–1916 | 57–66 | 7.1 | 10.6 | 3.5 |

SOURCE: Hauser and Featherman, "Equality of Schooling: Trends and Prospects," 110.

males, by year of birth, for 1973. In this table, a comparison is made between blacks and a category called "other" males, excluding hispanics. The latter category does include some nonblack and nonhispanic minorities, but it is overwhelmingly white (probably over 95 percent). Thus, the comparison between the black and the "other" group in Table 1 can be thought of as a black-white comparison. The classification according to year of birth enables us to view the differences in education among persons of different ages, so that we can observe the historical differences in schooling completed between the two racial groupings among their surviving members.

Two very important patterns emerge from these data. First, there seems to be a rather pronounced convergence in educational attainments between the races among young males relative to older ones. While younger members of both groups have experienced increases in schooling in comparison with their older counterparts, the difference in the average amount of schooling between races has declined from about 3.5 years in the oldest group to slightly more than one year in the youngest. That is, younger black and white males tend to look more alike in terms of their average amount of schooling than older ones. This leads to the second conclusion, that even among younger males there is still a substantial difference in educational attainments. To get some idea of the magnitude of the difference, black males in their midtwenties have about the same level of education as "other" males in their midforties. Stated another way, young blacks in 1973 were obtaining about the same amount of schooling as young whites had obtained some two decades before.

The same type of convergence is observed when we examine estimates of the amount of schooling completed at the time of labor market entry as shown in Table 2. As we would expect,

TABLE 2  Years of School Completed at Estimated Time of Labor Market Entry, for Males, 1930–1970

| Item | Year of Labor Market Entry | | | | |
|---|---|---|---|---|---|
| | 1930 | 1940 | 1950 | 1960 | 1970 |
| Mean schooling of blacks | 5.9 | 8.0 | 9.9 | 11.1 | 11.4 |
| Mean schooling of whites | 9.6 | 11.1 | 12.0 | 12.6 | 12.6 |
| Proportion of blacks with less than 9 years of school | .78 | .58 | .31 | .15 | .11 |
| Proportion of whites with less than 9 years of school | .42 | .22 | .15 | .10 | .07 |
| Proportion of blacks with more than 12 years of school | .03 | .07 | .13 | .19 | .19 |
| Proportion of whites with more than 12 years of school | .08 | .20 | .32 | .37 | .38 |

SOURCE: Smith and Welch, *Race Differences in Earnings: A Survey and New Evidence*, 10.

some persons who enter the labor market have not completed their schooling, a factor that probably explains the relatively lower values for comparably aged males in Table 2 in comparison with those in Table 1. Again, we observe a converging pattern of attainments over the period of analysis, with both groups increasing their schooling at the time of labor market entry. While the average schooling of white labor market entrants was more than 3.5 years greater than for their black counterparts in 1930, the difference had declined to little more than a year by 1970. However, even in 1970 the average amount of schooling completed by black labor market entrants was only slightly better than that of whites entering the labor market in 1940. Further, although about 38 percent of white labor market entrants had achieved more than twelve years of schooling in 1970, only 19 percent of blacks had achieved this level. Thus, the black figure for 1970 had risen only as high as the proportion of whites with twelve years or more of schooling for 1940.

In at least one respect the gap between blacks and whites has not narrowed in recent years. The proportion of the black population 25–34 years of age who completed at least four years of college rose from about 4.1 percent in 1960 to about 8.1 percent in 1974. However, the comparable figures for whites in the same age group were 11.9 percent in 1960 and 21 percent in 1974.[7] These changes in college completion rates between the two races meant that the white advantage rose from about eight percentage points in 1960 to about a thirteen percentage point difference by 1974.

But, in general, the data suggest that both black and white educational attainments have risen, with average black attainments improving at a faster rate than white ones. The result of these trends has been a rather constant diminution of the black-white educational gap. This convergence in educational attainments between the races should not make us lose sight of the fact that the average amount of schooling completed by blacks is still at that level completed by whites some two or three decades ago.

EQUALITY OF THE SCHOOLING EXPERIENCE. A major concern of *Brown* was the inequality of schooling experiences between blacks and whites. Presumably differences in the quality of schooling affect life chances in two ways. First, higher quality educational experiences could lead to the attainment of more schooling if those experiences improve the preparation of students for being admitted to and succeeding in subsequent levels of schooling. Second, better quality schooling could improve the preparation of students for employment and other postschooling opportunities at each level of education. That is, it is reasonable to believe that better schools increase cognitive skills and inculcate values and attitudes that are associated with higher occupational and economic attainments.

While it is not possible to explore directly the quality of the schooling experience between blacks and whites over the historical past because of a lack of data, it is possible to compare the schools that blacks and whites attended according to certain characteristics that are thought to be important educationally.[8] For example, Table 3 compares the average amount of instruction for each year of schooling by examining the length of the school year and the attendance rates of pupils by race. Up until 1953–1954, the data are divided according to "black schools" and "all schools." The black schools are those which were segregated in the dual school systems of the South. For the year 1965–1966 the data are taken from the landmark survey of *Equality of Educational Opportunity*, more commonly known as the Coleman Report.[9] These data correspond to the characteristics of schools attended by the average white or average black elementary school pupil in the sample, regardless of the racial composition of the school attended.

It is very clear that up until about 1950, the black schools had substantially shorter annual sessions than did schools as a whole

TABLE 3 School Term and Attendance for Black and White Students, 1919–1955

| | 1919–20 | 1929–30 | 1939–40 | 1949–50 | 1953–54 | 1965–66 |
|---|---|---|---|---|---|---|
| **Average Number of Days Schools in Session** | | | | | | |
| a) Black schools | 119 | 132 | 156 | 173 | 177 | — |
| b) All schools | 162 | 173 | 175 | 178 | 179 | — |
| c) Elementary schools attended by average black | — | — | — | — | — | 180 |
| d) Elementary schools attended by average white | — | — | — | — | — | 179 |
| **Percent of Pupils in Average Daily Attendance** | | | | | | |
| a) Black schools | 67 | 72 | 80 | 85 | 85 | — |
| b) All schools | 75 | 83 | 87 | 89 | 89 | — |
| c) Schools attended by average black | — | — | — | — | — | 93 |
| d) Schools attended by average white | — | — | — | — | — | 95 |

SOURCE: Compiled by Welch, "Black-White Returns to Schooling," 900 from various issues of U.S. Department of Health, Education, and Welfare, *Biennial Survey of Education* for 1919–20 to 1953–54. Data for 1965–66 are taken from Coleman, *et al.*, *Equality of Educational Opportunity,* Supplemental Appendix, 1966.

in the United States. To a large degree this pattern conformed with the needs for black farm labor and the length of the growing season in the rural South. As blacks moved from rural to urban areas and as the states standardized the length of the school session, the two patterns tended to converge. The 1949–1954 period shows little difference between races on this measure, and the 1965–1966 Coleman data are almost identical for the two groups. A similar convergence is found for the rate of attendance for white and black students. The percentage of students in average daily attendance rose for both groups, with a more rapid rise for black students and a tendency toward convergence. Although there was an eight to eleven percentage point difference in this measure in favor of whites in the 1920–1930 data, there was only a two percentage point difference in 1965–1966 with attendance rates having risen for both groups substantially.

The convergence of schooling characteristics is also evident in an examination of patterns of remuneration of instructional staff and of instructional expenditures in Table 4. The early salary data suggest that teachers in segregated black schools were receiving considerably lower salaries than those in southern white schools. By 1965–1966, the Coleman data suggest, salary levels of instructional staff in the South and for the country as a whole were similar between schools attended by the average white and black student.

Since much of the difference in school expenditures is determined by salary levels, it is not surprising to find that school expenditures followed a similar pattern, particularly for schools in the South. In 1931–1932 the average per-pupil expenditure in black schools was only about one-third of that of southern white schools, and even the latter was only about one-half the national average. By the time of the *Brown* decision, the average per-pupil expenditure in black schools had risen to about 60 percent of that in southern white schools, and the expenditure in the latter schools was about two-thirds of the national average. According to the

TABLE 4   Average Instructional Salaries and Expenditures for Negro and White Students, 1919–1966

| | 1919–20 | 1929–30 | 1939–40 | 1949–50 | 1953–54 | 1965–66[c] |
|---|---|---|---|---|---|---|
| **Average Salary Per Instructional Staff Member** | | | | | | |
| a) Black schools | $ — | $ — | $ 601 | $ 2143 | $ 2861 | — |
| b) Southern white schools | — | — | 1046 | — | 3384 | — |
| c) All schools | 871 | 1420 | 1441 | 3010 | 3285 | — |
| d) Average black student in South | — | — | — | — | — | $ 5221 |
| e) Average white student in South | — | — | — | — | — | 5053 |
| f) Average black student | — | — | — | — | — | 6121 |
| g) Average white student | — | — | — | — | — | 6155 |
| **Current Expenditure Per Pupil in Average Daily Attendance** | | | | | | |
| a) Black schools | $ — | $ 15[a] | $ 19 | $ — | $ 110[b] | — |
| b) Southern white schools | — | 49[a] | 59 | — | 181[b] | — |
| c) All schools | — | 87 | 88 | 209 | 265 | — |
| d) Average black student in South | — | — | — | — | — | $ 293 |
| e) Average white student in South | — | — | — | — | — | 287 |
| f) Average black student | — | — | — | — | — | 386 |
| g) Average white student | — | — | — | — | — | 427 |

[a] Refers to 1931–1932.   [b] Instructional expenses only.   [c] Elementary level.

SOURCE: Compiled by Welch "Black-White Returns to Schooling," 900 from various issues of U.S. Department of Health, Education and Welfare, *Biennial Survey of Education* for 1919–20 to 1953–54. Data for 1965–66 are taken

Coleman data, the average current educational expenditures for black students in elementary schools in the South had risen to about the same level as that for whites by 1965–1966. There was still a difference in favor of whites, though, on a national level.

That lower instructional salaries and expenditures for black pupils were translated into poorer quality educational services is documented by Horace Mann Bond and others. Bond reported on the rather dismal educational provisions that blacks faced in the 1930s. The data collected by Bond and those available from other sources are consistent in showing that black schools typically had poorer physical plants, fewer staff relative to enrollments, inadequate instructional materials, and less-qualified teachers than did the white schools. For example, while about 60 percent of teachers in the white schools of the South had at least four years of college in 1939–1940, only about one-third of teachers in the black schools had this level of preparation. In Mississippi the disparity was greater with 62 percent for the white schools and 9 percent for the black ones.[10]

The pattern of educational resources between schools serving blacks and whites seems to have been one of large divergences in favor of whites up to the thirties, with a rapid convergence towards equality by the fifties and sixties. Whether the tendency toward equality suggested by the Coleman data is accurate is a matter of some controversy. For example, the Coleman data for school expenditures have been questioned because they are based on school district averages that mask differences among schools within a district.[11] To the degree that higher salaried teachers and more of other resources were being allocated to those schools with predominantly white enrollments within school districts, the school district averages would not uncover the true inequalities favoring white students. Studies of intradistrict school resource allocation in Chicago and in Washington, D.C., in the sixties found that expenditures were higher in schools attended by whites.[12] Further, an extensive reanalysis of Coleman data for the large cities found that the per-pupil expenditures on teachers' salaries were directly related to the proportion of whites enrolled in the school.[13]

Nevertheless, a large number of resources in the Coleman study were measured on a school-by-school basis, and most of these suggest a general parity between schools attended by whites and blacks. With the possible exception of teacher race and teacher verbal score, there did not appear to be significant differences in resources in the original Coleman analysis or in the subsequent reanalysis.[14] However, there may still have existed important differences in school expenditures favoring whites within large cities, and on a national basis the Coleman data suggest that school expenditures for the average white student exceeded those of the average black student by about 10 percent.

There have been no systematic studies of school characteristics, by race, that would enable us to ascertain what has happened in the last decade. Since 1965–1966, the Elementary and Secondary Education Act has provided compensatory education expenditures for children from low-income backgrounds, and the states have provided such programs too. These programs would likely have an equalizing effect on educational expenditures between blacks and whites, because a higher proportion of black students are from families that meet the criteria for eligibility. However, there is considerable evidence that local school districts have substituted compensatory educational funds in place of support that would have been provided from state and local sources.[15] Thus, the degree of equalization or even the possibility of higher spending for blacks for such funding is not possible to ascertain. Many of the states have been pressed by the courts to provide fairer systems of state educational finance among districts.[16] To the degree that higher proportions of blacks live in those districts that will benefit most from the new arrangements, there may be a recent tendency towards greater parity for black students. Finally, the general diffusion of black college students from the traditional black colleges to a broader range of colleges and universities has probably had the effect of improving the quality of instruction for black college students in the last fifteen years. The majority of the black colleges were struggling and underfinanced alternatives to the white-segregated systems of higher education that typified the South and border states.[17] While they served a very important and heroic role in providing postsecondary opportunities for black youth who were neglected by other institutions, their material poverty has been a tremendous handicap in providing first-rate instructional opportunities.[18]

A final indicator of the quality of the schooling experience for blacks is the degree to which their education has taken place in a desegregated environment.

The historical pattern of school segregation and desegregation for the United States has really been two different patterns, one for the North and one for the South. At the time of the *Brown* decision, laws of some seventeen southern and border states as well as the District of Columbia required segregated schools. Until the end of World War II a number of other states practiced school segregation as well. In the decade following *Brown*, very little progress was made in the South towards desegregation. The Supreme Court did not rule on how desegregation was to be implemented until the second *Brown* decision in 1955. That edict declared that desegregation should take place under the jurisdiction of federal district courts "with all deliberate speed," and it permitted delays if local school boards could "establish that such time is necessary in the public interest."[19]

Even without this basis for delay, the states and local school districts that were affected by *Brown* tried all kinds of ploys and circumventions to avoid the implementation of *Brown*. The decade from 1954 to 1964 was a decade of recalcitrance and noncompliance by southern school authorities, with the greatest resistance in the states of the Deep South. In 1964, only about 9 percent of the 3.4 million students in the southern and border states were attending desegregated schools, and only 1.2 percent of the students in the eleven states of the South were enrolled in desegregated schools.[20] By 1968 the situation had improved substantially, as reflected in Table 5, which shows the racial composition for schools attended by blacks from 1968–1972. In 1968, some 18 percent of black pupils in the South were in such schools.

In contrast, the post-1954 years saw the development increasingly in the North and West of migration patterns of whites from central cities to suburbs and blacks from the rural South to the cities of the North and South. These migration patterns created heavy concentrations of blacks and other minorities in the northern cities, so that the enrollments of the large city schools began to reflect these racial compositions. Further, often blacks resided in "ghettos" far removed from the white areas of the cities and school districts, so that neighborhood schools were far more segregated than even the overall composition of population might reflect. For 1965 the Coleman survey found that the average black sixth-grader was in a school in which over three-quarters of the students were black.[21]

Moreover, the tendency towards greater racial concentration in the schools of the North was portended by a continuing outflow of whites from the cities, partially a response to efforts made to desegregate the city schools through busing and the use of other approaches.[22] As Table 5 indicates, in 1968 only about 28 percent of black students in the thirty-two states of the North and West were attending schools with minority enrollments of less than 50 percent. But by 1970, the progress in the South had created a higher level of desegregation in the South than in the North. Although individual northern districts had engaged in desegregation efforts, others were becoming more segregated over time. Thus, the overall picture did not change appreciably between 1968 and 1972.

While the schools of the South have experienced extensive desegregation over the last decade or so, the schools of the North

| Geographic Area | Total Pupils | Black Pupils | | Black Pupils Attending Schools Which Are: | | | | | |
| | | | | 0-49.9% Minority | | 50.0-79.9% Minority | | 80-100% Minority | |
| | | Number | % | Number | % | Number | % | Number | % |
| Continental U.S. | | | | | | | | | |
| 1968 | 43,353,568 | 6,282,173 | 14.5 | 1,467,291 | 23.4 | 540,421 | 8.6 | 4,274,461 | 68.0 |
| 1970 | 44,910,403 | 6,712,789 | 14.9 | 2,225,277 | 33.1 | 1,172,883 | 17.5 | 3,314,629 | 49.4 |
| 1972 | 44,646,625 | 6,796,238 | 15.2 | 2,465,377 | 36.3 | 1,258,280 | 18.5 | 3,072,581 | 45.2 |
| 32 North & West[a] | | | | | | | | | |
| 1968 | 28,579,766 | 2,703,056 | 9.5 | 746,030 | 27.6 | 406,568 | 15.0 | 1,550,440 | 57.4 |
| 1970 | 30,131,132 | 3,188,231 | 10.6 | 880,294 | 27.6 | 502,555 | 15.8 | 1,805,382 | 56.6 |
| 1972 | 29,916,241 | 3,250,806 | 10.9 | 919,393 | 28.3 | 512,631 | 15.8 | 1,818,782 | 55.9 |
| 11 South[b] | | | | | | | | | |
| 1968 | 11,043,485 | 2,942,960 | 26.6 | 540,692 | 18.4 | 84,418 | 2.8 | 2,317,850 | 78.8 |
| 1970 | 11,054,403 | 2,883,891 | 26.1 | 1,161,027 | 40.3 | 610,072 | 21.1 | 1,112,792 | 38.6 |
| 1972 | 10,987,680 | 2,894,603 | 26.3 | 1,339,140 | 46.3 | 690,899 | 23.8 | 864,564 | 29.9 |
| 6 Border & D.C.[c] | | | | | | | | | |
| 1968 | 3,730,317 | 636,157 | 17.1 | 180,569 | 28.4 | 49,417 | 7.8 | 406,171 | 63.8 |
| 1970 | 3,724,867 | 640,667 | 17.2 | 183,956 | 28.7 | 60,256 | 9.4 | 396,455 | 61.9 |
| 1972 | 3,742,703 | 650,828 | 17.4 | 206,844 | 31.8 | 54,749 | 8.4 | 389,235 | 59.8 |

[a] Alaska, Arizona, California, Colorado, Connecticut, Idaho, Illinois, Indiana, Iowa, Kansas, Maine, Massachusetts, Michigan, Minnesota, Montana, Nebraska, Nevada, New Hampshire, New Jersey, New Mexico, New York, North Dakota, Ohio, Oregon, Pennsylvania, Rhode Island, South Dakota, Utah, Vermont, Washington, Wisconsin, Wyoming.
[b] Alabama, Arkansas, Florida, Georgia, Louisiana, Mississippi, North Carolina, South Carolina, Tennessee, Texas, Virginia.
[c] Delaware, District of Columbia, Kentucky, Maryland, Missouri, Oklahoma, West Virginia.

SOURCE: U.S. Commission on Civil Rights, *Equality of Educational Opportunity*, 48.

have threatened to become increasingly segregated. Certainly, this is the long-term trend in the northern cities, and it is argued that efforts to desegregate schools in those cities have simply served to increase the rate of "white flight." An expert on this subject, Karl Taeuber, has argued that: "Until there is a much more even distribution of blacks and whites among central cities and suburbs, segregation indexes for metropolitan areas cannot fall."[23]

A summary of the educational experiences of blacks would suggest a convergence of school characteristics between those attended by black and white students over the last four or five decades. Based on such measures as teacher salaries, length of school session, attendance patterns, and expenditures, there was a movement towards equality even in the pre-*Brown* era. Since 1954 there seems to have been a continuing dimunition of the gap between schools attended by blacks and those attended by whites for those characteristics that are measurable. With respect to the racial composition of school environments, there has been a strong movement towards desegregation in the South with relatively little movement in the North and a long-run tendency in urban areas towards resegregation in both North and South. In 1972, almost half of all black students were attending schools that were between 80 percent and 100 percent minority according to Table 5.

A final concern on inequalities in educational experiences is the degree to which they have affected such outcomes as student achievement. In this respect we are handicapped in a number of ways. First, long-term studies of student achievement between blacks and whites are not available. Second, although the test scores of black students tend to be lower than white ones, it is not clear that the measures are racially unbiased. Finally, the statistical evidence on the relation between test scores and earnings is weak for both races, but it appears to be virtually nonexistent for blacks on the basis of recent studies.[24] That is, differences in measured achievement seem to have little power in explaining differences in earnings.

CONVERGENCE IN EDUCATION. Based on both the analysis of educational achievement as reflected in the amount of schooling completed and the characteristics of that schooling, it appears that there has been a strong tendency for the education of blacks and whites to converge. However, average educational attainments for black males are still about two or three decades behind those of white males. While school characteristics experienced by the two races have tended to converge, there was still an apparent expenditure gap in favor of whites in 1965–1966, and in 1972 almost two-thirds of blacks were attending schools that had student bodies composed of at least 50 percent minority students. Thus, while substantial equalization in educational attainments and experiences has occurred between the races, according to several measures there still exists a serious gap.

## Racial Differences in Earnings

The purpose of this section is to present the relative pattern of earnings for black and white males for the recent past in order to compare this trend with that in education. Before displaying information on this phenomenon, it is important to point out the reasons for restricting the analysis to earnings data for males rather than such alternative measures as family income or income and earnings for both races. As we noted in a previous section, the focus on male earnings is based on the fact that women are less likely to participate in labor markets and are more likely to work on a part-time basis as well as on a periodic basis over their adult years. The result is that historical patterns of earnings data for women will display cultural changes in labor force participation and work patterns that are more likely to confound the interpretation of historical trends in earnings between the two races. In contrast, male labor force behavior tends to be more clearly stable over time.

Second, the analysis will be limited to earnings rather than total income. Total income is derived from both property ownership and from the labor market. Since the direct effect of education on income will be attributable to its impact on labor earnings of an individual, it is important to restrict the analysis to earnings (which comprise about four-fifths of total income). Finally, it is important to note that the trends that are observed for males may differ considerably from those for females and especially for families. For example, family income depends not only on the earnings and other income of individual breadwinners, but also on the sex and number of breadwinners in the family. Even if there were increasing parity in the earnings and incomes of blacks relative to whites, a relative increase in the number of families that are headed by a single breadwinner and especially a female breadwinner could reduce the incomes of black families relative to white ones. This explains the apparent paradox that although the earnings of both black males and females have risen relative to their white counterparts since 1964, the relative incomes of black families have fallen over part of this period.[25]

Table 6 shows the ratios of median wage and salary income, by race, for years for which data are available between 1947 and 1975. In interpreting this table it is important to recognize that traditionally the relative economic status of blacks has risen and fallen with the vicissitudes of the business cycle. In times of prosperity and high employment, blacks have been more likely to obtain full-time jobs and occupational mobility than when economic conditions were bad, a manifestation of the "last-hired and first-fired" syndrome.[26] Thus, particularly during World War II and the Korean War with their surges in employment levels, blacks advanced economically relative to whites only to fall back in the postwar years.

What is striking about the pattern of earnings is the degree to which relative wages and salaries of blacks have risen since the early sixties. Although even in 1975 the average earnings of black male workers were only about 73 percent of those of their white counterparts, the figure was only 57 percent as late as 1963. Somewhat more encouraging is the fact that there seems to be no evi-

TABLE 6    Ratios for Median Male Wage and Salary Income by
Race for Selected Years, 1947–1975

| Year | Wage and Salary Earnings[a] | |
|---|---|---|
| | All Workers | Full-Time Workers |
| | Black Males[b] | Black Males |
| | White Males | White Males |
| 1947 | .543 | .640[c] |
| 1951 | .616 | N/A |
| 1955 | .688 | .635 |
| 1959 | .580 | .612 |
| 1963 | .568 | .654 |
| 1967 | .639 | .675 |
| 1969 | .666 | .694 |
| 1973 | .695 | .719 |
| 1974 | .709 | .736 |
| 1975 | .734 | .769 |

[a] Data are for all individuals fourteen years old and over.
[b] Black refers to Negro and other races.
[c] Data refers to 1946 urban and rural nonfarm.

SOURCE: U.S. Department of Commerce, Bureau of the Census, Current
Population Reports as summarized in Smith and Welch, *Race Differences in
Earnings*, 3.

dence of a relative decline in the black/white earnings ratio for
the recession of the early seventies, a performance that has defied
the traditional movement of earnings between the races over the
business cycle.[27] That is, it appears that the upward trend in the
late sixties was not merely cyclical.

In summary, the earnings of black males have risen dramatically relative to those of white males, especially since 1963. However, as with the educational pattern, the advantage of whites is
still considerable. Further, there exist differences in the black/
white earnings ratios of males according to region, education, and
age of workers.[28] Table 7 shows such ratios by age and region for

TABLE 7   Black/White Earnings Ratios of Males by Age and Region (All Workers) for Selected Years, 1967–1974

| Age | 1967 | 1970 | 1972 | 1974 |
|-----|------|------|------|------|
| All Regions | | | | |
| 21–30 | .715 | .715 | .765 | .760 |
| 31–40 | .584 | .631 | .654 | .688 |
| 41–50 | .558 | .580 | .622 | .628 |
| 51–60 | .528 | .583 | .593 | .606 |
| 21–60 | .591 | .626 | .658 | .667 |
| Northeast | | | | |
| 21–30 | .819 | .774 | .789 | .793 |
| 31–40 | .671 | .697 | .707 | .749 |
| 41–50 | .616 | .680 | .606 | .706 |
| 51–60 | .602 | .618 | .635 | .745 |
| 21–60 | .667 | .690 | .681 | .742 |
| North Central | | | | |
| 21–30 | .834 | .855 | .806 | .738 |
| 31–40 | .732 | .707 | .732 | .765 |
| 41–50 | .676 | .685 | .723 | .765 |
| 51–60 | .627 | .764 | .744 | .734 |
| 21–60 | .713 | .748 | .755 | .795 |
| South | | | | |
| 21–30 | .637 | .631 | .729 | .688 |
| 31–40 | .486 | .572 | .633 | .622 |
| 41–50 | .490 | .505 | .561 | .554 |
| 51–60 | .481 | .512 | .530 | .511 |
| 21–60 | .519 | .555 | .614 | .593 |
| West | | | | |
| 21–30 | .781 | .830 | .906 | .783 |
| 31–40 | .685 | .760 | .610 | .772 |
| 41–50 | .765 | .690 | .735 | .675 |
| 51–60 | .678 | .730 | .619 | .630 |
| 21–60 | .711 | .756 | .727 | .733 |

SOURCE: U.S. Department of Commerce, Bureau of the Census, *Current Population Surveys*, 1968–1975 as summarized in Smith and Welch, *Race Differences in Earnings*, 7.

all workers for selected years from 1967–1974. Among the notice-able patterns are the relatively greater earnings parity among younger workers and within the regions outside the South. Thus, the convergence of earnings between the two races has affected different groups of workers differently, even though the overall movement is toward a closing of the earnings gap.

*Education and Other Causes of the Convergence in Earnings*
Before exploring the impacts of *Brown* on both education and earnings patterns, it is necessary to assess the possible causes of convergence in earnings in recent years between blacks and whites. Three principal explanations have been posited. First, as the quality and quantity of educational attainments and experi-ences have converged between the races, labor market productiv-ity (and hence earnings) has also become more nearly equal between blacks and whites. Second, as blacks have migrated from the lower-wage South to other regions of the country, their rela-tive earnings have improved because the wage levels and the re-wards for any particular level of education are greater outside the South. The third major explanation is that labor market dis-crimination against blacks has decreased substantially over time with a resultant improvement in their relative earnings. Let us address each of these in turn.

As we have noted, there has been a long-run tendency for black and white educational attainments and experiences to converge. Economists translate this phenomenon into a straightforward "human capital" explanation for declining earnings differentials.[29] Differences in the quality and quantity of education are assumed to represent human capital investments that create differences in labor productivity. Assuming competitive labor markets with full employment, very large numbers of potential employers and em-ployees, perfect information on alternatives, mobility of factors of production, and profit maximizing behavior among large num-bers of competing firms, it is presumed that individuals always receive the value of their contribution to production.

Of course, these assumptions omit the realities of racial discrimination, high levels of unemployment, relatively few employers in a particular labor market, trade unions, minimum wages, and other factors that impede perfect competition. In any event, the implication of the theory is that as the quality of education and the number of years of education have converged between blacks and whites, the relative productivity of blacks has risen and has been translated into higher relative earnings.

The migration explanation is also straightforward. Not only have the relative earnings of blacks been higher outside the South, but the absolute level of earnings has also been considerably higher. This means that a movement from the South to other sections of the country for blacks relative to whites would improve the black/white earnings ratio. At the turn of the century some 90 percent of blacks lived in the South, but by 1970 the proportion was slightly greater than half.[30] Especially between 1940 and 1960 there were significant outflows of blacks from the South to other regions. Likewise, the historical movement of blacks from rural to urban locations, especially within the South, would have a similar effect.

The third explanation is that labor market discrimination against blacks has diminished in the post-1964 period so that occupational opportunities and earnings have improved for blacks relative to whites.[31] It will be recalled that a number of important pieces of civil rights legislation were passed in the early sixties, most importantly the Civil Rights Act of 1964 which prohibited employment and wage discrimination on the basis of race. These laws were both initiated and supported in their implementation by civil rights political activists. Further, a variety of government agencies began to monitor hiring practices generally as well as to enforce policies of nondiscrimination in government hiring and promotions and in industries receiving government contracts.

WHICH EXPLANATION IS MOST CONSISTENT WITH THE EVIDENCE? On the surface, the evidence could easily support more than one explanation. All the historical changes have taken place simultaneously and in the same direction. That is, the relative improvements in education, the mobility of blacks from rural to urban areas and from the South to other regions, and the pressures to reduce racial discrimination have all been present through the period of analysis. For this reason, effects may be difficult to separate and an advocate of any particular view might weigh more heavily the effects of one trend than another in drawing conclusions. Certainly, this may be true in the present case where some analysts attribute most of the increase in relative earnings of blacks to the improvement in the quality of the black educational experience, while others attribute it to a reduction in labor market discrimination.[32]

In general, it is agreed that the least important explanation for the improvement in relative earnings in the post-1964 period is that of migration. To a large extent the major changes in the regional and urban-rural distributions of blacks had already taken place prior to the midsixties. While these movements are still evident, they have been much more gradual in recent years than the rather precipitous changes of the forties and fifties.

A major recent report has argued that the most important cause of the reduction in the black/white earnings ratio is the convergence in "human capital" between races, especially by way of education.[33] Since blacks have obtained relatively greater increases in educational attainments and educational quality over time with a resultant narrowing of the educational gap between races, it is expected that the ratio of black to white earnings would have risen. Statistical support for this expectation is found in the fact that younger blacks and whites show more nearly equal earnings than do racial comparisons among older groups of males, as reflected in Table 7. Further, even when we view the earnings differential at any particular level of educational attainment between the races, there is a smaller racial difference in earnings between the younger and more recently educated cohorts than among older cohorts whose educational quality is of a less recent "vintage."[34] It is argued that both these findings would be predicted by the human capital interpretation of racial differentials in earnings. That is, the youngest blacks show "productive" characteristics that are more similar to those of whites than among their older counterparts. Finally, there is some evidence of a rise in the earnings associated with additional education for young blacks at the college level relative to whites, reinforcing the view that the rising quality of black education is improving the relative earnings of black males.[35]

In contrast, the role of diminished wage and employment discrimination is dismissed as a salient explanation. Smith and Welch argue that indirect statistical tests for these effects are not supportive of changes in that relation. While acknowledging that isolated cases may exist in which reductions in discrimination (usually under the threat of legal action) and affirmative action might have been productive in improving the relative status of blacks, the authors assert that there was no widespread effect of any substantial magnitude. These conclusions are drawn on the basis of statistical analyses of the employment and wage patterns of government agencies and those private industries that are seen as most susceptible to government enforcement, firms that derive substantial portions of their sales from government purchases. The authors are neither impressed by their own evidence of rising proportions of blacks in government and private industries that are heavily dependent upon government sales, nor do they find a powerful statistical impact of those situations on the rising black-white earnings ratio. Indeed, they have argued against the validity of earlier studies that showed more powerful statistical evidence of reduced discrimination in accounting for rising black-white earnings ratios.[36]

While these results are plausible, they are not convincing. In fact, a reasonable scrutiny would show that they are internally inconsistent and represent only a selective interpretation of a relatively limited scope, while ignoring evidence that contradicts the human capital explanation. A more complete evaluation tends to support the view that a pervasive reduction in racial discrimination by employers in the late sixties and early seventies seems to dominate the observed patterns, although it is probable that some smaller portion of the equalization was attributable to the convergence in educational patterns between races.

More specifically, the convergence in educational patterns between the races has taken place for at least the last fifty years. For example, Table 3 shows a rather dramatic increase in the length of the school session and attendance of blacks relative to whites from 1920 to 1950, and there is good reason to believe that equalization of other school resources was taking place as well over this period. Further, the amount of schooling that was being completed by males between the two races was converging more rapidly in the decades prior to 1950 than in the subsequent period. If the human capital view is correct, there should have been a concomitant reduction in the earnings gap between the two races following the entry of relatively better educated blacks into the labor market and the earnings convergence should have begun far earlier in this century. Yet, economic historians Fogel and Engerman conclude that "the gap between wage payments to blacks and whites in comparable occupations increased steadily from the immediate post–Civil War decades down to the eve of World War II," and studies of the relative occupational positions of blacks from early in the century until 1960 show no improvement except in the tight labor market situation of World War II.[37] Thus, the human capital interpretation seems to be applied in an *ad hoc* fashion to 1964 and beyond, while ignoring the lack of earnings equalization during the first half of this century when the trend towards educational equalization was much more dramatic.

A second *ad hoc* argument is the support asserted for the human capital interpretation by the rise in returns to blacks for each year of college relative to whites in the post-1964 period. The human capital theory would predict rising relative earnings of blacks for each year of schooling completed, whether at the elementary-secondary level or college level, as long as there were a convergence of educational quality at both levels between blacks and whites. But the returns to elementary and secondary education between white and black males shifted from a situation of equal additional earnings for each year of elementary and secondary schooling between races in 1967 to a doubling of returns *in favor of whites* by 1974. Instead of the convergence predicted by human capital theory, there was a powerful divergence in the direction of higher white earnings. The 1960–1970 comparisons also show no tendency toward convergence.[38]

Additionally, one must question the literal translation of the higher returns for college training to blacks than to whites in 1970. The human capital explanation would imply that the quality of college experience of blacks had improved so immensely that it exceeded that of whites—that the labor market productivity of blacks with college training was greater than the productivity of their white counterparts. The facts hardly argue for the view that blacks were receiving superior college instruction.[39] A more reasonable interpretation is that black labor market entrants with college training benefited more from the affirmative action efforts in the workplace of the post-1964 period than did blacks with only elementary or secondary school experience.

A third challenge to the human capital explanation is found in Table 7 which presents the black/white earnings ratios of males by age and region. If we examine the 51–60-year-old age group for all regions, we see that the black-white ratio rose from .528 to .606 (an increase of about 15 percent), while the ratio rose for the 21–30-year-old group from .715 to .760 (an increase of only 6 percent). Yet, it is hard to argue that in each successive year the blacks in the older population were obtaining more education relative to their white counterparts. Further, let us assume that the 51–60-year-olds in 1974 had the same educational composition between races as the 41–50-year-olds had in 1967. That is, by 1974 most of the 41–50-year-old group from 1967 would have joined the 51–60-year-old group. Using the human capital interpretation, we would expect the 51–60-year-old group in 1974 to have the black-white earnings ratio of the younger group some seven years earlier, or .558, by assuming that the higher black-white earnings ratio for the 41–50-year-old cohort in 1967 is due to a closer parity between races in education than one would find for the 51–60-year-olds at that time. But, by the time most of the 41–50-year-olds in 1967 have joined the 51–60-year-olds in 1974, the black-white earnings ratio has risen far beyond .558 to .606. If we attribute the increases in the rate of .030 for the 51–60-year-olds from .528 to .558 to the better educational attainments and experiences of blacks, there is still a larger gap of .048 to be explained by an improvement that is independent of education. That is, at least 60 percent of the gain between 1967 and 1974 in the black-white earnings ratio for 51–60-year-olds cannot be attributed to black gains in education. This fact, in combination with the fact that older cohorts of blacks gained relatively more in this period than younger ones, suggests that an improvement in the position of blacks was far more pervasive than the educational explanation and would be far more consistent with a broad reduction in job discrimination for blacks generally.

Under this interpretation, the lower black-white earnings ratio for older males would be attributable to greater relative discrimination against blacks who are more experienced. At labor market entry, wages and salaries tend to be relatively more equal between races because of the equalizing effects of lower variance in starting salaries, the impact of minimum wages, and the possibility that whites are more likely to enter on-the-job training programs with relatively low wages until their training is completed. Over time the whites are more successful in obtaining occupational mobility and promotions, as much of the discrimination against blacks takes the form of not placing blacks in supervisory positions over whites. With a reduction in discrimination and an increase in affirmative action, there is improvement in the relative earnings of blacks among all age cohorts, but the basic structure of past discrimination in occupational attainments by race is still reflected in the data.

This interpretation is also reinforced by the fact that earlier studies of occupational attainments and earnings of blacks showed less systematic relations between education and work experience than more recent ones. It is not that blacks simply were receiving lower returns to education and to experience in the pre-1964 period. Rather, these factors seemed to figure less systematically into the determination of labor market success for blacks than for whites, a pattern that is consistent with discrimination against race *per se*. Thus, Hanoch in his study of earnings found highly irregular statistical patterns for blacks relative to whites in the relations between earnings on the one hand and education and age on the other. Duncan and his associates found a similar weakness in attempting to explain occupational attainments of blacks relative to whites in 1962. But, in their data collected in 1973, Featherman and Hauser found that the power of family background variables and schooling to explain occupational attainments of blacks had approached that for whites.[40]

Finally, if much of the improvement of earnings for black males is attributable to a general decline in job discrimination against blacks, the technique of comparing firms that are most susceptible to government-enforced affirmative action with other firms is not an appropriate test. That is, if the values and attitudes of employers towards racial discrimination have been changing throughout the society, then such a comparison will always understate the reduction in discrimination. This problem has long existed in the analysis of the effects of unions on wage levels. If enough firms in an industry are unionized, the nonunion firms may have to raise wages to compete for workers with the union firms. Accordingly, a comparison of wages between unionized and nonunionized firms may show no difference, even though both sets of firms have higher wages than they would in the absence of unions. If most employers were stimulated by civil rights activity, by antidiscrimination laws, and by basic changes in public opinion into modifying their racial hiring policies, then a comparison of employment and wages—by race—of government agencies and government contractors with other firms may show little difference in racial employment and wage practices.

In summary, it appears that the improvement in the black-white earnings ratios cannot be easily explained by the human capital interpretation, in which most of the gains are attributed to better education. Even when educational experiences were unaltered between races, the gains in favor of blacks were large, and there are many contradictions to the application of the human capital paradigm. Rather, the improvements in the black-white earnings ratio were pervasive and the shift appears to have been an abrupt one coinciding with the intense civil rights activity and passage of major civil rights legislation in the early and middle sixties. In the next section we will explore the possible effects of the *Brown* decision on these changes.

## The Impact of Brown

We have noted the comparative improvement in educational attainments and experiences of black Americans over several decades, as well as the dramatic rise in the relative earnings of black males since 1964. I have argued that the particular pattern of convergence of black and white earnings appears to contradict the human capital interpretation that the black economic gains were derived primarily from the educational ones. In this section, we will turn to the role of the *Brown* decision and its impact on both educational and economic changes between the races.

*Brown* has been viewed traditionally as first and foremost a school desegregation decision. I will call this the orthodox view of

*Brown.* According to this criterion, the appropriate evaluation of the impact of *Brown* would consist of an assessment of the degree to which it desegregated the schools; the economic, political, and psychological costs of such desegregation; and the impact of the desegregation on student achievement and attitudes, as well as on residential location decisions. I will suggest that much of the present frustration and disillusionment with *Brown* and the recent criticisms of the Warren Court more generally are functions of this narrow social interpretation of the decision.[41]

In contrast, I will suggest a much broader impact of *Brown* by arguing that *Brown* was the catalyst that set off the enormous political, social, and economic changes in race relations of the late fifties and the sixties. I will attempt to trace briefly the nature of the activities that followed *Brown* and their relation to these changes. These include the southern reaction to *Brown*, the rise in black political activism, the passage of civil rights legislation guaranteeing equal access to education, jobs, and housing, and the major improvements in opportunities and outcomes for black Americans, including the shifts in race relations and in public opinions.

Before proceeding, it is important to point out the long history of institutional injustices leading up to the *Brown* decision.[42] Despite the passage of the Thirteenth, Fourteenth, and Fifteenth Amendments to the federal Constitution and of the Reconstruction Act, the South was intent on setting out its own laws which would continue to maintain blacks in subservient positions, economically politically, legally, and socially. Although many blacks had obtained election to political offices in the decade or so following the Civil War, this progress came to an end in the last quarter of the nineteenth century. Through the use of the poll tax, literacy tests, the gerrymandering of political districts, physical intimidation, and voting fraud, the black became effectively disenfranchised throughout most of the South. Segregation had become the rule, and the relation of the "freed" blacks to whites was not unlike that experienced under slavery, with harsh sharecropping and leasing arrangements creating a subsistent and dependent black populace.

Discriminatory laws were given constitutional approval by the well-known decision in *Plessy* v. *Ferguson* in 1896, in which it was decided that separate accommodations for blacks and whites in transportation facilities met the constitutional test as long as such accommodations were similar for each race. Barely more than three decades after emancipation, the highest court of the land had sanctioned the separation of the races and the institutions that were to serve them. Neighborhoods, schools, churches, public places, and transportation facilities were divided along racial lines in which blacks were separated from whites by the official doctrine of the state. The symbol of these separate institutions was the black bird or Jim Crow. The armed forces of the nation were segregated as well as every other public institution, and blacks had access only to the most menial jobs.

In every way the institutions were separate, but they were hardly equal. We noted the inequalities in education that characterized Jim Crow, and these were also reflected in virtually all the other institutions that served blacks. Second-class citizenship was enshrined in the daily experiences of white and black Americans, and many of the stigmas and experiences made their way North where a less formal system of segregated institutions was maintained. The acceptance of the system by both whites and blacks was heavily related to the attitudes and values and consciousness created by a way of life that seemed inevitable by both the dominant and the dominated. And he who violated the system was subject to physical and economic sanctions or worse. Throughout the first four decades of the twentieth century, the changes were few.

With the coming of World War II, labor markets became very tight. Jobs opened for blacks that had not been available before. With the availability of jobs came increased migrations from rural to urban areas and from South to North. Large numbers of black soldiers served in the armed forces, although in segregated units. Following World War II, blacks began to lose many of the economic and occupational gains obtained during the war, as labor markets slackened. Although the white primary had been declared unconstitutional and black voter registration had risen, most blacks were still without the franchise. President Truman took a few steps toward racial equality by establishing the Committee on Civil Rights and desegregating the armed forces. Yet, Jim Crow was still firmly entrenched. Few of President Truman's proposals from his Committee on Civil Rights emerged from congressional committees, and none was passed. While the stage had been set for massive change, the event or events that would trigger it had not arrived.

Leading up to *Brown*, the early fifties were characterized by a total system of domination, accepted by both whites and blacks, partially because of familiarity and partially because of inevitability and the accompanying belief system that what is familiar and inevitable must not be challenged.[43] And the outrage necessary to provide the momentum for change was not yet evident. In his recent work *Injustice: The Social Bases of Obedience and Revolt*, Barrington Moore, Jr. concluded:

People are evidently inclined to grant legitimacy to anything that is or seems inevitable no matter how painful it may be. Otherwise the pain might be intolerable. The conquest of this sense of inevitability is essential to the development of politically effective moral outrage. For this to happen, people must perceive and define their situation as the consequence of human injustice: a situation that they need not, cannot, and ought not to endure. By itself of course such a perception, be it a novel awakening or the content of hallowed tradition, is no guarantee of political and social changes to come. But without some very considerable surge of moral anger such changes do not occur.[44]

My contention is that the *Brown* decision was central to eliciting the moral outrage that both blacks and whites were to feel and express about segregation, and this new awareness set the stage for the changes that were to follow.

The initial NAACP attacks on Jim Crow schools started in the thirties. The attempts in those early years were to equalize educational facilities and salaries.[45] That is, the goal was to get the states to live up to the equality component of the "separate but equal" doctrine with the hope that ultimately the state would find the maintenance of an equal, dual school system too costly to maintain. It was expected that the state might seek to integrate the schools as the costs of resource equality for the separate systems mounted. By 1950 it was clear that both the equalization strategy and the integration one were failing, and the NAACP moved directly to constitutional challenges of the segregated institutions themselves.[46]

When the *Brown* decision was announced in 1954 there was great support by northerners, the northern media, and academics, but the decision was met by open statements of defiance and rancor throughout the South. While black expectations for the dismantling of Jim Crow institutions began to rise, the South was planning strategies to resist school desegregation. After fifty-four weeks, the Supreme Court handed down its decision on how *Brown* was to be implemented. Placing enforcement under the aegis of the federal district courts, local school boards were to be given responsibility to desegregate their schools "with all deliberate speed," and the boards could obtain delays if they were necessary in the "public interest."

The language was ideal for the tactics of state and local governments in the South and their substantial numbers of white supporters. Instead of responding to the letter and spirit of the Supreme Court's interpretation of the Constitution, the South reacted with a vengeance to any and all black constituents who might push for redress under the law. Local blacks who signed as plaintiffs faced economic sanctions and physical threats, and night-riders and the Klan reminded the blacks that the old order was not to be destroyed by a decision from a court in Washington, D.C. Blacks were dropped from voting rolls in some states, and all the South sought methods to circumvent the *Brown* ruling.[47] The South was making it clear to blacks that a new day was not dawning, and repression was the solution to any challenge to Jim Crow.

But if blacks could not get the federal Constitution and the NAACP to redress the injustices except through the lengthy process of litigation, a new tactic had to be found. In the anger and frustration of the immediate aftermath of *Brown*, the only response could be direct and collective political action. Six months after *Brown II*, a black seamstress and NAACP member, Rosa Parks, refused to move to the back of a municipal bus to make room for a white passenger. Under the leadership of Mrs. Parks's pastor, Martin Luther King, Jr., the blacks of Montgomery, Alabama, retaliated by staying off the buses to boycott the system.[48] The boycott lasted for over a year, and by its end the Supreme Court had struck down the legal segregation of transportation, overturning the *Plessy* v. *Ferguson* decision of 1896. This was the new media age, with television permeating virtually every community in America. The courage and persistence of the blacks who boycotted the public transportation system of Birmingham had two effects. First, they inspired a new strategy to complement the fruits of litigation, direct political action at a grassroots level.[49] Second, these actions made it very clear to whites outside the South what Jim Crow was about. Most northerners had not grown up in a society where discrimination and repression of blacks were so blatant, for discrimination in the North was much less tied to a formal social contract than an informal one. This morality suggested that blacks must be given equal rights under the law, but prejudice within society was a fact of life that was less assailable.

Thus, a new coalition of blacks and whites emerged to push

for civil rights legislation. And what could not be achieved just a decade before under Truman was accomplished:

In 1957 Congress passed its first civil rights bill in eighty years, and in the next decade went on to pass three more. Even the barrier of the Senate rules could not restrain the momentum of the Civil Rights movement—propelled by the Supreme Court decision outlawing school segregation, by the nonviolent "Negro revolution," and by instances of white brutality witnessed by an entire nation on television. By 1966 the Negroes' right to equal treatment in most aspects of the national life was established in law—with the notable exception of fair housing legislation which was not enacted until 1968. After that, there remained the harder problem of converting equal rights into truly equal opportunity.[50]

And rising to the challenge of "enforcing" the law were the direct political actions of sit-ins, boycotts, marches, legal challenges, and the use of the media to tell the nation "how it is." The Congress of Racial Equality (CORE), which had been at an ebb in 1954 after depletion from McCarthyism and other troubles, began to experience a resurgence.[51] The NAACP had little difficulty in finding plaintiffs to initiate litigation against Jim Crow. The Southern Christian Leadership Conference (SCLC) and the Student Nonviolent Coordinating Committee (SNCC) led new challenges and voter registration drives. The southern blacks had come alive to carry their own fight, and the civil rights movement was in full swing.[52] Northerners joined freedom marches to the South and assisted in voter registration drives, and the southern reaction of indifference, intimidation, or outright brutality just served to cement the public opinion of northern liberals, some white southerners, and blacks throughout the nation as to the righteousness and inevitability of change.

The 1957 Civil Rights Act, which owed its proposal and passage largely to Attorney General Herbert Brownell, provided only for the creation of a Civil Rights Commission with advisory powers,

a Civil Rights Division of the Justice Department, and the right
of the Justice Department to instigate litigation in behalf of Negroes who were denied their voting rights. In 1960, a second civil
rights law was passed broadening the powers of the federal government to protect the voting rights of blacks in the South.[53] By
1961, under John Kennedy and his brother Robert Kennedy, the
attorney general, a slightly more vigorous approach was taken toward pushing the civil rights issue. Nonviolent protest as a strategy for change had become firmly entrenched. Student representatives from the southern black colleges were especially active, and
while NAACP continued to push at the legal battleline, CORE,
SNCC, and SCLC were following the Martin Luther King strategy
of nonviolent protest in the form of boycotts, sit-ins, marches, and
the picketing of Jim Crow establishments.

By this time an estimated 300,000 persons belonged to the Ku
Klux Klan and White Citizen Councils actively opposing any in-
roads into segregation. Racial violence, murders, beatings, and
bombings had become a relatively common hazard for protesters.
Yet, the black activists and their allies moved on inexorably with
the advent of "freedom rides" and the beginning of desegregation
of several southern universities.[54] Black voter registrations increased, and the momentum was clearly on the side of the civil
rights groups. By 1963, King felt that the protesters could take on
the institutions of a major Jim Crow city, Birmingham, Alabama.
The responses to the demonstrations were the brutal bludgeoning
of and use of firehoses and police dogs on defenseless children
and adults who were marching and singing hymns. The televised
brutality of Public Safety Commissioner Bull Connor and the
police of Birmingham, as well as the March on Washington of
over 200,000 civil rights workers, underlined the urgency for
further federal action. In 1964, a third civil rights act was passed
with provisions for equal opportunity in employment, equal access
to public accommodations, further protection for black voting

rights, and desegregated education. And by 1968 housing discrimination was also prohibited.[55]

With each wave of legislation, the civil rights activists were given more rights to demand and to defend, and the government was provided with agencies to enforce the new laws. Thus, there was a powerful interplay between the three forces of litigation, direct political action, and pressures for new legislation. The legislation of the Great Society further reinforced these changes with its Equal Opportunity Act of 1964 and all of the programs that became known as the War on Poverty.[56] In the schools and in the workplace changes were occurring as local groups pushed for equality and fair employment practices. For example, local civil rights groups in Chicago were able to pressure that city's school authorities into equalizing educational spending among racial groups.[57] Likewise, local civil rights groups initiated litigation and direct political pressures in response to firms and government units that practiced discrimination in employment. These pressures went much further than the acts of the Equal Employment Opportunity Commission or the attempts of the Civil Rights Division or of contracting agencies of the government to reduce discrimination.[58] For example, in the late sixties, black student unions at the major universities pressed successfully for greater numbers of black faculty and administrators—long before the Department of Health, Education and Welfare began to push for racial parity and affirmative action.

What is important to note is that *Brown* had broken the piecemeal paralysis of incremental change by initiating both directly and indirectly the events that would address the entire relation of blacks and whites. As Myrdal emphasized so clearly: "Behind the barrier of common discrimination, there is unity and close interrelation between the Negro's political power; his civil rights; his employment opportunities; his standards of housing, nutrition and clothing; his health, manners, and law observance; his ideals and ideologies. The unity is largely the result of cumulative causation binding them all together in a system and tying them to white discrimination."[59]

The response to *Brown* addressed this entire *gestalt* and system of relations and institutions. Both the attitudes of blacks towards themselves and their rights and those of whites towards blacks were inexorably altered. Despite the turmoil faced by whites in the demonstrations, urban riots, and school busing, attitudes towards integration by whites became more and more favorable. In 1942 about 44 percent of the white population endorsed integrated transportation, a figure that rose to 60 percent by 1956 and 88 percent by 1970. Although only 4 percent of southerners accepted integrated transportation in 1942, the number rose to 67 percent in 1970. In commenting on this change, the public opinion experts concluded: "In less than 15 years—since Martin Luther King's historic boycott in Montgomery, Ala.—integrated transportation has virtually disappeared as an issue."[60]

In 1942 only 2 percent of whites in the South favored school integration, and by 1956 the figure had risen to only 14 percent. By 1970 almost half the southern white population favored integrated schools. For the nation's whites as a whole the figure rose from about 30 percent favoring integrated education in 1942 to almost 50 percent in 1956, to 75 percent in 1970. These trends are also supported by other public opinion polls that show improving attitudes towards school integration continuing into the seventies.[61]

Although *Brown* did not have the dramatic effect that was expected in desegregating the schools, it has had a powerful effect in many other ways in improving the education and training of black Americans. As we have noted, it created the impetus for the direct political action and solidarity of blacks in demanding improvements from their state and local schools. Second, the tremendous crescendo of civil rights activity that it detonated became a stimulus and backdrop for the large number of educa-

tion and training programs of the War on Poverty and for helping
the disadvantaged. Such programs as Head Start, Title I of the
Elementary and Secondary Education Act of 1965, the expansion
of the training programs under the Manpower Development
Training Act for blacks and other disadvantaged, the Job Corps,
and many other efforts were initiated during the early and middle
sixties and have expanded and continued in the seventies.[62] Even
the present challenges to the methods by which states finance
their schools can be traced to the *Brown* decision. Most of the
states have traditionally provided greater educational funding for
students in wealthy school districts than in poorer ones, and the
constitutional challenge is based heavily upon the "equal protection" arguments in *Brown*.[63]

In summary, the effect of *Brown* has been much wider than
just that of school desegregation. It is difficult to conceive of the
civil rights movement arising when it did and all of the associated
legislative gains of the sixties in the absence of *Brown*. It is equally difficult to conceive of the educational, employment, and earnings gains of blacks without the flurry of protest, litigation, and
legislation that *Brown* unleashed. And in the most human terms,
it has meant a major transformation in the place of blacks in
American society. As Kluger summarized:

Every colored American knew that *Brown* did not mean he would
be invited to lunch with the Rotary the following week. It meant
something more basic and more important. It meant that black
rights had suddenly been redefined; black bodies had suddenly
been reborn under a new law. Blacks' value as human beings had
been changed overnight by the declaration of the nation's highest
court. At a stroke, the Justices had severed the remaining cords
of *de facto* slavery. The Negro could no longer be fastened with
the status of official pariah. No longer could the white man look
right through him as if he were, in the title words of Ralph Ellison's stunning 1952 novel, *Invisible Man*. No more would he be a
grinning supplicant for the benefactions and discards of the master class; no more would he be a party to his own degradation.

He was both thrilled that the signal for the demise of his caste status had come from on high and angry that it had taken so long and first exacted so steep a price in suffering.[64]

## A Postscript

I have argued that the major changes in the economic position of black Americans since the early sixties have resulted from the overall impact of *Brown* in altering the nature of race relations rather than its narrow impact on school desegregation. By implication, *Brown* has had a very powerful effect on the functioning of our major social, political, and economic institutions, and the result has been a fairer society. This view contrasts sharply with those who see *Brown* as the classic example of how an "activist" Supreme Court cannot obtain changes that run counter to a deeply rooted system of social beliefs and without a mechanism of the Court to enforce its decisions.[65]

The main difference between my reading of history and theirs is that they tend to concentrate on the "official" purpose of *Brown*. Since *Brown* was ostensibly concerned with the desegregation of schools, they assume that the proof of its effectiveness must be in the extent, speed, and smoothness of the desegregation process. They find the extent of desegregation wanting, the speed of the process a snail's pace, and the nature of the process chaotic and ridden with conflict. What this narrow analysis tends to ignore is the larger impact of *Brown*, which goes far beyond the mere racial composition of student in the schools. I would ask that they answer the following: Is it possible to conceive of the major historical transformations of the late fifties and sixties in the absence of *Brown*? Further, using our hindsight, is there a different strategy that would have had similar effects? These are the key questions that must be raised in evaluating the impact of *Brown* and the role of the decision in bringing a greater measure of equality and justice to black Americans.

A second lesson that this interpretation would emphasize is that programs of social evaluation must always go beyond the "intended" consequences or the goals of the program or event that is being evaluated. To limit the impact of *Brown* to its effect on desegregation would miss completely the effects of the decision on the changes in political efficacy of blacks, improvements in their economic position, changes in white attitudes towards race, and so on. Evaluations should always start with the question of how the particular program or event changed processes and outcomes in all possible ways rather than only in the direction towards which the program or event was ostensibly tailored.[66]

Finally, the great strides made in the post-*Brown* era are reminders of the changes that *did not* take place as well as of the changes that did. Full equality for black Americans is still far from being achieved.[67] The unemployment rates of black males are double those of white ones, and family income of blacks is only about 60 percent of white families and possibly falling. Educationally, the attainments of blacks are still considerably below those of whites, with especially large differences in high school and college completion. Inequalities in housing opportunities and residential segregation are still a fact of life for blacks, and there seems to be little relief on the horizon. This paper, then, is not a plea for self-congratulations as much as a reminder that *Brown* initiated the first major and systemic phase of change in improving the status of blacks in the post-Reconstruction period. Perhaps some important lessons can be learned from this first stage that will enable persons of good will to carry out the final stage of the movement towards greater equality for blacks and for all Americans.[68]

# The White House and Black America: From Eisenhower to Carter

WILLIAM E. LEUCHTENBURG

To most black Americans in 1954, few places could have seemed more remote than the White House in Washington, D.C.; yet none had more potential for changing their lives. General Eisenhower in the executive mansion on Pennsylvania Avenue lived a world apart from the slumdweller in Harlem or Watts, and the black farmer in the Mississippi Delta had not even been able to cast a ballot in the election that put Eisenhower in office. Nonetheless, each of the six incumbents of the White House, from 1954 to this moment, has, in differing ways, shaped the destinies of black people in the United States. To be sure, presidents were not the only movers and shakers, and there were limits to what they could do as well as to what they would do. Furthermore, they often acted less on their own initiative than in response to pressures from blacks and their white allies. Nonetheless, no history of the quarter-century since the *Brown* decision[1] would be complete without an account of how the White House responded to the challenge and to the opportunity created by the Supreme Court's ruling.

It was altogether a misfortune for blacks in America that in the year the Supreme Court handed down the *Brown* decision, Dwight Eisenhower was president of the United States. That may seem a harsh judgment on a man who was so enormously popular at the time, and is remembered now as so goodhearted, but I think it is an assessment that Eisenhower has earned. There are many functions a chief executive may perform to further the interests of blacks. He may take full advantage of his role as chief legislator to foster meaningful civil rights laws; he may use his appointing power to name blacks to high offices in the government; he may employ his executive authority to administer civil rights statutes vigorously and to issue effective executive orders; and, above all, he may invoke his moral authority as leader of the nation to educate the country in what is expected of its citizens in according to all Americans their constitutional rights. Eisenhower did none of these things. Theodore Roosevelt once described the White House as a "bully pulpit." When Eisenhower was president, it was an empty pulpit. It is not too much to say that a great deal of the violence as well as the pitifully slow rate of compliance after 1954 may be laid at Eisenhower's door.

President Eisenhower approached the question of civil rights with a number of considerations in mind. He comprehended in a general way that blacks were denied equality, and he understood, too, that in a struggle with the Soviet Union for the allegiance of the Third World evidence of racial discrimination in the United States was a decided handicap. Both of these concerns led him toward a wider role for the White House. But other emphases, far more forceful, drove him in a contrary direction. He had a markedly circumscribed view of the powers of his office; throughout his reign, he sought to return the presidency to the role it had played in the era before Franklin Roosevelt and to divest the national government of authority that he thought had been usurped from the states. He had a limited notion, too, of how much one could advance civil rights by coercion. When Eisenhower was asked how he felt about the fact that his secretary of labor had endorsed an equal opportunity bill, he voiced his disapproval of "punitive or compulsory Federal law," and through most of his first term, the president strongly opposed the introduction of civil rights legislation. He insisted that "the final battle against intolerance is to be fought—not in the chambers of any legislature—but in the hearts of men."[2] Eisenhower ignored altogether the data that showed that when laws were enacted people altered their behavior in conformity to the statute and their attitudes also changed. Furthermore, there were political apprehensions. In 1952 Eisenhower had achieved great success in breaking the Democratic hold on the South, and he did not want to do anything to jeopardize those gains. Perhaps most salient was Eisenhower's attitude toward race, for he never showed much empathy for the plight of blacks in America. In 1948 the general had frowned upon complete integration of the armed forces, and during the 1952 campaign, the *Courier*, which rated Eisenhower "a sorry last" of all candidates on the issue of civil rights, was appalled by his "complete ignorance on the subject." One of his aides has concluded, "President Eisenhower, during his presidential tenure, was neither emotionally nor intellectually in favor of combating segregation."[3]

Eisenhower regarded the *Brown* decision with ill-concealed dismay. His attorney general, Herbert Brownell, had appeared as *amicus curiae* in the case only over the president's objections, and Eisenhower had not lifted a finger.[4] When two days after the *Brown* ruling a reporter inquired whether the president had any counsel for the South, he answered, "Not in the slightest." Three months later, when Eisenhower was asked if he had thought about submitting legislation to buttress the decision, he retorted, "The subject has not even been mentioned to me."[5] Again and again Eisenhower was urged to speak out on behalf of the Court, but he refused to do so, because, in truth, he did not believe in what the justices had done. "I am convinced that the Supreme Court decision *set back* progress in the South *at least fifteen years*," he said to one of his campaign aides in 1956. "The fellow who tries to tell me that you can do these things by *force* is just plain *nuts*."[6]

Despite these sentiments, Eisenhower did act in those few areas where federal authority was undoubted. On the very day after the *Brown* decision he summoned the commissioners of the District of Columbia to his office and told them he hoped that the capital would become a model for the nation in integrating its schools. Even before the Supreme Court's ruling, the Eisenhower administration had desegregated navy yards and army post schools, and Attorney General Brownell had argued successfully in the Supreme Court against a lower court decision sustaining segregation in Washington's restaurants. When I worked in Washington in 1946 as the only white on the field staff of one of the early civil rights lobbies, it was necessary to walk nearly twenty blocks to the Phyllis Wheatley YWCA to have lunch with other members of the staff, for there was not a restaurant, a hotel, or a soda fountain in the downtown district of the nation's capital that would serve blacks. Under Eisenhower, the White House brought pressure on owners of such establishments as restaurants and hotels in the District of Columbia to desegregate, and the district integrated swimming pools and parks as well. In addition, the President's Committee on Government Contracts under Vice-President Richard Nixon ended segregation in the telephone company serving Washington, D.C., and created job opportunities for black workers on buses and streetcars in the capital.

More than that, though, Eisenhower would not do, particularly with respect to integration of the schools, and when the president failed to take the lead, other groups moved in to fill the vacuum. In 1954, the first chapter of the White Citizens' Councils was organized in Sunflower County, Mississippi, Senator James Eastland's home county, and under the influence of such groups, states and school districts mounted so massive a defiance of the Supreme Court that in the Eisenhower years almost no school desegregation at all took place in the Deep South.[7] Not infrequently, antipathy to the *Brown* decision or to the exercise by blacks of their constitutionally guaranteed right to vote found violent expression. In Lincoln County, Mississippi, a man who was encouraging blacks to register to vote was murdered on the lawn of the courthouse before many eyewitnesses and no one was ever brought to trial; in Montgomery, Alabama, snipers fired on integrated buses and black churches were bombed; in Clinton, Tennessee, and Bessemer, Alabama, black neighborhoods were dynamited. Angered by these events, a group of prominent black leaders called together by Martin Luther King asked Eisenhower to "come immediately" to a city in the South to urge an end to such outrages and to ask for obedience to the Supreme Court's decisions, but when a reporter inquired about this request, Eisenhower revealed his utter ignorance by engaging in embarrassed whispering with his press secretary. When the question was raised again two weeks later, Eisenhower commented, "As you know, I insist on going for a bit of recreation every once in a while," adding, "I don't know what another speech would do." Not even at a formal White House press conference would he say a word against violence or the widespread use of economic reprisals. Nor for many years would the president even meet with a delegation of blacks. When he finally did, he instructed blacks to be "patient" and not to be too forward in seeking their rights.[8]

However, for all his reticence about endorsing the *Brown* decision and for all his reluctance to infringe upon the rights of the states, Eisenhower discovered that he could not avoid a major confrontation over school integration. The crisis that developed in Little Rock in 1957 came in a city with a measure of good will, and support from the White House for the moderate leadership might have made a difference. But Eisenhower offered none, and he even referred to the "mongrelization of the race."[9] When he did finally act, it was less because of solicitude for the rights of blacks than over the need to counter a challenge by the governor of Arkansas to his own prerogatives.[10] By federalizing the Arkansas National Guard and dispatching paratroopers to Little Rock, Eisenhower went well beyond the constitutional limits he had previously insisted upon, but with small benefit to blacks. In the following year, Little Rock's high schools were completely closed down, and Virginia carried a similar policy of massive resistance so far that the governor of that commonwealth even ordered the American flag taken down from the state capitol.[11]

The remainder of Eisenhower's years in office saw nothing of substance to alter this situation. To be sure, Congress did enact the first civil rights legislation of the twentieth century in 1957 and 1960 with White House approval. But neither law contributed anything to carrying out the *Brown* decision, nor very much toward voting rights.[12] Furthermore, the administration enforced the 1957 act with so little enthusiasm that when its impact was assessed two years later, it was found that it had not added one black voter to the rolls. Despite the authorization of the statute, the Eisenhower administration filed no voter-discrimination suit in Mississippi at all, although in Mississippi, where blacks composed 41 percent of the state's population, less than 4 percent could vote. Conditions, grumbled one federal official, "could hardly have been worse had Eastland himself been in charge." As late as 1959 Eisenhower was still saying, "I happen to be one of those people who has very little faith in the ability of statutory law to change the human heart, or to eliminate prejudice." As a consequence, in Eisenhower's last years in office, the rights of blacks in America were, in the words of the staff director of the Civil Rights Commission, a "White House orphan."[13]

In defense of Eisenhower, it was often said that he merely reflected the temper of the times, but the 1960 campaign made clear that the president was behind the times. The sit-in demonstrations of 1960 showed with painful clarity what a short way the United States had come toward achieving racial equality, and both of the major party platforms that year reflected growing recognition that justice delayed was justice denied.[14] South Carolina's Senator Strom Thurmond called the 1960 Democratic civil rights plank "the most extreme, unconstitutional, and anti-

Southern ever conceived by any major political party." It was difficult, he maintained, "to imagine how a more obnoxious and punitive approach could have been composed. Even the NAACP, in all its fervor, has never proposed more drastic steps." The platform, Thurmond protested with his usual hyperbole, was "a chart for amalgamation of the races and a reduction of the individuals of which our country is formed to the lowest common denominator."[15]

Although John Kennedy ran for election on this platform, no one could be certain what he would do with respect to civil rights. In 1957, against the advice of his retinue, he had responded to a taunt from the Republican chairman in Mississippi by saying to a Democratic gathering in Jackson, "I have no hesitancy in telling the Republican chairman the same thing I said in my own city of Boston, that I accept the Supreme Court decision as the supreme law of the land," and won deafening applause from his listeners for his courage and political skill. One Mississippi congressman remarked, "I never thought I'd see anybody in Central Mississippi speak up for integration and get a standing ovation." On the other hand Kennedy had never been so identified with the civil rights cause as Hubert Humphrey had. After talking to Kennedy in 1960, Jackie Robinson decided to back Nixon instead. He reported: "John Kennedy said, 'Mr. Robinson, I don't know much about the problems of colored people since I come from New England.' I figured the hell with that. Any man in Congress for fifteen years ought to make it his business to know colored people.' "[16]

Once in office Kennedy moved so cautiously that he reinforced those doubts Robinson had expressed. Like Eisenhower, Kennedy felt constraints with regard to civil rights, but they were of a different sort. Unlike his predecessor, he held an expansive view of the powers of the presidency, thought racial discrimination was an anachronism in the modern world, and had no difficulty in subscribing to the *Brown* decision. But unlike Eisenhower, he had been elected not by a landslide but by the narrowest margin in many years; he knew that he could claim no mandate and that it would entail a delicate balancing act to encompass in his coalition both Senator Eastland and the NAACP. Given the precarious Democratic margin in Congress, Kennedy feared that if he threw his weight behind civil rights legislation, he not only would fail to get it, but in the process would alienate enough marginal southern Democrats so that much of the rest of his program, some of which would benefit blacks, would go down to defeat too. In truth, he had good reason for such worry, but his hesitancy opened him to attack from liberals in his own party and from moderate Republicans. "On civil rights," Senator Prescott Bush of Connecticut commented in September, 1961, "the Administration has flunked out very badly."[17]

Kennedy claimed that he could achieve more by using his executive authority than by a futile effort to win approval for civil rights legislation, but his critics complained that even in the executive realm the president did not move decisively enough. In the 1960 campaign, he had said that "the stroke of a presidential pen" could end discrimination in federally financed housing, but not until November, 1962, did he issue an order, and that was a weak one.[18] After Kennedy's housing edict, Martin Luther King observed, "If tokenism were our goal, the administration moves us adroitly toward it." Some critics thought, too, that Kennedy could have given more federal backing to civil rights workers who were risking their lives in the Deep South, and they deplored a number of his appointments. Though Kennedy named the first blacks ever to serve on U.S. district courts in the continental United States, he also elevated outright segregationists to the federal bench, including Mississippi's Judge William Harold Cox, whose behavior on the bench—which even included using racial epithets— brought him a reprimand from the American Bar Association. Kennedy did better the Eisenhower record on integration of the schools—in 1960, the last Eisenhower year, only 17 school districts in the entire country desegregated; in 1963, the final Kennedy year, 166 did so. Yet when the school year opened in September, 1962, the ninth since the Supreme Court had handed down its *Brown* decision, not a single black went to the same school as a white, at any level from kindergarten to law school, in three states (Alabama, South Carolina, and Mississippi), and at the end of the Kennedy era, only 1 percent of black children in the states of the former Confederacy attended school with white pupils. In 1963, Dr. King declared that, though Kennedy was some improvement on Eisenhower, "the plight of the vast majority of Negroes remains the same."[19]

Though much of this criticism is well-reasoned, it has to be weighed against the many ways that Kennedy progressed beyond Eisenhower. The obsession of Kennedy and his circle with the Cold War gave an urgency to the issue of civil rights that the Eisenhower administration, even at the height of the Dulles messianism, never felt.[20] Under John F. Kennedy the appointment of . blacks to the higher civil service ranks nearly doubled in two years, and the president made no secret of the fact that he planned to select Robert Weaver as the first black Cabinet official. The Department of Justice under Robert Kennedy contrasted noticeably with that in the Eisenhower years, for the Kennedys recruited a dedicated cadre of men—Burke Marshall, Ramsey Clark, John Doar, and Nicholas de B. Katzenbach, among others—who took their responsibilities in the civil rights area seriously. In a Law Day address at the University of Georgia in May, 1961, Attorney General Kennedy said boldly: "You may ask, will we enforce the Civil Rights statutes? The answer is: 'Yes, we will.' "[21] In fact, appreciably more suffrage rights suits were instituted by the Justice Department under Robert Kennedy than had been begun in the Eisenhower era. In July, 1961, for the first time a voting rights suit was filed in Mississippi, and, after some hesitation, the government brought suit even in Jim Eastland's Sunflower County. In the spring of 1961, the Kennedys sent hundreds of federal marshals to protect freedom riders in Alabama, where rioters had set fire to one bus and had brutally beaten travelers on another bus.[22] In addition, the Kennedy administration took steps to end segregation in interstate railroad and bus terminals and at airports.

Unquestionably, still more could have been done, but consider what it necessitated from the White House under John Kennedy and the Department of Justice under Robert Kennedy to enroll one black student at this university. Recall that on the very day of Kennedy's inauguration, James Meredith applied to the University of Mississippi, and for nearly two years, with the support of the NAACP, Meredith made a determined endeavor to gain admission, only to meet continued recalcitrance from both university officials and the government of the state of Mississippi.[23] So the Justice Department intervened on Meredith's behalf, and finally, in September, 1962, a federal court order cleared the way for Meredith's admission. On September 20, Meredith came to the Ole Miss campus to register; he was accompanied by agents of the Kennedy administration, including a United States attorney and the chief United States marshal, but he was turned away by Governor Ross Barnett and jeered at by a crowd of two thousand white students. Twice more, the Justice Department went into court to get an order to make possible the admission of Meredith; twice more, Meredith and federal officials traveled to Oxford; and twice more, they were repelled, once by the governor, once by the lieutenant governor. "I won't agree to let that boy get to Ole Miss," Governor Barnett said. "I would rather spend the rest of my life in a penitentiary than do that."[24]

On September 30, 1962, the crisis reached a climax. For a fourth time, the Justice Department got a federal court order, and for a fourth time, Meredith came to Ole Miss, but this time the White House had resolved that he would come with sufficient backing. In a graduated series of steps, President Kennedy federalized the Mississippi National Guard, beefed up the force of deputy U.S.

marshals, and created a staging base at the Memphis Naval Air Station. On the night of September 30, some twenty-five hundred students and other rioters charged the cordon of U.S. marshals, hurled rocks and bricks, and fired rifles and shotguns into the Lyceum where the marshals were penned in. During the night two people were killed, one shot in the back, one shot in the head, and more than fifty were injured, including twenty-five U.S. marshals. By daybreak, there were several thousand troops in Oxford, among them a unit of armored cavalry. When Meredith went to his first class, he was accompanied by seventy-five marshals. Over the ensuing weeks, Ole Miss students burned Meredith in effigy, flung racial epithets at him, harassed him at meals, and ostracized and tormented white students who sat with him.[25] When the second semester opened, soldiers still patrolled the Ole Miss campus, and as late as March, 1963, Attorney General Kennedy was obliged to write Governor Barnett that military personnel would be withdrawn only when he and other officials gave "adequate assurance by deed and word" that they would accept "responsibility for the personal safety of James Meredith as well as for the safety of persons and property of other citizens in Mississippi."[26] Such was the exertion needed by the White House and the Justice Department to permit one black student to attend an American university.

President Kennedy's intervention entailed a high political cost, for it made his name and that of his brother anathema in Mississippi and through much of the Deep South. Three days before the Ole Miss crisis, an Alabama publisher who in 1960 had aligned newspapers in his state behind Kennedy wrote the attorney general that, though he deplored the Mississippi situation, he hoped that armed force would not be used. "We here in Alabama are having a harder fight with Republicans than at any time in my life," he explained. "And . . . one of our best arguing points is to the effect that Eisenhower sent troops into a Democratic state and not only humiliated the Governor, but used the bayonet on a few of the citizens of the community." By disregarding such counsel, Kennedy virtually conceded a large swath of the Gulf states to Barry Goldwater, who was expected to be the Republican nominee in the next election. On the night of the Ole Miss tragedy, students chanted, "2-4-1-3, we hate Kennedy," and when I came to Mississippi in the fall of 1964 to do research at this university, one could still see fading signs along the roadway with the inscription "Down with the Kennedys."[27]

Kennedy's critics do not deny that he sometimes acted effectively, but they assert that he did so not on his own but reactively, in response to the initiatives of the civil rights movement. I think that this generalization in its crudest form misses the subtleties of the interaction between the White House and the movement, in particular the way in which Kennedy gave young people the sense that their efforts would make a difference and thereby fostered a civil rights activism that in turn brought demands on him to respond. Nonetheless, I think the generalization is for the most part correct, at least for Kennedy's first two years in office. Without the demonstrations led by SNCC and the Southern Christian Leadership Conference, there would not have been a consensus for change that made it possible for Kennedy to act. Without the bravery of the freedom riders, there would have been no occasion for a federal presence in Alabama. Without the enterprise of James Meredith and of such NAACP leaders as Aaron Henry and Medgar Evers, there would have been no Mississippi crisis. And without such white people as a former professor of this university whom I am proud to call my friend, Jim Silver, the hope for a decent outcome would have been much harder to sustain.[28] To be sure, Kennedy had also provided an essential ingredient in showing that the White House would be attentive. Yet even after the Ole Miss confrontation, the president still seemed reluctant to commit himself fully to the cause of civil rights.

It required the events of the spring of 1963 to persuade Kennedy to go much farther down the road toward far-reaching civil rights legislation. Some of the process of education took place in Mississippi—in Clarksdale, flaming gasoline bombs were hurled into Aaron Henry's home—but this time the eyes of the country focused not on Mississippi but on Alabama. The demonstration led by Martin Luther King, Jr., in Birmingham in April, 1963, was met by such vicious counteraction, including the use of police dogs, electrified cattle prods, and high-pressure water hoses, all directed by the city's police commissioner Eugene "Bull" Connor, that the attitude of both the administration and the country was transformed. Kennedy himself gave sardonic recognition to this fact when he told civil rights leaders in 1963, "I don't think you should all be totally harsh on Bull Connor. . . . After all he has done more for civil rights than almost anybody else."[29]

In June, 1963, the Alabama situation came to an inevitable culmination, for Alabama was now the only state in the country where, from the lowest grade to the highest professional school at the state university, segregation was total. In his inaugural address as governor, George Wallace had announced, "I draw the line in the dust and toss the gauntlet before the feet of tyranny and I say segregation now, segregation tomorrow, segregation forever."[30] Wallace had promised the voters that he would stand in the doorway to bar any black student from registering at the University of Alabama. But the White House refused to capitulate. President Kennedy federalized the Alabama National Guard, and when Wallace made only a farcical show of resistance in Tuscaloosa, Jim Crow was a dying buzzard.

By now Kennedy had made a commitment on civil rights that he had been hesitant about making before. Two hours after Wallace's surrender, Kennedy, in an eloquent televised address to the nation, declared:

If an American, because his skin is dark, cannot eat lunch in a restaurant open to the public, if he cannot send his children to the best public school available, if he cannot vote for the public officials who represent him, if, in short, he cannot enjoy the full and free life which all of us want, then who among us would be content to have the color of his skin changed and stand in his place? Who among us would then be content with the counsels of patience and delay?

One hundred years of delay have passed since President Lincoln freed the slaves, yet their heirs, their grandsons, are not fully free. They are not yet freed from the bonds of injustice. They are not yet freed from social and economic oppression. And this Nation, for all its hopes and all its boasts, will not be fully free until all its citizens are free.[31]

On the same night on which the president spoke, an event in Mississippi gave heightened meaning to Kennedy's words. In the driveway of his home in Jackson, Medgar Evers, the longtime field secretary of the NAACP, was murdered, shot in the back from ambush. One week later, Kennedy, proclaiming that "the time has come for . . . making it clear to all that race has no place in American life or law," called upon Congress to approve the most sweeping civil rights legislation in the country's history, a measure that Senator Eastland castigated as a "complete blueprint for a totalitarian state."[32]

Kennedy never lived to see the enactment of his civil rights bill, but the sorrow at his death indicated what a deep mark his brief tenure had left. Blacks felt an especially keen sense of deprivation at the news of Kennedy's murder. A decidedly higher proportion of blacks than of whites reported that they were more troubled than "most people" by the president's death, and in Detroit 81 percent of black schoolchildren who were studied "felt the loss of someone very close and dear," again a higher proportion than for white pupils.[33] When Anne Moody, a young black woman from Mississippi, heard the shocking news, she experienced a momentary loss of consciousness, but when she walked into the dining room of the New Orleans restaurant at which she was working, she had a different feeling. She later recalled:

"When I turned around and looked at all those white faces—all of those Southern white faces—fire was in my eyes. I felt like racing up and down between the tables, smashing food into their faces, breaking dishes over their heads, and all the time I would shout and yell MURDERERS! MURDERERS! MURDERERS!" After work, while riding on a streetcar, she studied the countenances of blacks, "who had so many hopes centered on the young President," and reflected, "I knew they must feel as though they had lost their best friend—one who was in a position to help determine their destiny. To most Negroes, especially to me, the President had made 'Real Freedom' a hope."[34]

Kennedy's assassination had an unanticipated and ironic consequence: it abetted the cause of civil rights. It removed from office a northerner and brought to the White House a southerner, one who identified not with Jim Eastland and Ross Barnett but with those who believed deeply in equality of the races. Furthermore, Lyndon Johnson knew how to exploit to the fullest the nation's grief for the fallen president. At Ole Miss, a scene of violence only months before, more than twelve hundred people went to a memorial service for President Kennedy, and in Jackson over two thousand, black and white, gathered in the cathedral for an interfaith service that was one of the most integrated convocations in the state's history. In his first address to Congress, Johnson called for the enactment of the civil rights bill as a memorial to Kennedy. "We have talked long enough in this country about equal rights," Johnson stated. "We have talked for one hundred years or more. It is time now to write the next chapter, and to write it in the books of law."[35] As early as December, 1963, Senator John Stennis was informing his constituents about the new chief executive: "We in Mississippi, of course, are deeply interested in his position on those domestic issues of most vital concern to us and our people. Unfortunately, it is already abundantly clear that his position on civil rights is extreme."[36]

By the following summer, Johnson, with the cooperation of

leaders of both parties, had driven through the Civil Rights Act of 1964. In his State-of-the-Union message, the president declared, "As far as the writ of Federal law will run, we must abolish not some, but all racial discrimination,"[37] and during the next six months he used every resource as a legislative leader to break a civil rights filibuster for the first time in history. The Civil Rights Act of 1964 did almost as much as any federal statute could to fulfill Johnson's goal of wiping out "*all* racial discrimination." It barred discrimination in public facilities like motels, restaurants, soda fountains, and sports stadiums; extended still further national efforts to assure the right to vote; forbade job discrimination by employers or unions; authorized the attorney general to initiate school desegregation suits; allowed the Justice Department to sue to desegregate state and local facilities like swimming pools; and provided that federal funds would be withheld from any state agency that discriminated.

The ink had hardly dried on the Civil Rights Act of 1964 when its effects could be discerned. Georgia's Senator Richard Russell, who had fought strenuously against the legislation, provided a model for the citizens of his state in calling for acceptance of the law,[38] and in Jackson, Mississippi, the Chamber of Commerce issued a similar statement, to good advantage. Though one of Jackson's hotels, the Robert E. Lee, closed down rather than abandon its all-white tradition, blacks in Jackson stayed at the city's leading hotels and teed off at the municipal golf course, while in Vicksburg blacks ate at what had been a whites-only lunch counter. The University of Mississippi was one of 199 southern colleges that pledged compliance with the act. In McComb, a city notorious for bombings and burnings, 650 residents signed a statement in November calling for respect for law. On the next day, restaurants were desegregated peacefully and blacks, led by Medgar Evers's brother, Charles, registered at the Holiday Inn without molestation.

Not everyone, though, would accept change peacefully. When

in the summer of 1964, white and black students worked together in Mississippi to register blacks at the polls, they met unremitting violence.[39] During that summer, twenty-four black churches were burned in the state of Mississippi, and, in a deed that horrified the nation, three of the volunteers—James Chaney, Andrew Goodman, and Michael Schwerner—were murdered in cold blood. Despite the provisions of the 1964 act, many blacks were still denied the right to vote. In Mississippi, to qualify to register, blacks often had to pass impossible tests, such as being able to recite letter-perfect the entire state constitution. It was clear that yet another act of Congress was needed, and once again Martin Luther King took the lead by organizing demonstrations in a city that symbolized obdurate resistance to the rights of blacks— Selma, Alabama. Less than two months after he got the Nobel Prize, the youngest American ever to achieve this honor, King was in a Selma jail.[40]

King could succeed only if he had the cooperation of the White House, and, as he had before, President Johnson came through in a cleverly orchestrated interaction between the White House and black leadership. In February, 1965, Johnson stated at a news conference that "all of us should be concerned with the efforts of our fellow Americans to register to vote in Alabama," and he made clear his intention to see that the right to vote was secured. When Sheriff Jim Clark's deputies and Governor Wallace's state troopers attacked demonstrators, the president, on March 9, decried the "brutality" against blacks, and when on that same day a white minister from Boston was clubbed to death, Johnson expressed deep personal concern and sent a jet plane for his widow.[41] On March 9, too, the president put seven hundred federal troops on alert for deployment in Alabama.

Six days later Johnson delivered a nationally televised address before an unusual evening session of Congress. "Rarely in any time does an issue lay bare the secret heart of America itself," he declared. "The issue of equal rights for American Negroes is such an issue. And should we defeat every enemy, should we double our wealth and conquer the stars, and still be unequal to this issue, then we will have failed as a people and as a nation." The president asserted: "The real hero of this struggle is the American Negro. His actions and protests, his courage to risk safety and even to risk his life, have awakened the conscience of this Nation. . . . And who among us can say that we would have made the same progress were it not for his persistent bravery and his faith in American democracy?" Johnson announced that he was sending a new voting rights bill to Congress that would provide for intervention by the federal government to assure the right to vote. He added bluntly: "To those who seek to avoid action by their National Government in their own communities, who want to and who seek to maintain purely local control over elections, the answer is simple: Open your polling places to all your people." It was a remarkable speech, and one sentence in particular caught the imagination of the country. That came when the president, deliberately aligning himself with the civil rights movement by quoting directly from its anthem, assured the assembled members of Congress: "And we *shall* overcome."[42]

Johnson lost no time in making good his promise. On March 17, he sent his voting rights proposal to Congress, and on the following day no fewer than sixty-six senators sponsored the bill. As Congress considered the controversial legislation, Dr. King stepped up the level of public involvement by arranging a march from Selma to the steps of George Wallace's state house in Montgomery, and once more King and the president worked in tandem. On the night of March 18 Johnson summoned reporters to the White House and read to them a telegram in which Governor Wallace, who had condemned the march as a Communist conspiracy, said that he could not provide protection for the marchers. "If he is unable or unwilling to call up the Guard and to maintain law and order in Alabama," the president warned, "I will call the Guard up and give them all the support that may be required." When Wallace continued to refuse to meet his obligations, Johnson on March 20 federalized the Alabama National Guard and told the secretary of defense to use however many federal troops he might "deem necessary" to safeguard the demonstrators, and the march was able to take place.[43] That summer, after extended debate, Congress passed the voting rights bill, and on August 6 in the President's Room in the Senate, where more than a century before Lincoln had put his name on legislation freeing slaves, Johnson signed the Voting Rights Act of 1965.

In a ceremony before the statue of Abraham Lincoln in the rotunda of the Capitol, the president stated, "This good Congress . . . acted swiftly in passing this act. I intend to act with equal dispatch in enforcing this act."[44] Little more than a day after the bill was signed, the Justice Department filed its first suit—in Jackson, Mississippi, to have the poll tax invalidated as discriminatory. Two days later Attorney General Katzenbach announced that he was appointing federal examiners to register eligible black citizens in nine counties, two of them in Mississippi. In contrast to the previous literacy stipulations, the federal government insisted only that a prospective voter be able to make his mark. On a national television program, Katzenbach explained that since states like Mississippi had been "registering white illiterates" all along, "it is not unfair to say . . . 'Now you have got to apply that same standard to Negroes.'" Did he mean by that, he was asked, "that you are going to register all Negroes, Negroes who can't read or write?" The attorney general answered, "Yes, absolutely."[45]

Under that kind of administration in the Johnson era, the Voting Rights Act of 1965 brought rapid results. In less than a year registration by blacks in Mississippi quadrupled. Today, one out of four registered voters in Mississippi is black, 325,000 in all, nearly fifteen times as many as in 1964. Before 1965 there were fewer than 100 black officeholders in the entire South; today there are well over 2,000, including the mayors of the old Confederate capital of Richmond and Scarlett O'Hara's Atlanta. Georgia has 21 black legislators, and in Alabama, where George Wallace and Bull Connor once reigned supreme, 13 blacks sit in the legislature in Montgomery, "the Cradle of the Confederacy."[46]

The Voting Rights Act of 1965 brought the wave of cooperation between the White House and the civil rights movement to a crest, from which it immediately began to recede. That same summer came the riots in Watts and the divisions over Black Power; within months the civil rights movement was moribund. Where once there was unity, there now was fragmentation; the national director of CORE denounced Johnson as a racist. As the demands of blacks moved beyond those easily resolvable by statute, whites dug in their heels. When Martin Luther King went to Chicago in the summer of 1966 to attempt to open housing in white neighborhoods to blacks, he met such antagonism from mobs that he said the response was worse than anything he had encountered in the Deep South. By January, 1967, the country was preoccupied with the Vietnam war, and in his State-of-the-Union message that month, the president gave only a few sentences to civil rights. There would be one last hurrah in 1968, with the enactment of the open housing law, but the halcyon days were over.

Johnson's immediate successors in the White House, beginning with Richard Nixon, did little to advance the cause of civil rights and quite a bit to set it back. After winning election in 1968 with only a small proportion of black votes but with a number of states from the once-solid South in his electoral column, Nixon, prodded by his attorney general, John Mitchell, deliberately pursued a "southern strategy" in his nominations for the Supreme Court and in his attitude toward racial issues. Under Nixon, Whitney Young of the Urban League complained, southerners thought all previous policies could be "diluted, rescinded, or revoked." Nixon compelled the outspoken chairman of the United States Commission on Civil Rights to resign, and his administration enforced civil rights statutes with so little resolution that the commission rebuked it three times in the same year. When the government was asked to create a national biracial agency, Vice-President Spiro Agnew offered the complacent observation that "the main area of activity must remain on the local level." In 1969 Nixon even opposed extension of the Voting Rights Act of 1965 in its original form. In the light of such developments the legislative director of the NAACP charged that Nixon had "consigned Negroes to a political doghouse whose roof leaks," and the historian John Hope Franklin commented that Nixon would "never be forgiven by blacks" or "by any segment of the population."[47]

As had been the case in so many earlier instances, the state of Mississippi provided the locale for the most important event in civil rights in the Nixon administration. In the summer of 1969 both the Department of Justice and HEW, allegedly under pressure from Senator Stennis, stunned civil rights groups by asking a federal court to postpone the desegregation of Mississippi's schools. The NAACP's legal entity showed how much the White House had been transformed when it asked that the United States be switched from plaintiff to defendant in this action, because the national government no longer championed the rights of black children. In two separate rulings the Supreme Court upset Nixon's plans when it insisted that desegregation must take place "at once," which meant that, as *Time* wrote, "For Mississippi, an era had ended."[48] By then, though, black leaders had lost what little confidence they had ever had in Nixon's intentions.

Yet, paradoxically, some of the greatest gains for blacks, especially in carrying through the implications of the *Brown* decision, came under Nixon. In 1968, for all of the good will of the Kennedy and Johnson administrations, 68 percent of black students still went to all-black schools. In 1970, in Nixon's second year in office, this proportion had plummeted to 18 percent. "Around 1970 the desegregation called for initially in *Brown* versus *Board of Education* was largely realized in the South," one recent survey has noted. "By that year there was less racial isolation in southern schools than in any other region."[49] To no small extent, this was the result of forces already unleashed by Johnson, or because of independent action by the federal courts.[50] However, it also owed a lot to the initiative of the federal government under Nixon. For example, the Nixon administration brought suit against the entire state of Georgia. Much of this activity came not because of the enterprise of Nixon and his immediate aides but rather from momentum developed by the federal bureaucracy, a momentum which no president could easily halt.

Not surprisingly, the policy pursued by Gerald Ford differed little from that of Richard Nixon. In 1972, Nixon had asked Congress to place a moratorium on school busing orders by federal courts, and Ford, when he succeeded Nixon, called Cabinet members to the White House to organize a drive behind an administration bill to curtail sharply the use of court-ordered busing to achieve racial desegregation.[51] Nonetheless, it was Ford's conservative solicitor general who argued in the Supreme Court for the outlawing of all-white private schools, and under Ford, as under Nixon, the HEW continued to draft and administer guidelines to which institutions in local communities had to adhere.

By the time Jimmy Carter took office in 1977, the pertinence of the White House to black America had been amply demonstrated. No president, not even Lyndon Johnson, did as much as he might have; none acted without some attention to the political consequences; and all needed prodding from pressure groups. Frequently, the role of a chief executive was less decisive than that of the civil rights movement or the federal courts or congressional leaders like Hubert Humphrey or socioeconomic forces. Yet there was a great deal that American presidents contributed—in appointing blacks to high office, in employing troops to support judicial edicts, in issuing directives to desegregate facilities, in sponsoring civil rights legislation and administering it, and in arousing the nation to moral imperatives. Presidents have had an important effect, too, at different times in the period since 1954, even when they did not act. By refusing to speak out against flagrant discrimination, they sent signals to the American people that nothing was to be done about the persistence of racism in the United States. President Carter inherited both of these legacies—the positive and the negative.

In the short while that Jimmy Carter has been in the White House, he has changed things—but not much. He has departed from Nixon and Ford mainly in the appointments he has made. Carter named a black to the Cabinet post of secretary of housing and urban development, a black secretary of the army, a black solicitor general, a black assistant secretary of education, the first black head of the Civil Rights Division in the Department of Justice, black United States attorneys in California, Ohio, Illinois, Oklahoma, and North Carolina (the first black to hold that post in a southern state), black United States marshals in twelve states, a black ambassador to the United Nations, and six black ambassadors to foreign countries. He has also attracted to Washington whites considerably more sympathetic to black aspirations than Mitchell or Haldeman or Ehrlichman. As a consequence, civil rights statutes have been administered with more conviction than under his immediate predecessors. Still, though there have been these changes in emphasis, Carter has done very little to ameliorate the economic predicament of blacks in America, and he has failed to make that conundrum one of central concern.

To be sure, Carter could not be Lyndon Johnson even if he wanted to be. Carter is without the kind of consensus for action on civil rights that Johnson had. The controversy over the *Bakke* decision revealed a deep rift among liberals with respect to "reverse discrimination," and many who had no trouble seeing that every black is entitled to equality of treatment in public facilities harbor grave misgivings about racial quotas.[52] Even more pertinent is the fact that the march of events in 1978 is vastly different from when Johnson took office in 1963. There are no longer the vivid issues that so captured the hearts and minds of the country then. And so much has changed. Who would have imagined at the height of the Ole Miss crisis that in less than fifteen years Colonel Rebel would be a black student? (Or that, after such a brief interval, this symposium would be taking place here.) No longer is racist rhetoric a staple of southern politics, and, as one recent account acknowledged, "Like the segregated lunch counter and the 'colored' drinking fountain, the lily-white voting list has disappeared."[53]

Some, indeed, go so far as to say that race has vanished as a discrete problem in America and that, as a result, the White House has no specific relevance to blacks in this country anymore; but I think that those are serious misconceptions. Too many blacks continue to be trapped in fetid urban ghettos, and the unemployment rate for black teenagers hovers at an appalling 40 percent. The increase in black voting has not automatically meant a proportionate change in the distribution of power, and many of the old folkways survive.[54] When a black reporter for the Atlanta *Journal* traveled through the Southeast this summer, he found that "the old barriers of segregated lunch counters, public restrooms and other facilities have gone the way of the passenger pigeon," but he also recognized that a subtle racism persisted. He concluded: "It would seem that Martin Luther King, Jr., countless sit-ins, boycotts, freedom rides, marches, civil rights acts, voting rights laws and millions of federal dollars would have set things straight. But the truth is, that just ain't so."[55]

Even in 1978, there is a role for the White House to play, and it is an important role. We live today in an era where the common wisdom is that one must be wary of the imperial presidency. And so we should. But we must be wary, too, of an enfeebled presidency. As Richard Kluger has written, "If Dwight Eisenhower and Richard Nixon had used the power of the White House to insist that the nation meet its moral obligations to black Americans, racism in the nation might long since have become a fugitive."[56] One cannot expect President Carter to do what Kennedy did, in very different circumstances, in 1963, or what Johnson did in 1965. What one can ask of him though is that he put the same kind of energy into arousing the nation to an awareness of the fact that we have not yet achieved racial equality that he has into the struggle for the Panama Canal treaty or the deregulation of gas. Given the mood of America today, that would not be a promising assignment. But it would not be the first time that Carter had pulled an improbable success out of a difficult situation. If the president were to go even part of the way toward addressing directly the prevalence of inequality of income and opportunity in this country, and toward conveying to the American people a heightened sense of their moral responsibility, he would both redeem his own pledges and demonstrate once again the significance of the White House to black America.

# White Attitudes and Black Rights from *Brown* to *Bakke*

ROBERT H. WIEBE

The modern movement for black rights came as part of a nationalizing process that rose in the 1940s and 1950s, peaked in the mid-1960s, and wobbled into the 1970s. The national government was its indispensable auxiliary, for initially the advocates of black rights were seeking reforms far beyond their own capacity to achieve and well beyond the willingness of most white citizens to grant. As long as a general faith in the national government remained strong, so did the movement for black rights. When the one waned, the other also weakened. The critical turn in this relationship occurred in the late sixties, a time of complex changes in the drive for black rights and a rapid erosion of confidence in Washington's management. What emerged in the seventies was a movement without a clear sense of direction still dependent on a government without the authority to alter its drift.

In the modern era the primary source of the government's authority lay in its promise to maintain a healthy economy. A loose linkage that had always joined the state of the economy with government policy was welded by the prolonged depression of the 1930s, but there was no accompanying revelation on which policies actually worked. Because the Roosevelt administration never solved this essential problem, uncertainty about the government's competence continued to plague the Truman administration after the Second World War. Then the prosperity of the postwar years and a rising faith in fiscal manipulation rather quickly generated the necessary confidence in the government's ability to care for the economy as a whole. When the Eisenhower administration accepted responsibility for correcting the recession of 1953–1954, the government finally secured its reputation in this crucial area. After a quarter-century's quest, success here established an impressively broad base of government authority throughout American society. The popularity of entire branches would fluctuate radically, but government in the broadest sense stood as the guarantor of security, order, and well-being in its citizens' lives. Respect for the law of the land may never have been higher than it was at midcentury.

Well before the government had fulfilled its promise to sustain the economy, reformers began to dream of extending Washington's responsibilities across broad realms of the nation's welfare. At their most ambitious in the midst of World War II, these schemes envisaged guarantees that ranged from the rights to a comfortable income and a comprehensive national insurance to the rights "to rest, recreation, and adventure" and even to an enjoyable life.[1] Although a conservative opposition and a general dislike for Washington's lumbering bureaucracy drastically reduced the range of these hopes during the forties, the basic urge remained. Narrowed versions of this reforming impulse found a particularly receptive audience when they followed the flow of America's international involvements. During the Second World War, for example, nothing symbolized the horrors of fascism more vividly than Nazi racism. In response, American propaganda drummed the virtues of religious freedom and helped to promote a nationwide drive against domestic anti-Semitism. When the Cold War brought what seemed to be a variation of the same struggle between freedom and tyranny, sensitivity to America's own record of freedom sharpened still more, and criticisms from abroad honed the edge. It required no peculiar insight to identify the oppression of blacks as the most flagrant violation of freedom in the United States.

The impetus for an official assault on black oppression came from President Truman's blue-ribbon Committee on Civil Rights in 1947. Earlier campaigns to outlaw lynching and enforce fair employment practices had been dwindling, and that October the committee's report arrived as a fresh departure for national policy. By proposing an end to racial segregation in schools, housing, and public facilities, equal access to jobs, and equal voting rights, the committee established nationally visible goals that the movement for black rights would be seeking for approximately the next twenty years. The prominence of civil rights in the 1948 elections, the gradual desegregation of the armed forces, and several mildly encouraging decisions from the Supreme Court provided just enough boost to keep the movement from stalling before it could start. Anticipation everywhere in the nation that the long legal battle against Jim Crow would eventually triumph added considerably to the momentum.

Above all, the morale of the movement depended on the conviction that history was its ally. As the more sophisticated advocates of black rights interpreted America's development, racism and segregation had already become anachronisms. First and most important, the solid core of American values supported black equality. Almost as soon as Gunnar Myrdal's comprehensive *An American Dilemma* was published in 1944, it framed the understanding of how these values and the achievement of black rights were inextricably fused. Americans, according to Myrdal, shared a common belief in equality, justice, and opportunity for all. Properly activated, this creed could serve as a giant national lever to remove its one great contradiction, racial discrimination. Second, the increasing homogenization of American life also promoted black equality. Mass education, mass media, and mass consumerism, the assimilation of the New Deal and the mobilization for containment, all argued that old distinctions were blurring and ancient prejudices dissolving. Finally, even changes in the South favored reform. Yesterday's raucous racists—Bilbo, Rankin, Gene Talmadge—were disappearing. New state laws banned the voodoo masks of the Ku Klux Klan. As a modern economy spread throughout the region, southern liberals spoke more boldly and southern moderates gained more power. Jim Crow would soon become obsolete in its own home. Combining the assumptions behind these three lessons in contemporary history, the Committee on Civil Rights confidently advised, "It is sound policy to use the idealism and prestige of the whole people to check the wayward tendencies of a part of them."[2]

During these same years, history was revealing its lessons very differently to millions of white Americans whose lives were still rooted in their local, personal worlds. Race, religion, and nationality remained fundamental here. Their broad strength, for example, stood behind the large congressional majority reasserting discriminatory immigration quotas in the McCarran-Walter Act of 1952. In vague but powerful ways, locally oriented Americans saw the nationalizing and homogenizing trends that encouraged a cosmopolitan minority as an attempt to clamp alien rules and values on their America. From this pool of vulnerability and suspicion came the popular force behind the anticommunist movement that swept the United States in the postwar years. "Well, around here," an Alabama farmer told the novelist John Dos Passos, "communism's anything we don't like. Isn't it that way everywhere else?"[3] It certainly was, as the gaudy parade of state and local committees pursuing liberalism, collectivism, and subversion of the American Way of Life demonstrated. Although the official doctrines of the Cold War spoke to other issues, they still gave national legitimacy to these varied, parochial concerns.

In May of 1954, as the Supreme Court prepared to issue the *Brown* decision, forces that would shape its meaning sent signals that they, too, were ready. President Eisenhower had just resolved the last important doubts about the government's commitment to manage the economy, and a line of prosperous years stretched ahead. The stalwart of popular anticommunism, Senator Mc-Carthy, was embarked on his last crusade, and his large, scattered following would soon be seeking new causes and heroes. Far from the centers of legal segregation, five black families had recently moved into the Trumbull Park Housing Project, a white domain next to the steel mills of south Chicago, and their new neighbors were greeting them with curses, rocks, and occasional bombs.

When the *Brown* decision did arrive, no one seemed to know what to do. Its very sweep—the categorical repudiation of segregated education and the clear prefiguring of Jim Crow's collapse —created a sudden vacuum that neither its partisans nor its opponents were prepared to fill. Southern resistance gathered first. After an interlude of compliance along the borders of the South, strict segregationists rallied to dominate debate for the balance of the fifties. Their call to arms, accented by a distinctively southern defensiveness, expressed the same blend of subversion, invasion, and local jeopardy—often in the same language—that characterized popular anticommunism. The "home-grown variety of Communists [who] clustered in Washington, in the colleges, universities, churches, on the lecture platform and in other strategic places in this country" formed the army of their enemies: "Red," "Yankee," and relentless. Waverers in the defense of the South were "soft on integration." The NAACP, the CIO, and "Communist-infiltrated" merged together, as did "Integration, Social Gospel, Collectivism." To implement the schemes of these radicals, the *Brown* decision now gave "the central government a power it had never before possessed—the power to put its grasping and omnipotent hand on a purely local function."[4] If liberals thought these segregationists were condemning themselves as demented bigots, the segregationists believed liberals were condemning themselves as eager fellow travelers.

Massive resistance in the fifties gave a deceptive impression of power and cohesion.[5] Locally oriented Americans never welcomed extensive, systematic organizations, and other than on election days, southern segregationists remained an array of units that functioned best in such tight little ventures as the long school closing in Prince Edward County, Virginia, or the persecution of neighboring black activists. Each unit was about as strong as its own resources made it. Leaders of the resistance further weakened it by entwining segregation with a number of unpopular causes. The overlap between officials of the White Citizens' Council and members of the John Birch Society highlighted their tactical problems, for no broad southern constituency wanted to abolish graduated income taxes or eliminate the welfare state. Moreover, the same unyielding policies that secured a short-run advantage for the strict segregationists proved in the not very long run a grave deficiency. With even a moderately serious enforcement of the law their brittle program would simply snap. An all-or-nothing defense left them no room for retreat.

Law in general was the central and unsolvable problem of massive resistance. The solid citizens in charge of the movement had grounded their careers in the intricacies and authority of the law. Just as they turned naturally to it in an attempt to destroy such local enemies as the NAACP, so they struggled mightily with it to avoid the stigma of an illegal cause, leaving an elaborate trail of homemade constitutional law for their efforts. Though many of them recognized its quixotic qualities, the temper of the nation as well as their own values made it an essential enterprise. Outside the South, the strongest flow into the vacuum behind the *Brown* decision was a sense that the law of the land had invested blacks with new rights and that these rights must somehow be honored. Mandatory school integration, a cause without a focused constituency before 1954, won support at a steady three-to-one ratio for the balance of the decade. An even larger majority sided with the government's enforcement of the law in the crisis of 1957 over integrating Little Rock High School.[6]

With rights came stature. A remarkable shift in white attitudes began to occur in the wake of the *Brown* decision. Equal access to public transportation, a prospect that could never muster a majority of whites during the forties, now had three advocates for every opponent outside the South. In 1942, 84 percent had endorsed segregated housing for blacks; by 1958, three out of five could accept the thought of a black moving next door. Most striking of all, a poll in 1959 of white parents outside the South registered over 90 percent willing to send their children to integrated schools.[7] No doubt these attitudes changed more readily in the late fifties because very few whites had to test them in practice. Nonetheless, something akin to the plan behind the civil rights movement was unfolding. With the national government as monitor, millions of whites were recognizing for the first time a natural connection between the rights of blacks and the American Creed of equality and justice for all. As the pressures on southern segregation mounted, who could fault the strategy of using "the idealism and prestige of the whole people to check the wayward tendencies of a part of them"?

It was this strategy that Martin Luther King, Jr., translated with such genius and flair. Like the NAACP before him, he compartmentalized southern racism as America's great aberration. Appealing to the "heart and conscience" of whites everywhere, King turned the image of the patient southern Negro into a tactic for winning immediate benefits and a justification for demanding more. He invariably combined his civil disobedience with an open respect for the law and an acceptance of its punishments. Always when he addressed whites the value of equality and justice—the American Creed—appeared at the forefront of his message. Blacks wanted nothing more than the "rights [that white Americans] have already enjoyed." "Nonviolent direct action . . . ," King wrote, "found its natural home in [America], where refusal to cooperate with injustice was an ancient and honorable tradition."[8] In 1963, with America's ear attending, King rolled to the climax of his remarkable Washington speech: "I have a dream that one day this nation will rise up and live out the meaning of its creed."

The momentum of the early sixties made the dreamers look like cool-eyed realists. As blacks applied King's tactics in a wholesale assault on Jim Crow, national publicity neatly contrasted the quiet self-discipline of the protesters with the explosive brutality of their opponents. The South stood doubly condemned as lawless. Not only had it defied the word of the courts, it had also twisted the instruments of local justice into implements of oppression. President Kennedy's careful pattern of actions, including prominent offices for blacks, selective use of federal marshals in the South, and timely statements in support of civil rights, set the authority of a popular administration behind the blacks' cause. The façade of strict segregation crumbled. As the White Citizens' Council disintegrated, a network of state and local Republicans, far more adaptive to change, took its place. Now the revolution in attitudes was sweeping the South. In 1963, an astonishing 88 percent of southern whites approved voting rights for blacks, three out of four endorsed integrated public transportation, and only one in five opposed equal job opportunities.[9] King reached the pinnacle of his prestige. By January, 1964, three out of five Americans favored a comprehensive civil rights law, and that July they got one, followed the next year by an elaborate act to ensure the black franchise.[10] With a broad base of public support to sustain it, Congress fulfilled the agenda of Truman's Committee on Civil Rights and brought the first phase of the movement for black rights to a triumphant conclusion.

By 1966, triumph had given way to anger and confusion. Two summers of urban rioting demolished the image of orderly black protest in a frightening cloud of fire and violence. As attention shifted from the South to the industrial cities, where a majority of the nation's blacks now lived, King lost control of his movement and groped for new issues, new ways to harness the rage of the ghettos. Competing black voices dismissed the American Creed as cant, declared racism the white man's faith, and demanded a revolution of their own making. "Backlash" was everybody's term for the white reaction. In Washington, Congress defeated President Johnson's open housing bill. That November, the headlines broadcast a string of conservative victories, led by Ronald Reagan's election as governor of California. Surveying the prospects for black rights in 1967, William Brink and Louis Harris, like so many other sympathizers with the movement, found that their assumptions could no longer explain the conflicts around them. "Americans are, on the whole, a tolerant people and a generous people . . . but they have not seen fit to grant America's 21 million Negroes [their] freedom. . . . Why?"[11]

Like numerous reform movements before it, the initial drive for black rights applied a set of principles to public policy until puzzling, unforeseen circumstances exposed their flaws. The same convictions that had once powered a movement for reform now stalled it. In response to a challenge that the reformers themselves had helped to create, they patched a bit here and adapted a bit there, but they simply could not build anew from fresh assumptions. The energy of the movement dissipated. In retrospect these deficiencies glared back at the historian as evidences of failure. Yet the impressive successes of the civil rights movement argued that its faith in the American Creed, the authority of government, and the peculiar susceptibility of the South to a campaign of national pressure had made a good deal of sense. Nothing unraveled the crucial revolution in white attitudes. Although a minority of segregationists became far noisier in the late sixties, they did not affect the base of opinions beneath the civil rights acts of 1964 and 1965. Backlash, rather than a reversal in white attitudes, was a recasting of them, a shift in emphasis that brought out of the shadows an existing pattern of reservations, doubts, and discontents.

The question of how rapidly to dismantle the structure of racial inequality lay dormant during the late fifties when the felicitous ambiguity of the second *Brown* decision—"with all deliberate speed"—and the sluggish pace of federal enforcement kept the issue from disturbing the changes in white attitudes. In the early sixties, however, a critical gap opened between the commitment to black equality on one side and the proper rate of achieving it on the other. As the snarling dogs of Birmingham and the peaceful March on Washington were preparing the way for the first major civil rights law, 64 percent of the nation's whites thought that blacks were pushing too fast for equality and a meager 6 percent believed that they were moving too slowly. When Johnson buried Goldwater in November, 1964, and looked toward a second major law, those opinions held at 62 percent to 9 percent, not appreciably different from the division of 70 percent to 4 percent during the turmoil of 1966. Responses to the rate at which the national government was pressing for desegregation were only slightly more favorable and equally consistent between the summer of 1963 and the elections of 1966.[12] Beginning with the sit-ins of 1960, each new tactic in the civil rights campaign sparked a negative reaction from whites, including a high percentage who blamed Communists and other "outside agitators." Both before and after the March on Washington, about two-thirds of the nation's whites disapproved such demonstrations. Indeed, they wanted blacks to stop all kinds of public protest. In December, 1966, after ghetto riots and fiery rhetoric had accentuated the moderation of King's strategy, ten whites thought he had hurt the blacks' cause for every seven who judged him a help.[13]

At the same time, whites neither repudiated the abstract right to agitate nor relinquished their commitment to legal equality. The majority condemning the Mississippi Freedom Summer of 1964, for example, was more than matched that year by a majority who believed the national government should enforce black voting rights and protect the activists in Mississippi.[14] At the height of resistance to the black protests in 1966, even larger white majorities continued to believe in such staples of the movement as equal voting and equal access to jobs, rights that quantities of blacks still did not have. A partial explanation for these conflicting attitudes lay in the racist assumption that blacks were simply not capable of using so much freedom all at once, an opinion that two out of three whites held during the heyday of the civil rights movement.[15] More important still was the belief that black equality should come voluntarily, that laws should never be forced on whites of good will. Voluntarism grew at the roots of the civil rights movement. Walter White had spoken its language. So had Eleanor Roosevelt. That spirit lingered through the fifties, and only the sudden acceleration in the early sixties disrupted its sleepy aura. Although almost no whites were being coerced to do anything for or with blacks, events now had an uncomfortable push about them, and whites responded by insisting that the whole movement slow down. Some freedom now. More later.

Racism was more intimately connected with a second major qualification to the new belief in black equality. No proposition had greater currency among white leaders in the civil rights movement than the conviction that closeness dissolved prejudice. There was "incontrovertible evidence," Truman's Committee on Civil Rights declared, "that an environment favorable to civil rights is fostered whenever groups are permitted to live and work together."[16] Chief Justice Warren's phrasing of the *Brown* decision fixed the principle in public policy, and much of the magic surrounding integrated schools drew on this faith. Yet no conclusion was clearer from the polls of the early sixties than the increasing wariness among whites, as equality implied greater intimacy with blacks. From an almost unanimous support for equal voting, the percentage of white approval for black rights descended step by step: equal employment opportunities, integrated public transportation, integrated schools, and then at the pivot between acceptance and rejection, integrated housing. While a slight majority of the nation's whites endorsed open housing in 1963, only 22 percent thought they would stay if many blacks moved into the neighborhood.[17] Even equality in employment presumed some separation. "It's the idea of rubbing up against them," said a white factory worker who considered himself a tolerant man. "It won't rub off but it don't feel right, either."[18] At the bottom rung, whites overwhelmingly opposed interracial dating and marriage. A strand of "amalgamation" fears from the nineteenth century had entwined itself in the twentieth-century movement for equality.

As the underside of white attitudes was being exposed, the tone and thrust of black demands changed dramatically. Looking at the rubble of hopes around him in 1966, a young Brooklyn black announced the next phase of the movement: "I don't think we need civil rights, we need human rights. . . . The trouble here is people have nothing to do."[19] The most expressive black voices of the late sixties called for fulfillment, the right to seize opportunities for a rich, open life as individuals and as blacks. The first phase of the movement had emphasized legal form and public equality; now the accent fell on human potential and personal freedom. In the civil rights movement, black progress was measured against a determinate base—the rights of white Americans. Fulfillment left that standard and stretched outward for room to grow. Like the pursuit of happiness, it beckoned people toward irresistible visions. As firmly as the objectives of the civil rights movement drew blacks and whites together, the preconditions of fulfillment separated them. Black Power and Black Pride required breaking loose from the white man's web to develop a distinctively black independence. What appalled an older generation of leaders resonated well with popular black sentiments. In the flush of the civil rights movement, when less than one black leader in ten thought whites were primarily motivated by a desire to oppress their people, almost half the nation's blacks expressed that grim opinion. Fifty-two percent of the leaders believed that above all whites wanted greater opportunities for Negroes; only one in four American blacks agreed. Judgments about an improvement, or lack of it, in recent white attitudes showed the same striking contrast between leaders and masses.[20] When the ghetto riots erupted, a large majority of urban blacks approved their spirit even as they deplored many of their consequences. Whatever else the riots meant, they marked the end of legal equality as a sufficient reform agenda.

Black militancy spread confusion among the white partisans of civil rights. Some felt cheated. Black Power, they charged, was reverse racism. They had expected legal equality to moderate sentiments, minimize disruptions, and stabilize society. Rioting and accusing blacks, by implication, had broken the rules. Many other whites sympathized with the cries for fulfillment. They read Malcolm X and Claude Brown appreciatively, applauded the sober liberalism of the Kerner Report on Civil Disorders, and recognized the need for far greater efforts. Yet they simply did not know what to do. Acknowledging the subtle pervasiveness of racism and the intolerable burdens of poverty did not create a new program. The cue words of the late sixties—compensation, reparations, affirmative action—suggested a way of thinking more than a line of policy.

To the degree that the civil rights movement had incorporated the yearnings toward fulfillment, it subsumed them under the broad expectations for integrated education. The rise of the movement from the late forties to the early sixties coincided with the years of greatest faith in the personal and social powers of quality education. It was the beanstalk in everyone's backyard: climb the ladder of special skills and reach the American Dream. Hence the *Brown* decision not only broke the wall of segregation; it also defined the promises on the other side. Although integration and education no longer roused the same fresh enthusiasm in the late sixties, they remained a primary continuity with the first phase of the movement, and policymakers plunged ahead in an effort to force a fast, high return from their investment. Stern court orders to integrate and busing to implement them, Head Start and Upward Bound programs, new attempts to reach black dropouts and recruit black graduate students, all reflected this urgent attention to the curative effects of education. Nevertheless, equality had forever lost its clarity. Equal opportunity, equal rights to dignity and growth, contained none of the specificity of a flat legal equality covering all citizens. Opportunity measured by the lives of which whites or what ideal? Who could even calculate dignity or self-realization? Just when the urban riots invested the issue of black rights with a sense of immediacy, well-intentioned white reformers could grasp neither the ends nor the means for an appropriate response.

A majority of whites had far less difficulty assessing the events of the late sixties. Mass media, which had been so favorable to the civil rights cause a few years earlier, spread terrifying images of inner cities in flames and black guerrillas in arms. Longstanding white concerns about law and order and about the speed and tactics of the civil rights movement swelled into harsh demands for repression. The way to stop riots, most of them agreed, was not to expand opportunities but to quash rioters. Even before Americans heard that Mayor Daley had instructed Chicago police to kill arsonists and maim looters, two-thirds of them advocated shooting anyone who threw a fire bomb during a riot. A majority of whites in every region, occupation, age-group, and political party welcomed the news of Daley's order. Under stress, it became more apparent than ever that most whites viewed the struggle for equality as an issue between blacks and other whites in other places. In their own communities, three out of four of them concluded, blacks were receiving the same treatment as whites. The next logical step was to relieve whites of any further obligations for black progress. After widespread rioting in the spring of

1968, only 24 percent thought that whites were more responsible for the blacks' problems than the blacks themselves.[21]

The less leeway that whites enjoyed in their own lives, the harder these attitudes toward blacks grew. At the lowest levels of income, education, and skills were concentrated the largest proportion of holdouts against black equality and the greatest anxiety about changes in race relations. When the normative attitude on open housing waffled between a tentative acceptance and a cautious rejection, for example, 58 percent of the blue-collar whites in Chicago fiercely resisted the prospect of any blacks in their neighborhoods.[22] Here black gains threatened white losses, and the movement for equality assumed the guise of a raid on their small storehouse of privileges. Blacks held no monopoly on the yearnings for fulfillment. Blue-collar whites also dreamed of breaking the box around their lives, and quite literally these black and white dreams might involve the same schools and jobs and houses.

Even among those whites who accepted black equality during the civil rights era, its most common translation read: a right to as much as I have—but no more. Hence the persisting uneasiness over the speed of the movement. In 1963, when a substantial white majority in favor of equal job opportunities had become well-established, a mammoth 97 percent opposed giving blacks any preferences in employment.[23] Once again, the intensity of these feelings deepened among poor whites. Seventy percent of the whites with incomes of $3,000 or less rejected the entire panoply of President Johnson's "War on Poverty" because they thought it benefited blacks at their expense. Blue-collar Philadelphians regarded federal aid to education as a ruse for ignoring them and helping blacks. In both cases this hostility was firmly tied to a belief that blacks were no worse off than they.[24] As the national government increasingly used affirmative action to answer the needs of blacks, only the diffuse, piecemeal nature of its actions avoided an angry confrontation with white opinion.

Precisely what angered whites grew less and less distinct during the late sixties and early seventies, for the resistance to an expansion of black rights was becoming submerged in a larger flow of resistance to national power. The Supreme Court, pioneer in applying the government's authority to black rights, also initiated the erosion of that authority. As early as 1957 the liberal bent of the Warren Court had started to cut into its national popularity, but an actual crisis in confidence did not begin until 1962, when *Engel* v. *Vitale* prepared the way for a ban on prayers and Bible-reading in the public schools and *Baker* v. *Carr* placed state reapportionment under the Court's jurisdiction. By the midsixties, campaigns to overturn the religious restrictions and modify the rule of one-person, one-vote were pushing hard for constitutional amendments. By then the Court had also completed its widely publicized framework to protect the rights of criminal suspects.

In the battle against Jim Crow, the national government's power and authority had meshed remarkably well. Outside the South a large majority of whites had perceived the southern segregationists as a deviant, lawless minority and the government as an impartial agent of law and order. By the early sixties, southerners who rejected segregation could take cover beneath this national consensus, leave unconverted whites even more isolated, and increase public pressures behind an enforcement of the law. Whatever their persuasions, southern whites came to accept as a fated fact that "the South [was] moving from segregation to integration."[25] No comparable climate surrounded the law of the land in the late sixties. Various majorities now perceived the national government as a source of lawlessness and disorder. It undermined religion, promoted pornography, and coddled crooks. A survey in 1968 revealed 70 percent who considered the Supreme Court a major cause of crime.[26] Meanwhile, the official lies and public tumult accompanying the Vietnam War deepened the identification of Washington with deception and disruption. Though these attitudes never combined into a single, simple judgment, a blend of them had a devastatingly corrosive effect on the popular faith in an impartial national government. At the core of the matter was a belief that national power was assaulting the inalienable rights and peaceful pursuits of its citizens.

Throughout the transition in attitudes toward the government, opposition to Washington and opposition to black rights persistently reinforced one another. Responding to *Baker* v. *Carr*, one Tennessee legislator declared that the "Supreme Court already has shoved integration down our throats, and now it is trying to do the same with reapportionment. . . . Apparently its formula is more Negroes and less money for rural areas."[27] Among those who resented the latest government programs in behalf of black equality, the objects and subjects of an intrusive national power merged in ever more visible ways: a bus for the school children, a federal registrar for the black voters, a local OEO office for the poverty programs. Bitterness toward welfare fed upon white images of lazy, irresponsible blacks. Stereotypically and statistically, the most likely criminal suspect in the major cities was a young black male, and the issue of police practices swirled around the ghetto riots. Interactions of this kind helped to erase the impression of sharp regional differences in white attitudes. Before Johnson's presidency, the most publicized debates over social policy gave the appearance of a southern camp versus a northern camp. The causes of the late sixties leveled these barriers. By 1964, Senator Everett Dirksen of Illinois was directing northerners and southerners alike against the Supreme Court's rulings on reapportionment and religious instruction, and Governor George Wallace of Alabama was leading a formidable revolt in the Wisconsin and Indiana presidential primaries. Wallace's net, once restricted to "segregation forever," had expanded to cover a national scope of fears about invasive powers. Left to its own inclinations, he declared that year, Washington would squire "out-of-state riff-raff, Communists, and fellow travelers, kooks, beatniks, prostitutes and bums" into every American community and cripple the "local law enforcement personnel who seek to prevent depradations against peace and order."[28] By the end of the decade, the contours of southern white opinion on race relations looked very much like those of national white opinion. Here as elsewhere integration was becoming another example of national coercion.

When Nixon and Wallace together won 57 percent of the presidential vote in 1968, Kevin Phillips, the troubadour of a coming Republican era, singled out "the Negro problem . . . [as] the principal cause of the breakup of the New Deal coalition."[29] At best it was a dubious guess. To the extent that black rights remained a separable issue, white attitudes on equal education, public accommodations, employment, and housing gradually and steadily liberalized from the mid-sixties to the early seventies. Even in the sensitive areas of interracial intimacy, significant shifts in opinion occurred. The majority support for antimiscegenation laws collapsed, and the belief that interracial dating and marriage were the coming trends won broad acceptance.[30] As these attitudes moderated, the issues themselves lost their salience. By 1971, only 20 percent of both whites and blacks listed racial equality among the nation's most important problems, a ranking far below questions of pollution, drugs, and crime.[31] Black rights alone could move no majority across party lines.

The upshot of these changing views on black rights was a rough three-way division in white attitudes. About a quarter of the nation's whites retained strong racist and segregationist convictions. They judged blacks innately inferior, criminally inclined, and insensitive to family feelings. None of their demands was justified, and Washington had no business enforcing them. Whatever the law said, whites had every right to exclude blacks from white neighborhoods.[32] Approximately another quarter of the white population were committed partisans of the black cause. They considered blacks generally oppressed, accepted most of their specific charges of discrimination, and endorsed the actions that blacks had taken in their own behalf. Neither the prospect of large numbers of blacks in their neighborhood nor the thought of busing white children to achieve integration disturbed them. The government, they believed, should hold Americans to the letter of the civil rights laws.[33] The remaining half of the whites slipped into the latest version of an American dilemma. They supported the original civil rights agenda, recognized that some of it had not been fulfilled, and acknowledged the need for national force to implement it. At the same time, they balked at almost every new measure to further black rights. Although most of them approved immediate school integration and the appropriateness of blacks living wherever they could afford to go, they opposed both mandatory busing and open housing laws. Unequivocally they condemned affirmative action. Skeptical about the severity of black hardships and the wisdom of black tactics, this segment of the white population contained the critical body of citizens who would have to be converted in any renewed drive for black rights.[34]

Instead, other issues were taking precedence, and to a striking degree they were augmenting the antigovernment movement. Legalized abortions brought new recruits. So did the sapping of confidence that accompanied the fall of Agnew and Nixon. Even the popular faith in Washington's economic management, the basic prop beneath its structure of authority, seriously weakened as government officials fumbled with the complex problems of stagflation. The consequences for black rights were uniformly depressing. White backlash, despite its racist sting, primarily sought limits to the pursuit of these rights. The broad movement against national intrusion, on the other hand, demanded an outright reversal of government policies, a removal of those powers restraining the free play of local values. Caught in its currents, the cause of black rights suffered more than it should have on its own merits. In countless ways during the fifties and sixties, prosperity had underwritten the drive for black rights, breeding optimism about more opportunities for everybody, generating funds for new programs, and justifying an expansion of the government's responsibilities. Economic uncertainty and political ineptness lowered expectations across a whole range of government programs and sharply diminished Washington's capacity to rally citizens behind any cause, let alone as difficult a one as black fulfillment.

Superficially, the government's policies on black rights entered the seventies intact. Congress finally banned housing discrimination in 1968, and the next year the Supreme Court replaced "all deliberate speed" with immediate compliance as the guide to school desegregation. As President Nixon took office, he promised special assistance for black capitalists. Clauses requiring some measure of affirmative action soon became commonplace in federal laws and contracts. Yet the entire process lacked thrust and imagination. The government demobilized the War on Poverty, and Nixon made it perfectly clear that no substitute was forthcoming. "Benign neglect," the administration's controversial slogan on the issue of black rights, deftly captured the haziness in national policy. In 1973, with rising violence over school integration in Boston and growing hostility to busing in Washington, the Supreme Court disapproved a metropolitanwide desegregation plan for Detroit because its white suburbs had shown no discriminatory intent. Chief Justice Burger's opinion conspicuously praised the principle of local control over education. Henceforth, busing orders would follow a cautious, case-by-case approach. Detachment accompanied drift. Income data became the new measure of black equality, superseding the legal standard of the civil rights era. Although these statistics unquestionably dealt with matters crucial to fulfillment, the graph-watching of the seventies usually implied a cool view of long-term changes, an absence of urgency about black progress, and a willingness to take satisfaction from almost any lessening of the racial gaps. No dots on the chart marked King's beatific vision or Detroit's smoldering ghetto.

Few whites fought hard against the drift in national policy. Without a new source of cohesion, veterans of the civil rights movement fragmented and dispersed. The marching, chanting college students disappeared, not simply because Black Power had driven them away but also because no magnetic goals drew them in. As the black population in industrial centers expanded, former white allies in the battle against urban decay abandoned both the programs and the cities to the blacks themselves. Union officials who had been wary of the movement for black rights since the midsixties now joined the opposition to affirmative action. Only black leaders consistently gave their own cause top priority, and even they experienced great difficulty in defining strategy.

As Ford succeeded Nixon and Carter Ford, nothing eased the anger at outside intrusions, the decline in government authority, or the confusion over black equality, and nothing better exemplified these trends than the inconclusive hullabaloo over *Regents of the University of California* v. *Bakke* (1978). Around Bakke's contention that a quota for minority students had unreasonably denied him entry to medical school, concerns about public policy radiated in wider and wider circles. Would the Court discourage blacks from mounting the educational ladder? Black leaders, sensitive to the continuing unpopularity of affirmative action, met *Bakke* like the devil's host.[35] What of affirmative action in other institutions? Resisting corporations and unions looked for a sign of relief. Where would the government turn if it could no longer use mild doses of affirmative action to answer almost every problem of black rights? The Justice Department requested a judgment that would leave maximum discretion to the government. How would this case affect the larger movement against government management? The National Association of Manufacturers and the United States Chamber of Commerce, inveterate enemies of government regulation, filed briefs in Bakke's behalf.

In two 5-to-4 decisions and six opinions, the Court stripped the case of its cosmic implications and made it a mirror for the blurred conditions surrounding black rights. One bare majority of justices declared the meaning of equality in its simplest civil rights sense no longer adequate: they upheld affirmative action. Another scant majority opposed a systematic program of formulas to engineer opportunities for blacks: they left quotas in limbo. Preserving the principle of affirmative action, the Court drained its value for general policy. As in the Detroit busing case, the Court linked the use of quotas to evidence of discriminatory intent, particularizing the issue and guaranteeing interminable, indeterminate litigation. Compensatory justice would redress one specific grievance at a time, not do battle with the accumulated sins of society.

Moderate voices from *Time*, *Newsweek*, and the *New York Times* praised the *Bakke* decisions for their intelligent restraint, if not their legal precision. In a pile of words, the Court gave acceptable expression to the caution and the muddle over an issue that a generation earlier had appeared so ready for bold, clear action. Once black rights had been defined as legal uniformity, and Americans could chart its progress on a master sheet of statutes. Now black equality blended with social opportunity and human fulfillment, and Americans could agree neither on its meaning nor on its wisdom. Once the national government had invested a surplus of authority in accelerating the civil rights movement. Now running a deficit, it could afford almost no risks in the blacks' cause. Once black rights had been understood as a peculiar problem of southern backwardness. In 1954, the name of the Topeka Board of Education opposite Brown had seemed an ironic quirk of legal history. Now southern white attitudes toward school integration no longer showed any traces of regional distinctiveness, and black children "were more likely to attend schools with substantial numbers of [white] children in the South than elsewhere in the nation."[36] In 1978, the regents of the University of California were logical mates to Bakke, for their state contained a thoroughly national mixture of conflicting attitudes and crosspatch inclinations toward black rights.

If anyone wanted to claim the role of seer in this transformation, the credits would divide about evenly between the radical Right and the radical Left. The archconservative cries of government tyranny that had sounded so cranky in the fifties proved to be harbingers of a majority sentiment for the seventies. Their anticommunism had been lost in the rhetoric of antibureaucracy, their Birchite economics had been softened for less affluent Americans, and their calls for freedom had been leavened with the language of local rights. Nonetheless, the hostility to an oppressive, invasive government ran a clear connecting line across the decades. The strength of that line also traced the progress of black rights. When the enemies of managerial government were relatively weak and scattered, the civil rights movement thrived. When resistance to Washington and resistance to black ambitions joined, the movement stalled. When the government's authority declined, no new movement could get underway. By the seventies, an American Creed that had once facilitated civil rights was slowing the drive toward black fulfillment, for the most popular enemy of equality and justice and freedom was now national power. In the same month of the *Bakke* decision, California contributed still another signal of the times when its voters endorsed a sweeping antigovernment attack on property taxes. Appropriately, the most dependable foes of this nationwide reaction were blacks and other racial minorities, whose opportunities suffered the most from the government's waning authority.

From the far Left had come warnings that class, not race, lay at the base of the blacks' problems. An analysis that seemed downright perverse during the civil rights era moved closer and closer to the heart of the matter as the goals of the movement shifted from legal equality to human fulfillment, for the essence of fulfillment was a cluster of aspirations common to working-class whites and blacks alike. Much of the indecisiveness besetting well-to-do whites after the mid-sixties reflected their uneasiness over demands that challenged not just American racism but the social order itself. The Second Reconstruction, like the first, faltered at a point where black rights blended with the needs of poor Americans generally. Affirmative action accepted the existing scale of incomes and opportunities, then tried to spread blacks evenly across it. From that vantage point the data watchers found encouragement in such evidence as the diminishing difference in black and white wages. Between 1955 and 1975, black men climbed from 64 percent to 77 percent of the level for white males, and black women rose from 57 percent almost to parity with white women. But because blacks concentrated where unemployment and family disorganization were endemic, their median family income in 1975 still hung near 60 percent of that for white families, a very modest improvement of about 10 percent over twenty-five years and a reminder of the trap that slums sprang on all their inhabitants.[37] Only an attack on the problems that bound blacks and whites together at the bottom of American society would budge this sticky curve.

In countless private decisions whites verified the new merger of race into class. Toward blacks as humans and as equals their attitudes had altered fundamentally. The basic civil rights laws became objects of national pride, and Martin Luther King entered the ranks of America's schoolroom heroes. With remarkably little fuss whites accepted the diffusion of blacks throughout the world of television, and the saga of *Roots* drew tears from interracial millions. Yet whites fled the cities as fast as possible, carrying with them an equation of black life with violence and crime, congestion and garbage, bad schools and blighted opportunities. Only those who could not afford the resegregation of the seven-tics remained behind with the blacks. "The vast majority of the members of the two races lived as far apart in the 1970s as they had in the 1940s," one expert has concluded.[38] What had not changed was the myth of middleclassness, the belief that American society had spaces for everyone to enjoy a comfortable competence with a pocketful of credit cards, a cart full of groceries, and an ample retirement plan. Black poverty cast the darkest single shadow across this vision, and conflicting white urges to escape it, eradicate it, condemn it, and evade it pushed the issue itself beyond the boundaries of effective policy.

# The Jurisprudence of *Brown*
# and the Dilemmas of Liberalism

MORTON J. HORWITZ

The decision in *Brown* v. *Board of Education* was not only a major event in the history of race relations; it was also a significant moment in American jurisprudence. It represented the beginning of the disintegration of a progressive consensus on the nature and function of law and of the role of courts and legislatures in our constitutional system.

This consensus—which I will call "liberal jurisprudence"—began to develop in the late nineteenth century and crystallized into a synthetic whole shortly after 1905, when the United States Supreme Court decided *Lochner* v. *New York*, which held that the state regulation of workmen's hours constituted a violation of a constitutional right to "freedom of contract."[1] The famous dissenting opinion of Justice Holmes in that case, which, with biting irony, accused the majority of enacting Herbert Spencer's *Social Statics* into law, became the rallying focus for fifty years of liberal jurisprudence. "The case," Justice Holmes protested, "is decided upon an economic theory which a large part of the country does not entertain."

After Justice Holmes's dissent, it became a standard point of argument among progressives to denounce the United States Supreme Court for enacting its own reactionary social and economic preferences into law. Constitutional law, they charged, had

been politicized. The only appropriate institution authorized under our constitutional system to make political choices, they maintained, was the legislature and not the courts. And out of this
progressive critique of the so-called "nine old men" came the
rallying cry of liberal jurisprudence—"judicial restraint."[2] For a
half-century until the decision in *Brown* v. *Board of Education*
the notion that courts should ordinarily defer to the policies of
the legislature became the principal article of faith of liberal
jurisprudence.

All of that changed with *Brown*. And for the last twenty-five
years liberal opinion has gradually tried to make jurisprudential
sense of its abandonment of the dogma of judicial restraint in that
case and many that followed.

Let me make my own position clear. I do not believe that the
classical liberal argument for judicial restraint ever really made
sense. It was an ideology designed for the particular purpose of
restraining conservative judges who were interfering too much
with a long overdue program of social reform at the beginning of
the twentieth century. Judicial restraint certainly never corre-
sponded to the realities of our actual constitutional traditions.
One was constantly amused to find that proponents of judicial
restraint like Justices Holmes, Brandeis, and Frankfurter also
numbered among their heroes Chief Justice Marshall, who certainly could never have been accused of modest exercises of
judicial power. Heroic judges, they seemed to be saying, should
be confined to a mythic past when judges were larger than life.
True, Chief Justice Marshall could dedicate his life to molding
American law in accordance with his own most fundamental visions of American society. But, these justices seemed to believe,
the age of heroic judges had passed and judicial modesty was
currently the only virtue.

The argument for judicial restraint did not arise from any clear
constitutional tradition of deference to legislatures. If anything,
the constitutional history of our first hundred years tended to

show the opposite. It was not history but theory that produced the progressive arguments for judicial restraint.

Simply put, the progressive argument was that judicial review of legislation was undemocratic and that it had been smuggled into American law without any constitutional justification by Chief Justice Marshall in *Marbury* v. *Madison*. Out of illicit beginnings, the argument went, judicial review continued to perform the undemocratic task of overruling legislative majorities. I think it is now quite clear that judicial review was solidly grounded in the understandings and assumptions of the Founding Fathers,[3] though we would still need to argue about whether it is any longer possible to believe in what the framers of the Constitution did believe in—that most constitutional commands were relatively clear and easy to apply without presenting the danger of too much judicial discretion. In any case, once the historical argument about the intention of the framers concerning judicial review drops out of consideration—on the basis of clear evidence that some sort of judicial review was assumed by many of them—we are still left with the question of whether judicial review is undemocratic.

That the question could have been put in this way is a measure of the myopia that those engaged in political struggle are willing to impose on themselves. How could the progressives of 1905— or anyone for that matter—ever have supposed that fidelity to majority rule was the only constitutional value in American society? Or for that matter, why did they not turn to the analogous question of whether the power of common-law judges to make law was undemocratic, which had been the central issue during the Jacksonian period seventy-five years earlier?

In short, it seems clear in retrospect that our constitutional system has always presupposed some system of higher law in which judges would on occasion interpret constitutional commands to limit the will of the majority.[4] Only the exigencies of political struggle—the desire to erect a theory which would delegitimate the reactionary decisions of the Court around 1900—led progressives to a theory of judicial restraint based on the notion that judicial review was undemocratic.

Another aspect of liberal jurisprudence was challenged in *Brown.* After 1905, a major element of progressive jurisprudence focused on the idea that law simply reflects social forces. What was wrong with the courts, this argument emphasized, was that law had become so formalistic and legalistic that it had lost touch with social realities. By the 1920s, this view had crystallized into the only native American school of jurisprudence—"legal realism."[5]

But legal realism had assumed that law simply reflects social forces, and that it was not either desirable or possible for it to serve as a catalyst for social change. Under the influence of legal realism, law had been emasculated of its traditional moral content, and progressives had lost faith in its utopian possibilities for defining the dreams, hopes, and aspirations of a community.

Judicial restraint was an inevitable consequence of this loss of faith in law.

But however weak and internally incoherent they may be, ideologies often take on a life of their own. And by the time *Brown* v. *Board of Education* was to be decided, almost two generations of liberals had imported into their own jurisprudence some version of judicial restraint. Thus, *Brown* truly represented one of the most agonizing moments in American jurisprudence. In some sense, all American constitutional law for the past twenty-five years has revolved around trying to justify the judicial role in *Brown* while trying simultaneously to show that such a course will not simply lead once more to another *Lochner* era.

After twenty-five years of debate, it would be presumptuous of me to suppose that I can, in a single stroke, resolve this dilemma. What I wish to do instead is present certain guidelines within which any discussion of the legitimacy of the constitutional role of the Supreme Court must function.

First, we must abandon the erroneous assumption that our constitutional tradition ever required that a temporary majority should be able to rule without constitutional restraint. If that is antidemocratic, so be it.

Second, we must abandon the assumption that we can easily distinguish between political and nonpolitical, neutral versus nonneutral, or result-oriented versus principled constitutional decision-making. In some sense, constitutional decision-making in America has always involved choices among ultimate values and goals by judges. That is inevitable with any system of judicial review, just as the common-law power of judges to decide contracts or property disputes also endows them with law-making power.

Third, we must abandon the silly notion that our constitutional text usually provides clear or self-executing constitutional commands which permit us to suppose that the process of constitutional adjudication is neutral and nonpolitical. Most searches for a clear "intent of the framers" end up in uncertainty and ambiguity. This is doubly true when we focus on such intentionally ambiguous constitutional phrases as "due process" or "equal protection of the laws." Though we may yearn to believe that in a world of flux and uncertainty at least legal principles are clear and unambiguous, such a situation has rarely existed, even though in some historical periods many people have actually believed it to be so.

What I am suggesting is that to some extent we must judge constitutional principles by whether they accord with our own substantive views of justice and not with some preordained abstract model of a neutral and nonpolitical judicial role.

And the reason why *Brown* v. *Board of Education* presented liberalism with such a deep jurisprudential dilemma was that liberalism, still fighting the last war, had developed a thoroughly simple-minded model of judicial restraint that ignored some of the underlying values of our constitutional system. And because the earlier attack on the *Lochner* Court had been framed, not in terms of substantive objections to that court's social and economic vision, but instead in terms of some abstract model of the properly neutral judicial role, liberalism was stuck with its own inadequate definition of the problem.

In this sense, apart from its enormous influence over our vision of race relations in this country, *Brown* stirred up a major jurisprudential debate over the nature and function of judicial review that has persisted through the present. What only a generation earlier had seemed like a settled question that yielded clear and indisputable answers has once more, as it has so many other times in American history, become a major subject of debate.

I would now like to turn to some of the actual substantive dilemmas presented by the decision in *Brown*. We have not been able, twenty-five years after *Brown* v. *Board of Education* was decided, to work our way clear of its basic dilemmas. For example, does it stand simply for color blindness—for the principle that it is constitutionally impermissible for the state to take race into account even for benign purposes—or instead does it stand as a barrier only to the use of racial classifications for the purpose of oppressing racial minorities? Should the principle of *Brown* continue to be directed only at governmental discrimination—so-called state action—or should it apply to private action as well? Does *Brown* require only that racial minorities be provided equality of opportunity? But what happens when even after all of the *formal* barriers of exclusion are dropped, the intangible culture of racism or the scars of a history of deprivation continue to produce racially unequal consequences? Is a racially discriminatory program one that is intended to produce unequal results or one that actually produces such results regardless of the intentions or motivations of its creators? Do such programs interfere with the constitutional rights of nonminority members who may be excluded because of minority preference for jobs, housing, or admission?

The entire history of the judicial battle against racial discrimination over the past twenty-five years has been dominated by several important factors:

First, by a political and legal culture of individualism that defines a problem exclusively in terms of the rights of individuals, not of groups.

Second, by a pervasive legalism, which has frequently undermined lawsuits challenging racial discrimination by confusing them either with criminal trials or with private lawsuits between individuals. As a result, there has been a series of embarrassing judicial fluctuations among different conceptions of the antidiscrimination lawsuit.

Third, there has been a periodic resurgence of extremely formalistic judicial decisions, usually for the purpose of vainly trying to maintain a coherent line between public and private or between political and social discrimination.

Finally, the struggle for racial equality initiated by *Brown* has brought to the surface a whole series of dilemmas concerning the precise nature of our commitments to social and economic equality.

At the heart of many of the confusions produced by an overly legalized approach to the problem of racial discrimination is the prevailing view that individual and not group rights are at stake in any lawsuit challenging racial discrimination. Justice Powell recently stated the dominant view in his decisive opinion in the *Bakke* case:[6]

. . . the difficulties entailed in varying the level of judicial review according to a perceived "preferred" status of a particular racial or ethnic minority are intractable. The concepts of "majority" and "minority" necessarily reflect temporary arrangements and political judgments. . . . the white "majority" itself is composed of various minority groups, most of which can lay claim to a history of prior discrimination at the hands of the state and private individuals. Not all of these groups can receive preferential treatment and corresponding judicial tolerance of distinctions drawn in terms of race and nationality, for then the only "majority" left would be a new minority of White Anglo-Saxon Protestants. There is no principled basis for deciding which groups would merit "heightened judicial solicitude" and which would not. Courts would be asked to evaluate the extent of the prejudice and consequent harm suffered by various minority groups. Those whose societal injury is thought to exceed some arbitrary level of tolerability then would be entitled to preferential classifications at the expense of individuals belonging to other groups. Those classifications would be free from exacting judicial scrutiny. As these preferences began to have their desired effect, and the consequences of past discrimination were undone, new judicial rankings would be necessary. The kind of variable sociological and political analysis necessary to produce such rankings simply does not lie within the judicial competence—even if they otherwise were politically feasible and socially desirable.

There is no question that within our political and legal tradition we have had difficulty in recognizing the existence of groups or classes. We are in part products of the history of the rise of liberalism which directed much of its energies to destroying a medieval corporate society that was organized into classes and guilds. The overthrow of legally established churches in America after the Revolution also contributed to the predisposition to view all legal as well as religious entitlements exclusively in terms of relations among atomized individuals. Thus, liberals came largely to conceive of groups as artificial aggregations of individuals having no real identities apart from those who happened to compose the group. As a result, our legal tradition has regularly tried to deny the significance or "naturalness" of group membership.

But this disposition to deny the significance of group rights—because, in Justice Powell's words, "the kind of variable sociological and political analysis necessary to produce such rankings does not lie within the judicial competence"—may at the same time involve an egregious denial of reality as well as of justice.

Justice Powell's view is predicated on the premise that there are, legally speaking, no "natural classes" obviously entitled by our history, culture, and law to distinctive treatment.[7] "[T]he recognition of special wards entitled to a degree of protection greater than that accorded others," Justice Powell writes, would turn "the clock of our liberties . . . back to 1868."[8] To the extent that there are differences in the treatment which our society has accorded various minority groups, he simply assumes they are differences of degrees, not of kind. He therefore supposes that, at most, there exists a continuum of unjustly burdened minority groups for which we might conceivably establish "rankings" of oppression only after an incredibly complex process of sociological and political analysis. Such a complex task, he concludes, is simply beyond judicial competence.

I submit that the issue is much simpler than that. There do exist at least two "natural groups" in American society that even a cursory study of American history would affirm. Both American Indians and blacks, because of a history of treatment which has both sought to promote and to remedy injustice and has been reflected both in culture and law, have been regularly accorded a distinctive place in American society and law. One might wish to argue about women as a third such class, but I prefer to pass for now on that question. This does not mean that, for example, affirmative action for Chicanos might not be justified under some other principles of justice. But to suggest, as Justice Powell does in *Bakke*, that the nature and quality of discrimination experienced by blacks in America is different only in degree from that suffered by Jews or Italian Americans is in my view an egregious misunderstanding of American history.

One hundred years ago, shortly after the Civil War and the passage of the Civil War amendments, it was abundantly clear, in the words of Justice Miller in the *Slaughter-House Cases*,[9] that the then recently enacted constitutional amendments "disclosed a unity of purpose" and contemplated "a grand yet simple declaration of the personal freedom of all the human race within the jurisdiction of this government—a declaration designed to establish the freedom of four million slaves." "[T]hat history," he wrote, "is fresh within the memory of us all." Only to the extent that we forget that history can we ever believe that blacks are just like any other burdened minority in American society.

Let me suggest that the classical liberal hostility to recognizing any groups as "natural" expresses other deep ideological tendencies in liberalism. Liberal thought has always resisted analysis of society in terms of social classes. From John Locke on, there has been a willingness to talk about the "sovereignty of the people," despite the fact that in Locke's time and for one hundred fifty years thereafter the disembodied abstraction he called "the people" still represented only a small property-holding elite entitled to vote.

At the foundation of the liberal emphasis on individualism is the view that the only legitimate standard for judging an individual is on the basis of his own energy and ability. Inequality of rewards has been regarded as a necessary and legitimate consequence even of equality of opportunity, since we are not all equally able or lucky. All that has been required is that each individual start the race of life equally.

But because of its attempts to create a radical distinction between the supposedly legitimate goal of equality of opportunity and the supposedly illegitimate goal of equality of condition, liberalism has faced a number of impossible dilemmas. The first is the obvious problem that in a substantially unequal society it is impossible to produce real equality of opportunity. Does it come as a surprise to learn that the life chances of a large number of persons are determined by the circumstances into which they are born or that the life expectancy of blacks is substantially lower than whites? If we were really serious about equality of opportunity wouldn't we at least impose a virtually confiscatory inheritance tax so that each person would get much less arbitrary advantage from the wealth of his parents than he does at present?

Nor has liberalism really been able successfully to explain why an unusually large number of members of particular groups seem regularly to come out at the bottom. Recent efforts to find a correlation between intelligence and racial groups—the so-called I.Q. controversy—are, in my opinion, but another symptom of the more general bankruptcy of liberal thought. Unwilling to accept the disturbing reality or the anti-individualist implications of a culture of group oppression and deprivation, and unwilling to confront the hypocrisy of any effort to radically distinguish between equality of opportunity and equality of condition, these social scientists have tried to find a supposedly scientific and non-political means of explaining group deprivation. Without a genetic explanation of group deprivation, the ideology of equality of opportunity is revealed as a fraud.

But above all, I wish to insist that we are able to believe that our commitment to equality of opportunity does not entail any commitment to equality of condition, only because we are able also to convince ourselves that individual opportunity has little relation to class or group background. Race in this country has always stood as a constant reminder of the fact that each individual is not judged solely as an individual.

In short, the ideology of individualism in the field of racial discrimination is imposed primarily in order to avoid having the issue of racial equality overflow its bounds and become involved with the cognate question of the legitimacy of social and economic inequality. In fact, however, most of the present distinctions in legal doctrine concerning racial discrimination are efforts to reinforce the political distinction between equality of opportunity and equality of condition.

However much it has been eroded in practice, prevailing constitutional theory continues sharply to distinguish between impermissible public discrimination and legitimate private discrimination. The doctrine of "state-action" still interprets the

Fourteenth Amendment to bar only discrimination through law. This public-private distinction was originally a creation of liberal political theory, which strongly took hold in America a half-century before the Fourteenth Amendment was drafted. It was designed to bridge a seemingly contradictory set of beliefs and values. How could one be in favor of equality before the law while also accepting substantial inequality in social and economic circumstances? The answer given was that all the law requires is that everyone be given an equal opportunity.

Tocqueville long ago observed that Americans have a penchant for turning such political questions into legal ones. The advantages of such a course are clear. The legal system can serve as a cushion or buffer which may diffuse and channel social conflict. And there is no question that the decision in *Brown* v. *Board of Education* both served as a catalyst for and a legitimation of social change. By turning a massive social revolution into legal channels, it ultimately traded on the American reverence for law and legal institutions. A traditionally conservative social institution—the law—was drafted into the cause of social change.

Yet, we have not given enough attention to the other side of the coin, to the tremendous price that legalization and judicialization of social change may have produced. By seeking legal solutions to the problem of racial discrimination, we have also gotten stuck with some of the worst features of any legal definition of a social problem.

As I have already indicated, our legal system is overwhelmingly geared to a conception of redressing individual grievances, not of vindicating group rights or of correcting generalized patterns of injustice. This perspective does not easily encourage judges to focus on the burdens, stigmas, and scars produced by history. Rather, each individual comes to court robbed of the special attributes of group membership, and hence denied the opportunity to say to society at large: "You owe me something as a fellow member of society, because you and your ancestors once deprived my people of their dignity and thus have scarred us all." Deprived of a group identity by a legal system that addresses only violations of individual rights, the minority plaintiff can raise no claim as a result of the injustices heaped on his ancestors and, through them, on him. The history and culture of oppression, transmitted through legally anonymous generations, is made antiseptic by treating each individual as a disconnected and separate being with no history.

There is another and more troubling consequence of the legalization of the problem of racial discrimination. Courts by their nature tend to limit and confine the scope of any conflict over fundamental principle. They also tend to decide questions on the narrowest available definition of principles. As a result, they frequently distort the true meaning of conflicts by supposing that a generalized and deep-seated social conflict is merely an individual legal controversy.

Courts have gone to incredible lengths to restrict the principles under which they have attacked discrimination. For example, they have increasingly insisted that when a racially unequal situation exists, there must also be a showing of discriminatory purpose or intent to discriminate before the unequal pattern is declared unlawful.[10]

The introduction of proof of intent serves several functions. First, it enables courts to introduce the "fault" principle into constitutional adjudication. Unless a governmental entity actually intends to produce a discriminatory result, how are we otherwise to distinguish between political and social inequality, or between the ordinary inequalities of condition and those that are racially motivated? The introduction of intent allows judges to say that they are not engaged simply in the task of redressing the general inequalities in social life but only those that are produced by racially motivated action.

Since proof of racial motivation is exceedingly difficult, the intent requirement seriously hampers the typical lawsuit attacking racial discrimination. But notice how courts, out of fear that the race discrimination lawsuit cannot be distinguished from the simple effort to correct social and economic inequalities, have tended to choose to make racial discrimination even more difficult to prove.

There is therefore a deep relationship between racial discrimination, on the one hand, and social and economic inequality on the other. Courts wish to radically distinguish between the two, in order to avoid tampering with mere social inequality or the existing distribution of wealth and privilege. And yet the best and often the only proof of racial discrimination is none other than proof of the connection between economic inequality and race. The legalization of the problem of racial discrimination, therefore, presents the liberal tradition with deep conflicts between its opposition to racial discrimination and its equally strong conviction that the courts ought not to be involved with the problems of social and economic inequality.

And it is in this way that *Brown* v. *Board of Education* has begun to overflow its originally circumscribed limits. While originally about the relatively narrow question of whether government could actually choose to discriminate by race, it has gradually come to involve the question of whether the government can passively sit by and acquiesce in a socially, economically, and legally unequal society, one of whose most dreadful consequences is a culture of racism.

Since the official American ideology accepts inequality as both an incentive and a reward for talent and industry, we are forced to distinguish between the indistinguishable. We are expected to accept social and economic inequality at precisely the moment that it is the best evidence of the existence of racial discrimination.

Another distortion has been introduced by turning the battle against racial discrimination into legal channels. The schools—the weakest and most vulnerable of American institutions—have been forced to bear the brunt of the social change required in the battle against racial discrimination, even though school segregation is now largely a function of discriminatory housing patterns which are, in turn, related to job discrimination.

It is in the nature of courts that they cannot take a systematic view and must therefore focus their energies on those institutions which are by history and legal tradition most amenable to judicial control. In the field of racial discrimination, with its constitutional prohibition only of "public" discrimination, the schools—the most "public" of American institutions—inevitably became the central target of legal strategies for change. The more intractable problems of jobs and housing—which were also far less "public" in terms of legal conceptions—were thus relatively immune from legal attack until recently.

We have thus been largely dealing with symptoms and not causes of racial inequality. And, as a result, the schools have had to bear a burden of social change that even less vulnerable institutions could not long endure. This particular distortion has been introduced primarily by the fact that the constitutionalization and legalization of the campaign against racial discrimination made schools a uniquely suitable target for courts.

In his wonderful book *The Problem of Slavery in the Age of Revolution*, David Brion Davis shows how even during the American Revolution, those who defended or acquiesced in the institution of slavery saw a clear connection between the abolition of slavery, the threat to property, and the dangers of equality. The treatment of blacks in American society has always brought to the surface more general questions about the precise nature of our commitments to equality. And most of the jurisprudential dilemmas that grow out of *Brown* v. *Board of Education* derive, ultimately, from our uncertain commitments to equality.

# Have We Overcome?

LERONE BENNETT, JR.

I have been away from this state for a long time, and I hope you will permit me a personal remark or two. I grew up in this state in the thirties and forties when this institution was closed to me, and to my people, and when Mississippi occupied a position in the western world roughly equivalent to the position of South Africa today. And as I stand here tonight, I am reminded of Richard Wright and the other great sons and daughters of Mississippi who were lost to this state and this region because of that situation. And I am reminded also of other great sons and daughters of Mississippi—the James Merediths, the Fannie Lou Hamers, the Aaron Henrys, the Margaret Walker Alexanders, the brave children of SNCC—who stayed here and fought the good fight in the hope that Mississippi would one day come into its own and recognize its own. And it seems to me that whatever the difficulties of the moment, or the magnitude of the obstacles, that we should always remember the brave and beautiful few who brought us thus far along the way. For if it was possible for them to change what they changed in Mississippi, then there is absolutely no limit to what we can dream and hope.

It is in this connection, and in the context of what has been done, and what remains to be done, that I am reminded of the story of a group of people who sought a great prize that was across a deep river, up a steep mountain, on the far side of an uncharted sea. The task before them was almost impossible, but they were a brave people, and history had given them big hearts. And so they embarked, in the white of the night, and reached the middle of the river, where a great storm arose. The storm lashed their little boat and washed many overboard, but they managed somehow to reach the other side, losing many of their friends on the way. When the boat touched dry land, they held a symposium of sorts, and a select group went to the captain and said: "We did a great thing in crossing that river, and we believe we will dig in and rest for a while in this new and desegregated place." And the captain said: "This thing that you did in crossing the river was splendidly done, and deserves praise. But there is no rest for us, or safety, short of the grail freedom. So sing, shout, and rap tonight, for tomorrow the journey continues. *We crossed a river, and now we've got to cross a sea.*"

The words speak to us all. They speak to white Americans, who crossed many rivers in the last two hundred years, and now face the necessary task of reinventing themselves in a world that is overwhelmingly red, brown, and black.

*We crossed a river, and now we've got to cross a sea.*

The words speak to black Americans, who crossed ten thousand Jordans in the years of the movement and who now face the necessity of dealing with the gravest crisis we have faced as a people since the end of slavery time.

*We crossed a river, and now we've got to cross a sea.*

The words speak to us all, and define us all. And it is within the context of these words that I approach the topic assigned me tonight:

"Have we overcome?"

I could, and should, say no and sit down and save your time. But this is a scholarly setting, and a scholarly no requires—I am told—at least one hour of disputation and on-the-other-handing. Let me try then to earn my keep, and let me begin by questioning the question.

The question is have we overcome?

And my question is how are we to understand that dangerous word *we*?

And what does it mean *to overcome*?

Well, in the context of the song and the struggle, *we* means black people and—watch this interpretation—white people who are committed to and involved in the struggle for equality and racial justice. And *to overcome*, again in the context of the song and the struggle, means the act of transcending and destroying all racial barriers and creating a new land of freedom and equality for all men, all women, and all children.

"Oh, deep in my heart I do believe we shall overcome," we shall overpass, triumph over mean sheriffs, robed riders, assassins of the spirit, segregation, discrimination, hunger, poverty, and humiliation.

Have we done it? No, a thousand times no.

We were there, some of us, and we sang the song, some of us, and saw the blood, some of us. And we know—deep in our hearts —that what the singers and dreamers and victims hoped for . . . what they struggled and died for . . . has not happened yet. Because of the passion and the pain of the singers and victims and dreamers, we have, in the past twenty-four years, crossed many barriers . . . but we are nowhere near the end of our journey, and we have miles to go before we sleep.

And so, it is necessary to say here, in the name of the dreamers and victims, that we have not yet started the process of grappling with the depth and the height of the dream. As a matter of fact, we haven't even defined what we must do in order to overcome. To cite only one point, the admission of a handful of gifted black students and athletes to a white university in which all the lines of authority and power are still controlled by whites is not—re-peat—*not* integration. It is at best desegregation and a prelude, perhaps a necessary prelude, to that great American dream which was written down on pieces of paper, which was promised, and which has never existed anywhere in America, except in the hearts of a handful of men and women.

By any reasonable standard, then, we have failed to meet the goal. And to understand the magnitude of our failure, and the dangers that failure poses to all Americans, it would be helpful, I think, to go back for a moment to the beginning, to Monday, May 17, 1954, when some man believed the millenium was around the next turning.

According to news reports of that day, the Supreme Court decision was immediately hailed by a wide variety of black voices as "a second emancipation proclamation," which was, in the words of the *Chicago Defender*, "more important to our democracy than the atom bomb or the hydrogen bomb." In Farmville, Virginia, for example, a sixteen-year-old student named Barbara Trent burst into tears when her teacher interrupted class to announce the decision. "Our teacher told us," she told a reporter, "it may cost her, her job . . . we went on studying history, but things weren't the same and will never be the same again."

There were, of course, cynics and dissenters, most notably Langston Hughes, who put the following words in the mouth of his fictional character, Simple:

White folks are proud, But I don't see nothing for them to be proud of just doing what they ought to do. If they was doing something extra, yes, then be proud. But Negroes have a right to go to decent schools just like everybody else. So what's there to be proud of in that they are just now letting us in. They ought to be ashamed of themselves for keeping us out so long. I might have had a good education myself had it not been for white folks. If they want something to be proud of let them pay me for the education I ain't got.

Simple's views were shared apparently by many blacks, but in the first flush of victory most people focused on the silver lining in the cloud. The most widely quoted man of the day was the architect of the victory, NAACP counsel Thurgood Marshall. Here is an excerpt from an interview with Marshall that appeared in the *New York Times* on Tuesday, May 18, 1954: "Mr. Marshall, asked how long he thought it would be before segregation in education was eliminated, replied it might be 'up to five years' for the entire country. He predicted that, by the time the 100th anniversary of the emancipation was observed in 1963, segregation in all its forms would have been eliminated from the nation."

Not only Marshall but significant sectors of the white population said the struggle would soon be over. Earl Warren recalled later that it was suggested at the Supreme Court that the processes set in motion on this day would be completed by the centennial of the Fourteenth Amendment—1966.

Thus America, thus the petitioners and dreamers, on a day of hope and triumph and innocence.

How remote, how unimaginably distant and remote that May day seems in this October of our years. The events of the intervening years—Montgomery, the sit-ins, the freedom rides, the marches, and urban rebellions—came so suddenly, so dramatically, that our sense of time has been distorted and incidents and personalities of only a few years ago have been pushed into the distant past.

For this reason, among others, it is difficult to put this period into proper perspective. For this reason, among others, it is difficult to orient and situate the young. It is a fact, worthy of long thought, that there is a whole generation of young blacks and whites who have never seen a Jim Crow sign and who express astonishment when told that they once existed.

The Jim Crow signs are gone now. There are black mayors in Alabama and black representatives in the Mississippi legislature, and there are children, and even some adults, who seem to believe that it has always been this way. But it hasn't always been this way, and it would be well for us to remember tonight that this October and the Octobers of yesterday are linked and separated by a great crossing and a great hope. During that crossing, a revolution . . . it is not too strong a word . . . in the courts and a rebellion in the streets destroyed the legal foundations of segregation and moved the racial dialogue to a new level.

The internal and external changes flowing from this event have been profound and dramatic. So have the costs. Martin Luther King, Jr., is dead; Malcolm X is dead. Whitney Young, Medgar Evers, Fred Hampton, James Earl Chaney, Viola Luizzo, Fannie Lou Hamer, the four Birmingham girls: they are all dead. And the movement they led and symbolized has foundered on new realities.

What makes this all the more disconcerting is that the gains for which they died are threatened by a new mood of bakkism and reaction in white America. And there is the further fact that the gains of the green years, important as they were, did not go to the root of the matter, the neocolonial relations between the black and white communities of America and the institutionalized unfavorable balance of trade of black America.

It is true, and important, that blacks are going places today they couldn't go twenty-four years ago. *Everything, in fact, has changed in Mississippi and America, and yet, paradoxically, nothing has changed.*

Despite the court orders and civil rights laws, blacks are still the last hired and the first fired. They are still systematically exploited as consumers and citizens. To come right out with it, the full privileges and immunities of the U.S. Constitution do not apply to blacks tonight, in Mississippi or in Massachusetts, and they never have. You want to know how bad things are? Listen to the facts cited by Robert B. Hill of the National Urban League in a recent booklet, entitled *The Illusion of Black Progress.*

Contrary to popular belief, the economic gap between blacks and whites is widening. Between 1975 and 1976, the black to white family income ratio fell sharply from 62 to 59 percent.

Not only is black unemployment at its highest level today, but the jobless gap between blacks and whites is the widest it has ever been . . . .

The proportion of middle-income black families has not significantly increased. In fact, the proportion of black families with incomes above the labor department's intermediate budget level has remained at about one-fourth since 1972.

The proportion of upper-income black families has steadily declined. Between 1972 and 1976, the proportion of black families above the government's higher budget level dropped from 12 to 9 percent.

The two black societies thesis of a widening cleavage between middle-income and low-income blacks is not supported by national income data. The proportion of black families with incomes under $7,000, as well as those with incomes over $15,000, has remained relatively constant in recent years.

The statistical evidence strongly contradicts the popular belief that high unemployment among black youth is primarily due to their educational or skill deficiencies—when job opportunities are greater for white youth with lower educational attainment. White high school dropouts have lower unemployment rates (22.3%) than black youth with college education (27.2%).

These figures are terrible, and the reality is worse. How did this happen? How is it possible for black America to be in so much trouble after all the demonstrations, and marches, and court orders? What is the meaning of this terrible indictment?

The short answer to these questions is that we stopped marching too soon. The long . . . and scholarly . . . answer is embedded in the history of our journey.

We started out, twenty-four years ago, in the white of night. We crossed large bodies of water, marched day and night, were pushed back and advanced again, singing and shouting and stepping over the bodies of our brothers and sisters. By these methods . . . and others . . . we arrived, after indescribable anguish and pain, at this place.

But where precisely are we? What have we gained and lost?

Did we go wrong somewhere? Or is this a necessary historical detour leading to a higher level of development. What, in short, is the meaning, the sense, the signification, of the twenty-four years of the great crossing struggle?

There can be no easy answer to that question, for we are too close to that event to situate it globally. But it is possible, indeed likely, that the post-*Brown* struggle, despite its limitations, was a necessary stage in the social maturation of black people. And there can be little doubt that it created black America's finest hours and one of the finest hours in the history of the republic.

It is fashionable nowadays to heap scorn on the old civil rights movement and the so-called "Hamburger War." But this is a misreading of the historical process that advances on the crest of succeeding waves, which rise and fall, over and over again, with the ebbing and flowing of the energies of the people. From this vantage point, history is a dialogue, and the movement of the last twenty-four years was a vast and leaping wave in a continuous flow of energy that started with the first revolt on the first slave ship and will not end until America deals with the revolutionary mandate of its birth.

Because of that struggle, we have made significant gains on the political front and in the middle sectors. The movement changed, destroyed, wiped out the visible and dramatic signs of racism, but it did not and perhaps could not at that time deal with the subtle forms of institutional racism. Nor did it change or even make a dent in the economic inequities of a society that can make work for black men inside prisons after they commit crimes but cannot find work for black men outside prisons before they commit crimes.

And so, as a result of the failure of the movement to make a total breakthrough on the racial front, we find ourselves tonight in the postrevolutionary phase of a revolution that never happened, the postrevolutionary phase of a revolution that turned sour because it could not be accomplished historically at that particular time under the prevailing ratio of forces.

Does this mean that the movement was a failure? By no means. As a result of that struggle,.one-third of this nation—the South— was changed, perhaps forever, and the rest of the nation made its first tentative steps toward democracy. Beyond all that, the movement created the foundations for future departures, which will depend on the maturation of social forces and the courage, vision, and perseverance of black people.

The important point here, as elsewhere, is that the movement was historical. It had historical roots, its direction and limitations were historically determined. It rose and fell according to the laws of motion . . . I almost said . . . the laws of being of the political economy of blackness.

One way to avoid the implications of this fact is to focus, as so many people do, on ephemeral aspects of the movement, such as the personalities. And so we find people saying almost everywhere that the main problem was leadership. Or we find them saying— and you've heard them say it—that the movement failed because the leaders were integrationists or separationists or because they didn't brush with Crest. This is a Walt Disney approach to the historical process. The leaders didn't start the Montgomery boycott: the people started it. The leaders didn't start Watts: the people started it. And when the energy of the people ran out, when they had tried everything, or almost everything, when they had demonstrated, petitioned, rioted, prayed, and consulted astrologers, and when every new advance revealed a new all, the people withdrew to retool and rethink. And what we've got to understand tonight is that this temporary withdrawal was and is natural under the circumstances. The law of history is that people cannot live forever on the heights. The law of history is that a people advance and retreat, advance and retreat, advance and retreat, until they reach a collective decision to go for broke.

Since 1900, the black movement in America has been characterized by this rhythm of advances and withdrawals. And this entitles us to say, I think, that if the sun continues to shine and the wind continues to blow, the movement of the sixties will reemerge in America on a higher level of development.

And the task we face tonight is the task of consolidating our gains and preparing the ground for the next departure which will come, as surely as night follows day, if we stop cursing history and learn from history how to make history.

One of our problems in the sixties—certainly one of my problems—was that we underestimated the resiliency of the system. For a moment there, we thought we had the cat. For a moment there, we thought the promised land was around the next turning. But that was an illusion, and the mandate we have tonight from the dreamers and victims is to learn from our illusions and prepare ourselves for a long-range struggle for the transformation of this society.

This, in my opinion, was one of the four great lessons of the sixties, which taught us, in many a hard classroom, that the struggle to overcome is not a hundred-yard dash but a long-distance run involving phases and characteristics that have no precedent and cannot be predicted. We must prepare, therefore, for the long haul. We must prepare for a struggle of five, ten, fifteen, or even fifty years.

The second lesson, growing out of the first, is that people change only when they have to change, and that it is the task of the oppressed to do whatever is required to force change. The lesson of the sixties, and of this hour, was anticipated more than one hundred years ago by Frederick Douglass, who said:

Let me give you a word of the philosophy of reform. The whole history of the progress of human liberty shows that all concessions yet made to her august claims, have been born of earnest struggle. If there is no struggle, there is no progress. Those who profess to favor freedom and yet deprecate agitation, are men who want crops without plowing up the ground, they want rain without thunder and lightning. They want the ocean without the awful roar of its many waters.

This struggle may be a moral one, or it may be a physical one, and it may be both moral and physical, but it must be a struggle. Power concedes nothing without demand. It never did and it never will. . . . Men may not get all they pay for in this world, but they must certainly pay for all they get.

Struggle: that's the second lesson, and the third is that we cannot overcome and the gains of the post-*Brown* years cannot be preserved without a total struggle for a fundamental transformation of institutional structures. It should be clear by now, to almost everyone, that the white problem cannot be solved and black America cannot be saved without a total struggle for a fundamental transformation of American society, without real changes in the tax structure and the relations between the private and public sectors, without a redefinition of values, and a redistribution of income.

This need is particularly acute in the South. In my travels through the land of my birth, I have been struck repeatedly by the gains white southerners have made in the areas of personal relations. I have also been struck repeatedly by the same structural faults that led to the failure of the First Reconstruction. It is admitted now, by almost everyone, that the First Reconstruction was doomed from the start by the failure to provide blacks with economic as well as political votes. If we hope and intend to overcome, and if there is still time, somebody, somewhere is going to have to come up with the twentieth-century equivalent of forty acres of land and a mule.

Finally, and most importantly, the white South and white North are going to have to deal with themselves. The great lesson of the sixties, a lesson heeded almost nowhere, is that there is no Negro problem in Mississippi and in America. The problem of race in Mississippi, and in America, is a white problem, and we shall not overcome until we confront that problem. Somebody, somewhere is going to have to tell poor whites the truth about their lives. Somebody, somewhere, is going to have to assume responsibility for educating white people about the political, economic, and social realities of the twentieth century.

This is the challenge, this is the danger, this is the hope. It is the next great barrier, the sea beyond that we must cross together, before we can reach a place of safety where we can speak, with truth, to our graves and say: "You did not dream or die in vain, for we have finally and at long last overcome."

The whole wide world around, the whole wide world around, the whole wide world around someday.

# Selective Bibliography

The purpose of this bibliography is to provide the reader with a general, working guide to the topic of race relations since *Brown*. It is not intended to be complete. Anyone interested in the sources cited by the individual authors should consult the footnotes for each paper.

Abraham, Henry J. *Freedom and the Court: Civil Rights and Liberties in the United States.* New York: Oxford University Press, 1967.

Allen, Robert L. *Black Awakening in Capitalist America.* Garden City, N.Y.: Doubleday, 1961.

Allen, Robert L., and Pamela P. Allen. *Reluctant Reformers: Racism and Social Reform Movements in the United States.* Washington, D. C.: Howard University Press, 1974.

Aptheker, Herbert, ed. *A Documentary History of the Negro People in the United States.* New York: Citadel Press, 1951.

Ashmore, Harry S. *The Negro and the Schools.* Chapel Hill: The University of North Carolina Press, 1954.

Baldwin, James. *Nobody Knows My Name.* New York: Dial Press, 1961.

Bardolph, Richard A., ed. *The Civil Rights Record: Black Americans and the Law, 1844–1970.* New York: Crowell, 1970.

Barron, Milton L., ed. *Minorities in a Changing World.* New York: Knopf, 1967.

Bennett, Lerone. *Confrontation: Black and White.* Chicago: Johnson Publishing Company, 1965.

————. *The Challenge of Blackness*. Chicago: Johnson Publishing Company, 1972.

Bergman, Peter N. *The Chronological History of the Negro in the United States*. New York: Harper and Row, 1969.

Berman, Daniel M. *It Is So Ordered: The Supreme Court Rules on School Segregation*. New York: Norton, 1966.

Bickel, Alexander M. *Politics and the Warren Court*. New York: Harper and Row, 1965.

Blaustein, Albert P., and Clarence Ferguson, Jr. *Desegregration and the Law: The Meaning and Effect of the School Segregation Cases*. New Brunswick, N.J.: Rutgers University Press, 1962.

Brauer, Carl M. *John F. Kennedy and the Second Reconstruction*. New York: Columbia University Press, 1971.

Brink, William, and Louis Harris. *The Negro Revolution in America*. New York: Simon and Schuster, 1964.

Broderick, Francis L., and August Meier, eds. *Negro Protest Thought in the Twentieth Century*. New York: Bobbs-Merrill, 1965.

Campbell, Angus. *White Attitudes Toward Black People*. Ann Arbor, Mich.: Institute for Social Research, 1971.

Carmichael, Stokely, and Charles Hamilton. *Black Power: The Politics of Liberation in America*. New York: Random House, 1967.

Carter, Hodding. *The South Strikes Back*. Garden City, N.Y.: Doubleday, 1959.

Chalmers, David M. *Hooded Americanism: The History of the Ku Klux Klan*. Garden City, N.Y.: Doubleday, 1965.

Clark, Kenneth. *The Negro Protest*. Boston: Beacon Press, 1963.

Conrad, Earl. *The Invention of the Negro*. New York: P. S. Eriksson, 1966.

Farmer, James. *Freedom—When?* New York: Random House, 1969.

Franklin, Raymond S., and Solomon Resnik. *The Political Economy of Racism*. New York: Holt, Rinehart and Winston, 1973.

Frazier, Edward Franklin. *Black Bourgeoisie*. Chicago, Ill.: Free Press, 1957.

Greenberg, Jack. *Race Relations and American Law*. New York: Columbia University Press, 1959.

Gossett, Thomas F. *Race, The History of an Idea in America*. New York: Southern Methodist University Press, 1973.

Killian, Lewis. *The Impossible Revolution?* New York: Random House, 1968.

———. *White Southerners.* New York: Random House, 1970.

Killian, Lewis, and Charles Grigg. *Racial Crisis in America: Leadership in Conflict.* Cliffwood, N.J.: Prentice Hall, 1964.

King, Martin Luther, Jr. *Stride Toward Freedom.* New York: Harper, 1958.

———. *Where Do We Go From Here: Chaos or Community.* New York: Harper and Row, 1967.

———. *Why We Can't Wait.* New York: Harper and Row, 1963.

Kluger, Richard. *Simple Justice: The History of "Brown v. Board of Education" and Black America's Struggle for Equality.* New York: Knopf, 1976.

Lewis, David C. *King: A Critical Biography.* New York: Penguin Books, 1970.

Lincoln, C. Eric. *Martin Luther King: A Profile.* New York: Hill and Wang, 1970.

———. *My Face Is Black.* Boston: Beacon Press, 1964.

———. *The Black Muslims in America.* Boston: Beacon Press, 1969.

Loewen, James, and Charles Sallis, eds. *Mississippi: Conflict and Change.* New York: Pantheon Books, 1974.

Lomax, Louis E. *The Negro Revolt.* New York: Harper, 1962.

Lubell, Samuel. *White and Black: Test of a Nation.* New York: Harper and Row, 1964.

McMillen, Neil R. *The Citizens' Councils: Organized Resistance to the Second Reconstruction, 1954–1964.* Nashville, Tenn.: Vanderbilt University Press, 1971.

Masters, Stanley. *Black-White Income Differentials.* New York: Academic Press, 1975.

Matthews, Donald, and James W. Prothro. *Negroes and the New Southern Politics.* New York: Harcourt, Brace and World, 1966.

Meier, August, and Elliott Redwick. *CORE: A Study in the Civil Rights Movement, 1942–1968.* New York: Oxford University Press, 1973.

Miller, Loren. *The Petitioners: The Supreme Court and the Negro.* New York: Pantheon Books, 1966.

Miller, William. *Martin Luther King, Jr.* New York: Webright and Talley, 1968.

Moody, Anne. *Coming of Age in Mississippi.* New York: Dial Press, 1968.

Muse, Benjamin. *American Negro Revolution: From Nonviolence to Black Power, 1963–1967.* Bloomington, Ind.: Indiana University Press, 1968.

———. *Ten Years of Prelude: The Story of Integration Since the Supreme Court's 1954 Decision.* New York: Viking Press, 1964.

Myrdal, Gunnar. *An American Dilemma: The Negro Problem and Modern Democracy.* New York: Harper, 1944.

O'Neill, William. *Coming Apart: An Informal History of America in the 1960s.* New York: Quadrangle, 1971.

Orfield, Gary. *The Reconstruction of Southern Education: The Schools and the 1964 Civil Rights Act.* New York: Wiley-Interscience, 1964.

Parmet, Herbert. *Eisenhower and the American Crusades.* New York: Macmillan, 1972.

Pettigrew, Thomas F. *A Profile of the Negro American.* New York: Van Nostrand, 1964.

———. *Racially Separate or Together?* New York: McGraw Hill, 1971.

Reddick, Lawrence. *Crusader Without Violence.* New York: Harper, 1959.

Roland, Charles. *The Improbable Era: The South Since World War II.* Lexington, Ken.: The University Press of Kentucky, 1975.

Sarratt, Reed. *The Ordeal of Desegregation: The First Decade.* New York: Harper and Row, 1968.

Silver, James W. *Mississippi: The Closed Society.* New York: Harcourt, Brace and World, 1966.

Sobel, Lester A., ed. *Civil Rights, 1960–1966.* New York: Facts on File, 1967.

Sowell, Thomas. *Race and Economics.* New York: D. McKay Company, 1975.

Sundquist, James. *Politics and Policy: The Eisenhower, Kennedy, and Johnson Years.* Washington, D.C.: Brookings Institution, 1968.

Taylor, Clyde, ed. *Vietnam and Black America.* New York: Anchor Press, 1973.

Wilson, William. *The Declining Significance of Race.* Chicago: University of Chicago Press, 1978.

Wolk, Allan. *The Presidency and Black Civil Rights: Eisenhower to Nixon.* Rutherford, N.J.: Fairleigh Dickinson, 1971.

Woodward, C. Vann. *The Strange Career of Jim Crow.* New York: Oxford University Press, 1967.

Zinn, Howard. *SNCC: The New Abolitionists.* Boston: Beacon Press, 1964.

——. *The Southern Mystique.* New York: Knopf, 1964.

# Notes

Notes to THE NEW BLACK ESTATE: THE COMING OF AGE OF
BLACKAMERICA
*by C. Eric Lincoln*

1. Thomas F. Gossett's *Race, The History of an Idea in America* (New York, 1973) is still the most illuminating work on American self-perception in contrast to others in their world of contact.
2. See Albert Murray, "The Elusive Black Image," in *The Omni-Americans* (New York, 1970).
3. See Jack Greenberg, *Race Relations and American Law* (New York, 1959).
4. See, for example, Milton L. Barron (ed.), *Minorities in a Changing World* (New York, 1967).
5. See, for example, Earl Conrad, *The Invention of the Negro* (New York, 1966).
6. See, for example, the excellent essay by Elliot Zashin, "The Progress of Black Americans in Civil Rights," *Daedalus*, CVII (Winter, 1978).
7. See, for example, William Julius Wilson's study, *The Declining Significance of Race* (Chicago, 1978).
8. See Stokely Carmichael and Charles V. Hamilton, *Black Power: The Politics of Liberation in America* (New York, 1967).
9. See C. Eric Lincoln, "Color and Group Identity in the United States," in Robert K. Yin, *Race, Creed, Color, or National Origin* (Itasca, Ill., 1973).

Notes to SO MUCH HISTORY, SO MUCH FUTURE: MARTIN LUTHER
KING, JR. AND THE SECOND COMING OF AMERICA
*by Vincent Harding*

1. I have not yet discovered the original source of the Salvemini quotation, but I am grateful to Donna J. Benson—my research assistant while I was visiting at Duke University—not only for calling it to my attention, but for the important work she did in helping search out the documentation for

this paper. At the same time I cannot possibly overstate the immense debt I owe to my niece and administrative assistant, Gloria Jackson, for her skill, persistence, and devotion in helping move this document from my initial scribblings to the finished copy.

2. After having been expelled from Albany State College in 1961 for her early participation in the Albany movement, Bertha Gober joined the staff of the Student Non-Violent Coordinating Committee, and was a member of the original SNCC freedom singers. A small, frail, quiet young woman, with great courage and a magnificent voice, Bertha suffered many harsh wounds of the spirit, partly as a result of her experiences in the jails of southwest Georgia, and partly as a result of the often unbearable internal tensions of the struggle. She died in 1974. Ten years earlier, her creation, "We'll Never Turn Back" (which cannot possibly be appreciated apart from being heard in the context of struggle), had become the theme song of the Mississippi summer volunteers. This version of the text appears in James W. Loewen and Charles Sallis (eds.), *Mississippi: Conflict and Change* (New York, 1974), 262.

3. Loewen and Sallis, *Mississippi*, 263–65. Apropos of the question of overcoming, perhaps it would be important to note here that while this work by a team of historians, sociologists, and others is generally recognized to be the best interpretation of the history of the state, in the modern spirit, it has not been adopted as a text, nor has any public voice been raised on its behalf from scholars at the state's most prestigious university.

4. Frantz Fanon, *The Wretched of the Earth* (New York, 1963), 167. The eventual discovery of Fanon by many of the young people of the movement marked a critical turning point in their lives.

5. See C. Eric Lincoln, "The New Black Estate: The Coming of Age of Blackamerica," in this volume, pp. 3–30.

6. The references are to Malcolm X; Fannie Lou Hamer, Mississippi civil rights activist from 1962 until her death in 1977; Clarence Jordan, founder of Koinonia Farm, Americus, Georgia; Thomas Merton, Trappist monk and world-renowned advocate of peace and human rights; Ruby Doris Smith-Robinson, one of the founding members of SNCC and a bedrock of its Atlanta office staff. Like King and Hamer, all of these persons are now dead.

7. Herbert Lee, Medgar Evers, Mickey Schwerner, Jimmy Chaney, and Vernon Dahmer were among the best known of the martyrs to freedom's struggle in Mississippi; others like Henry, Turnbow, Meredith, Blackwell, Moore, Johnson, King, Brooks, and Robinson continue to live and work for change in the state; Moses was the courageous, indomitable and truly humble leader of the SNCC forces who eventually included among their members persons like Peacock, Block, Watkins, Travis, and Guyot—all native Mississippians, as well as those who came from elsewhere to join the struggle, like Diane Nash Bevel, Zellner, Forman, Cobb, and Mahoney. Many of that band of heroes who still live bear deep physical and psychic scars as marks of their participation in the battles to transform this state and this nation.

8. For accounts of the murders of George Lee, Gus Courts, and Herbert Lee, see Loewen and Sallis, *Mississippi*, 257–58. The special significance of Herbert Lee's life and death is noted in Bertha Gober's song, cited in the epigraph to this article, and is especially mentioned by Bob Moses in his oral

account, *The Story of Greenwood*, Folkways Record, ED 5593. James Forman, one of the most powerful shapers of SNCC's ideological direction, offers more details on Herbert Lee's case in his semiautobiographical, all-important study, *The Making of Black Revolutionaries* (New York, 1972), 231. Indeed, it is impossible to understand the meaning of Mississippi to the movement or the significance of SNCC to that state's struggle without a careful reading of Forman's work, especially pp. 215–310 and 354–457. Other important firsthand accounts of the Mississippi freedom movement of the 1960s may be found in Sally Belfrage, *Freedom Summer* (New York, 1965); Elizabeth Sutherland (ed.), *Letters from Mississippi* (New York, 1965); Anne Moody, *Coming of Age in Mississippi* (New York, 1968); Joanne Grant (ed.), *Black Protest*, 299–301, 303–308, 329–36, 415–16, 472–75, 498–506, and Len Holt, *The Summer That Didn't End* (New York, 1965).

9. On the Hamer and Ponder experiences, the two women (along with June Johnson of Greenwood, who was also beaten, and who continues to work for justice in her hometown) gave me their accounts in the summer of 1963, not long after the beatings. For a published account see Howard Zinn, *SNCC: The New Abolitionists* (Boston, 1964), 94–95. This was the first, and is still one of the best works on the student movement, especially its earlier phases.

10. Cleveland Jordan's statement comes from *The Story of Greenwood*. The Reverend White's experience was related to me in an interview, October 11, 1978. The prayer from Greenwood jail is reported by James Forman, "Some Random Notes from the Leflore County Jail," in J. Grant (ed.), *Black Protest*, 333–34.

11. The reference to Tupelo is, of course, a recognition of the powerful black organization of northern Mississippi, the United League, its campaign of boycotts and demonstrations in the cause of racial and economic justice, and the well-published response from the Ku Klux Klan, all in the course of 1977–1978. For examples of newspaper reports see Jackson (Miss.) *Clarion-Ledger and Daily News*, June 11, 1978, *Arkansas Gazette*, August 30, 1978, and Jackson (Miss.) *Advocate*, August 17–23 and September 7–13, 1978. I am indebted to Colia Lafayette, one of the veterans of the movement, and to Sandra Stell Rush for calling my attention to these accounts.

12. In his exemplary work, *Black Jacobins* (New York, 1963), C. L. R. James's specific reference was to another magnificent leader of a rather different black revolution, Toussaint L'Ouverture of Haiti. There, James's words were, "Great men make history, but only such history as it is possible for them to make."

13. The story of King's pre-Montgomery experiences has been told in many places and in many ways. His own brief autobiographical statement appears in Martin Luther King, Jr., *Stride Toward Freedom* (New York, 1958), 1–9. There are four standard biographical works: Lawrence D. Reddick, *Crusader Without Violence* (New York, 1959); Lerone Bennett, *What Matter of Man; A Biography of Martin Luther King, Jr.* (Chicago, 1964); William L. Miller, *Martin Luther King, Jr.* (New York, 1968); and David L. Lewis, *King: A Critical Biography* (New York, 1970). Largely as a result of his extensive interviews in Montgomery, Arthur Smith is especially helpful in pointing out the decisive role of the black community, especially its

women, in the development of the structure and momentum of the boycott. See Smith's *Rhetoric of Black Revolution* (Boston, 1969), 87 ff. The most recent bibliography of works by and about King appears in *The Journal of the Interdenominational Theological Center*, IV (Spring, 1977), 67–69.

14. King, *Stride Toward Freedom*, 10–38; Lewis, *King*, 46–61; Miller, *Martin Luther King, Jr.*, 30–41; Reddick, *Crusader*, 112–54. It is important to compare these with E. D. Nixon's contemporary account from another angle of vision, "How It All Got Started," *Liberation* (December, 1956), and to Rosa Parks's modest oral reflections four months after her arrest: "Montgomery Bus Boycott," in Joanne Grant (ed.), *Black Protest*, 276–80.

15. I am paraphrasing the original list of goals reproduced in Preston Valien, "The Montgomery Bus Protest As a Social Movement," in Jitsuichi Matsuoka and Preston Valien (eds.), *Race Relations: Problems and Theory* (Chapel Hill, N.C., 1961), 116.

16. In tracing his "Pilgrimage to Non-Violence" in *Stride Toward Freedom*, 72–88, King went into considerable detail about his earlier readings in the work of Thoreau, Hegel, Marx and particularly Gandhi, and how they joined his Christian vision of life. However, he was surprisingly brief in his account of the help he received from Glen Smiley of the Fellowship of Reconciliation, and said nothing at all—in the entire book—about the significant contribution of Bayard Rustin, who was at the time probably one of the two leading black theoreticians and practitioners of nonviolence and pacifism in the cause of radical social change. Both Smiley and Rustin spent considerable time with King during the early months of the boycott and probably contributed more to the practical working-out of his philosophy and strategy of nonviolence than King was prepared to admit. (Rustin had already begun to be Red-baited about his earlier political associations, and King, always sensitive to such matters, might not have been prepared to have the brilliant black Quaker appear to play an important role in the development of the movement.) William Miller, who worked closely with Smiley and Rustin, and who knew King, gives a fuller account of the role of the two men, saying, indeed, that Rustin "soon became King's secretary" (Miller, *Martin Luther King, Jr.*, 46–47). Some of Rustin's own contemporary understanding of the relationship may be found in his "Montgomery Diary," *Liberation* (April, 1956).

17. A transcript of a tape recording of the first bus boycott mass meeting, December 5, 1955, quoted in Smith, *Rhetoric*, 102–105.

18. Benjamin Mays was president of Morehouse when King was a student there, and set his powerful imprint on thousands of black young men; see his autobiographical *Born to Rebel* (New York, 1971). Mordecai Johnson was the first black president of Howard University. An eloquent speaker, socially concerned Baptist preacher, and world traveler, Johnson provided King's first real introduction to the life and work of Ghandi. Howard Thurman, father, advisor, and teacher of thousands of black and white religious seekers, was dean of the chapel at Boston University while King was there. One of the nation's great preachers, he was a friend and counselor to King. Nor is it accidental that Thurman's best-known among many books is *Jesus and the Disinherited* (New York, 1949). Vernon Johns, the powerful preach-

er who preceded King at Dexter Avenue, left a legacy of constant—usually unsuccessful—efforts to involve his middle-class congregation in the risky issues of freedom and justice for blacks in Montgomery. See Smith, *Rhetoric*, 98–99.

19. The bombing of King's house and his handling of the black community's enraged desire for retaliation are reported in Reddick, *Crusader*, 134–36; Miller, *Martin Luther King, Jr.*, 45–46; Lewis, *King*, 69–70. The railroad station incident appears in Glen Smiley, "A Man Remembered," *Fellowship*, XLIV (April/May, 1978), 6.

20. Among the many available accounts of the school desegregation and other of the earlier post-1954 struggles, three may offer helpful, complementary perspectives: Lerone Bennett, *Confrontation: Black and White* (Chicago, 1965) provides a powerful, engaged black overview; Anthony Lewis (ed.), *Portrait of a Decade* (New York, 1964) is a selection of *New York Times* accounts from many places, while Daisy Bates, *The Long Shadow of Little Rock* (New York, 1962) gives a thoughtful, poignant, firsthand account of one situation by one of the too-soon-forgotten heroes of the freedom movement. The role of Ella Baker as the elemental force behind the early developments of SCLC's structure has been too long overlooked or underplayed. See brief accounts of her role in Lewis, *King*, 108, 113, and Miller, *Martin Luther King, Jr.*, 84. She received much more adequate recognition in Zinn's *SNCC* and Forman's *Making of Black Revolutionaries*. Fortunately, work is now progressing which should bring forth both a book and a documentary film on the life of this woman who has influenced so many of the participants in the black freedom struggle since the 1930s.

21. The rise of the Muslims and the role of Malcolm X are most ably discussed in C. Eric Lincoln, *The Black Muslims in America* (Boston, 1962) and [Alex Haley], *The Autobiography of Malcolm X* (New York, 1964). Robert Williams tells his story (at least its pre-1960 stages) in *Negroes With Guns* (New York, 1962). James Forman became deeply involved in the situation with Williams and reports from his perspective in *Making of Black Revolutionaries*, 158–211.

22. *New York Times*, December 1, 1959, p. 23.

23. One of the best and earliest accounts of the first stages of the student movement is Dan Wakefield, *Revolt in the South* (New York, 1960). Two important documents from the Raleigh conference are in August Meier, Elliot Rudwick, and Francis L. Broderick (eds.), *Black Protest Thought in the Twentieth Century* (Indianapolis, 1971), 307–15. Zinn's *SNCC* is an invaluable report from a social historian who was one of the earliest adult advisors to the group. See also Forman, *Making of Black Revolutionaries*, 215–23. Jack Newfield, *A Prophetic Minority* (New York, 1966) states the crucial, direct connections between the rise of SNCC in the South and the development of the New Left white student movement in the North shortly thereafter. It is important to note, too, that all the above narrative accounts mention the fact that King and other SCLC leaders had expected to incorporate the student movement as the youth arm of the older organization and they seemed never to have forgiven Baker for encouraging the young people to stand firm in their quest for independence.

24. Among the best accounts of the freedom rides are James Peck, *Freedom Ride* (New York, 1962); James Farmer, *Freedom—When?* (New York, 1965), and August Meier and Elliot Rudwick, *CORE: A Study in the Civil Rights Movement, 1942–1968* (New York, 1973).

25. Much of the following account of the Albany movement is based on my own personal files, which I shall designate as Harding, Albany Files. The best initial published report on the early Albany movement situation was Howard Zinn, *Albany, A Special Report of the Southern Regional Council, Atlanta, Georgia, January, 1962*. See also Zinn's *SNCC*, 123–36. The Albany section of James Forman's *Making of Black Revolutionaries*, 250–62, is a crucial part of the story. The Albany story is also treated in some detail by Miller, *Martin Luther King, Jr.*, 112–29, as well as Lewis, *King*, 150–70, in his usual flippant style. King gave Albany very little sustained attention in his *Why We Can't Wait* (New York, 1964), 34–35. Unless otherwise cited, the Harding files and the Zinn and Forman works form the basis for the following treatment of Albany.

26. The critique of King and SCLC in Albany that appears in Forman's *Making of Black Revolutionaries*, 253–60 is crucial to an understanding of the continuing and deepening rift between SNCC and SCLC on many ideological and strategic grounds, and between Forman and King (perhaps Forman and other SNCC comrades had even more difficulty with the flamboyant Wyatt T. Walker) on personal grounds.

27. Rosemarie Harding and I have continued to revisit Albany and our friends there periodically since those early days of the movement.

28. As the best known of King's southern movement campaigns, the Birmingham action in the spring of 1963 has elicited an extensive literature, and there will be no attempt here to do more than mention a few crucial works. King's own statement of the campaign is found in his *Why We Can't Wait*, a book devoted almost exclusively to that experience. Expectedly, we find an important, though brief, counterpoint to King's views in Forman's *Making of Black Revolutionaries*, 311–16. In addition, there are several significant, but too often neglected accounts in Robert Brisbane, *Black Activism* (Valley Forge, Pa., 1970), 130–50; Smith, *Rhetoric*, which provided the results of extensive interviews with key SCLC organizers. The eloquent "Birmingham Manifesto" which signalled the start of the demonstrations appears in Staughton Lynd (ed.), *Nonviolence in America* (Indianapolis, 1966). I also rely heavily on my own Birmingham files, compiled during my participation in the activities of that spring and since then: Harding, Birmingham Files.

29. The information in this paragraph, including the "Commandments For the Volunteers," is based on Harding, Birmingham Files.

30. Many observers noted the powerful, militant spirit of the young people. See, for example Forman, *Making of Black Revolutionaries*, 313–14; Smith, *Rhetoric*, 127 ff, and Louis, *And We Are Not Saved*, 130 ff. Even Eugene "Bull" Connor, the notorious commissioner of public safety, was so impressed with the fervor and intensity of the young people who went off to his jails singing their songs that he said, "Boy, if that's religion, I don't want any." Lewis, *Portrait*, 182.

31. Published in many forms and languages, King's eloquent "Letter from Birmingham Jail" is most readily accessible and set in its context in *Why We Cant' Wait*, 77–100.

32. The night of violent rebellion and King's response to it are reported, among other places, in Smith, *Rhetoric*, 156–60, and Lewis, *Portrait*, 183–86.

33. The connection between the powerful outbreaks in Birmingham and those which took place in black communities across the nation is noted in many accounts. See especially Louis Lomax, *When the Word Is Given* (New York, 1964), 73–75; Smith, *Rhetoric*, 178; Louis, *And We Are Not Saved*, 130–37; and Lerone Bennett, *The Negro Mood* (Chicago 1964), 6. Bennett claimed, "The Bastille of Birmingham was a turning point in the Negro resistance movement. Sparks from the flame of Birmingham leaped from ghetto to ghetto, igniting flammable material that had been gathering for years, welding Negroes into a great black mass of livid indignation."

34. The changeabout of the Kennedys and King's ambiguous involvement with them were reported in both contemporary and historical accounts. For instance Donald M. Schwartz, "What Lies Ahead in Civil Rights Fight," Chicago *Sun Times*, February 2, 1964; Zinn, *SNCC*, 206, and Smith *Rhetoric*, 127 ff. Even more important in the long run were the forces which the Kennedys and their administration represented. For when the young people exploded across the city, calls came to the Birmingham businessmen not only from the Kennedys, but from Secretary of the Treasury Douglas Dillon and Secretary of Defense Robert McNamara. It is likely that such men were pressing for some kind of settlement not simply as temporary government officials, but also in their far longer-term roles as members of the powerful American-based multinational capitalist community, a community which was clearly disturbed about the possibilities of Birmingham's sparking a national black insurrection. See both Smith, *Rhetoric*, 127ff, and Bayard Rustin, "The Great Lessons of Birmingham," *Liberation*, VIII (June, 1963), 7–9, 31, on this critical long-range connection and concern. It is a connection that must be remembered when we later consider the response to King's eventual threat of national, massive, nonviolent civil disobedience.

35. On the unpublicized discussions of the nonviolent army, I am partially dependent on my memory and my files, including the Birmingham Files. See also Louis Lomax, *The Negro Revolt* (New York, 1962), 99. Walker's convention address is quoted in Bennett, *Confrontation*, 244.

36. Among the helpful discussions of the making and remaking of the march are Forman, *Making of Black Revolutionaries*, 331–37, and, almost inadvertently, Lewis, *King*, 210–32. Smith, *Rhetoric*, 186–89, includes some of the story of the restraining of the original idea, and quotes fittingly from a *New York Times* story on the great sigh of relief which arose from many quarters when the march was clearly domesticated. On August 29, 1963, Russel Baker's page-one story noted, "Instead of the emotional hordes of angry militants that many had feared, what Washington saw was a vast army of quiet middle-class Americans who had come in the spirit of the church outing." We may assume that Baker later discovered that in the presence of anger, militance, and deep emotions of hope and distress, church outings do not last very long.

37. On the situation of many voices and forces, James Baldwin, the novelist and essayist, had succinctly stated the issue that spring: "No man can claim to speak for the Negro people today. There is no one with whom the power structure can negotiate a deal that will bind the Negro people. There is, therefore, no possibility of a bargain." *New York Times*, June 3, 1963.

38. "*Playboy* Interview: Dr. Martin Luther King," *Playboy* (January, 1965), 65–68, 70–74, 76–78.

39. His increasing, self-conscious sense of responsibility to speak out on Vietnam and other issues of imperialistic exploitation and domination may be seen in "An Address by Dr. Martin Luther King, Jr. At the Synagogue Council of America," December 5, 1965—precisely a decade after his first Montgomery mass meeting address. Harding, King Files. King's father, a staunch Republican, found his son's increasingly radical antiwar position hard to take. Of course, the responses of the FBI and other federal agencies have become more fully known since King's death. David Lewis had begun to deal with Hoover's responses in *King*, 256–58. However, even King's earliest, more outspoken criticisms of the American involvement came later and were much more restrained than the position already taken by such movement activists as Bob Moses of SNCC and Jim Bevel of SCLC. Moses was a leader of the first major antiwar demonstration in August, 1965, in Washington, D.C. James P. O'Brien, "The New Left's Early Years," *Radical America*, II (May–June, 1968), 7.

40. The fact that the Selma march was anticlimactic in a larger, historical sense does not in any way diminish the long, hard, courageous voter-registration organizing work that had gone on there since 1963, beginning with the digging-in of Bernard and Colia Lafayette of SNCC. The Selma march itself is covered in Miller, *Martin Luther King, Jr.*, 204–21, and Lewis, *King*, 264–93, with Lewis proving, as usual, somewhat critical of King's role. Neither biographer brought the perspective, the personal involvement, or the bitterness to the history of that experience that is present in Forman, *Making of Black Revolutionaries*, 316–26, 345–54, 440–42. His view is essential to any full assessment. The "Wallace" song may be found in one of its textual variations in Guy and Candie Carawan (eds.), *Freedom Is a Constant Struggle* (New York, 1968), 168–69.

41. The overall ferment of the black struggle in this post-Selma period is handled with skill and analytical sophistication by Robert Allen, *Black Awakening in Capitalist America* (New York, 1970). James Boggs's *Racism and Class Struggle in America* (New York, 1970) is an important collection of essays on the significance of the period's developments. Also helpful as an overview is Robert Brisbane, *Black Activism*. The important role of Adam Clayton Powell is likely best grasped in his autobiographical *Adam by Adam* (New York, 1971). Julius Lester, "The Angry Children of Malcolm X," *Sing Out* (November, 1966)—more accessible in Meier, *et al.*, *Black Protest Thought*, 469–84—makes clear the power of Malcolm's death to the younger black community. See also Vincent Harding, "The Religion of Black Power," in Donald Cutler (ed.), *The Religious Situation, 1968* (Boston, 1968).

42. The actual experience of the Meredith March may be viewed from the perspective of some of the participants via Stokely Carmichael and

Charles Hamilton, *Black Power: The Politics of Liberation in America* (New York, 1967); Martin Luther King, Jr., *Where Do We Go From Here: Chaos or Community* (New York, 1967), 23–66; and Floyd McKissick, *3/5 of a Man* (New York, 1969). One of the best contemporary journalistic accounts is Paul Good, "The Meredith March," *New South*, XXI (Summer, 1966), 2–16. It is also treated in Lewis, *King*, 321–31, and Miller, *Martin Luther King, Jr.*, 241–49. Of course, the concept of Black Power was at least as old as nineteenth-century black nationalists like Martin Delany, and the term itself had been used by Richard Wright as a title for his book on the rise of blacks to power in Africa: *Black Power* (New York, 1954). More recently, Paul Robeson had spoken of the need for massive "Negro Power" in his *Here I Stand* (New York, 1957). In the North at least as early as 1965, a group of black radical activists had formed an "Organization for Black Power," directed by Jesse Gray of Harlem. "Jesse Gray," Vertical Files, Schomburg Collection, New York Public Library. It is likely, however, that Adam Clayton Powell's use of the idea and proximate use of the term was one of the most important immediate stimuli for the SNCC forces who had been developing their own ideas on the theme for more than two years earlier.

43. King's SCLC convention statement is found in Martin Luther King, Jr., "President's Annual Report . . . Jackson Mississippi, August 10, 1966," in Harding, King Files.

44. Most of the work cited in the first part of footnote 41 of this essay would be helpful here.

45. Much of this section is based on my own extended conversations with King and my preparation of memos on American involvement in Vietnam for his use as well as conversations on the relevance of nonviolence for the new period in the black struggle. See also his developing ideas on dealing with poverty in *Where Do We Go From Here*, 135–66.

46. Martin Luther King, Jr., "Beyond Vietnam," in Clyde Taylor (ed.), *Vietnam and Black America* (New York, 1973), 79–98. Taylor's anthology places King's crucial statement in its proper context—the larger black opposition to America's fight against Vietnam.

47. On the criticism of King's Vietnam stand within and outside the shattered civil rights establishment, see Miller, *Martin Luther King, Jr.*, 255–56; Lewis, *King*, 357–67.

48. Martin Luther King, Jr., *The Trumpet of Conscience* (New York, 1968), 59–60.

49. The statement, which appeared posthumously, was the most unequivocally positive public assessment King had ever made of the rebellions: "A Testament of Hope," *Playboy* (January, 1969), 175.

50. King, *Trumpet of Conscience*, 59–60. The italics are mine.

51. In the spring of 1967, King had used the term "revolution of values" several times in his conversations with *New York Times* reporter David Halberstam and in his "Beyond Vietnam" speech. See Halberstam's "The Second Coming of Martin Luther King," *Harper's* (August, 1967), 39–51.

52. King, "Beyond Vietnam," 97.

53. The difficulties King faced in bringing himself and his staff to work out a real plan for the campaign as well as to find a way to handle the constantly mounting criticism and self-doubt, are suggested in Lewis, *King*, 368–72, 259–68. The constant temptation, to which he often seemed under-

standably prepared to succumb, was to blunt the radical edges of his plans, to make the campaign another, longer, civil rights–type march rather than a revolutionary action of confrontation. I was involved in many of the conversations that went on that winter, and I am not convinced that David Lewis is correct in his statement that Lyndon Johnson's decision to refrain from seeking a second full term caused King to decide—just before Memphis—that he would at least postpone the Washington campaign. See Lewis, *King*, 384–85. Of course, King knew that neither he nor SCLC was ready.

54. The immediate, volatile black responses to the death of King—and the federal government's massive military responses—are documented in Jerome Skolnik, *The Politics of Protest* (New York, 1969), especially pp. 172–73. See also Louis, *And We Are Not Saved*, 343.

55. See Robert Allen, *Black Awakening*; Institute of the Black World, *Black Analysis for the Seventies, 1971–1972* (Atlanta, 1973). Perhaps the symbolic highpoint of this period of black solidarity—as well as the signal of its temporary nature and its structurally weak foundations—was the National Black Political Convention at Gary, Indiana in March, 1972. The "Gary Manifesto" is included in *Black Analysis*.

56. On the variegated social ferment of the late 1960s and early 1970s and its relationship to the black movement, see Vincent Harding, "The Black Wedge in America: Struggle, Crisis and Hope, 1955–1975," *The Black Scholar*, VII (December, 1975), 28–30, 35–46; also Howard Zinn, *Post-War America: 1945–1971* (Indianapolis, 1973). Two important additions to any thought about the connections between past and future struggles for revolutionary change in America and elsewhere are James and Grace Lee Boggs, *Revolution and Evolution in America* (New York, 1974), and James and Grace Lee Boggs, *Conversations in Maine: Exploring Our Nation's Future* (Boston, 1978). The latter book was developed by the Boggses in collaboration with Freddye and Lyman Paine.

57. King, "Beyond Vietnam," 97; Fanon, *The Wretched of the Earth*, 255.

## Notes to EDUCATION AND EARNINGS OF BLACKS AND THE *BROWN* DECISION
### by Henry M. Levin*

*The author wishes to express his appreciation to Cuir Riak, Christine Robinson, and Juanita McKinley for library assistance. He is also grateful to David Tyack and Jay Chambers for comments on the draft and to Sharon Carter for her tireless devotion in preparing the manuscript.

1. 347 U.S. 483 (1954).

2. For example, U.S. Commission on Civil Rights, *Racial Isolation in the Public Schools* (Washington, D.C., 1967); U.S. Commission on Civil Rights, *Twenty Years After Brown: Equality of Educational Opportunity* (Washington, D.C., 1975); U.S. Commission on Civil Rights, *Fulfilling the Letter and Spirit of the Law: Desegregation of the Nation's Public Schools* (Washington, D.C., 1976); Betsy Levin and Willis Hawley (eds.), "The Courts, Social Science, and School Desegregation," *Law and Contemporary Problems*, XXXIX (Winter/Spring, 1975); Gary Orfield, *Must We Bus?* (Washington,

D.C., 1978); Robert Crain, *The Politics of School Desegregation* (Garden City, N.Y., 1969); James Coleman, *et al.*, *Trends in School Segregation, 1968–1973* (Washington, D.C., 1975); Thomas Pettigrew and Robert Green, "School Desegregation in Large Cities: A Critique of the Coleman 'White Flight' Thesis," *Harvard Education Review*, XLVI (February, 1976); David Armor and Donna Schwarzbach, *White Flight, Demographic Transition, and the Future of School Desegregation* (Santa Monica, Calif., 1978).

3. U.S. Commission on Civil Rights, *Racial Isolation*; David Cohen, *et al.*, "Race and the Outcomes of Schooling," in F. Mosteller and Daniel Moynihan, *On Equality of Educational Opportunity* (New York, 1972), 343–70; David Armor, "The Evidence on Busing," *Public Interest* (Summer, 1972), 90–126; David Armor, "The Double Standard: A Reply," *Public Interest* (Winter, 1973), 119–31; Thomas Pettigrew, *et al.*, "Busing: A Review of 'The Evidence,'" *Public Interest* (Winter, 1973), 88–131; Levin and Hawley (eds.), "The Courts, Social Science, and School Desegregation."

4. Levin and Hawley (eds.), "The Courts, Social Science, and School Desegregation"; David Horowitz, *The Courts and Social Policy* (Washington, D.C., 1976); S. Michelson, "For the Plaintiffs—Equal School Resource Allocation," *Journal of Human Resources*, VII (Summer, 1972), 283–306.

5. Philip Kurland, "Equal Eductional Opportunity, or the Limits of Constitutional Jurisprudence Undefined," in Charles Daly (ed.), *The Quality of Inequality: Urban and Suburban Public Schools* (Chicago, 1968), 47–72; Alexander Bickel, *The Supreme Court and the Idea of Progress* (New York, 1970).

6. For a general picture of educational inequalities between blacks and whites, see U.S. Congress, Congressional Budget Office, *Inequalities in the Educational Experiences of Black and White Americans* (Washington, D.C., 1977). A comprehensive analysis of a major data set is Robert Hauser and David Featherman, "Equality of Schooling: Trends and Prospects," *Sociology of Education*, XLIX (April, 1976), 99–120.

7. Reported in Congressional Budget Office, *Inequalities in Educational Experiences*, 28.

8. For reviews of studies that seek to ascertain the relation between school characteristics and educational outcomes, see Harvey Averch, *et al.*, *How Effective is Schooling? A Critical Review and Synthesis of Research Findings* (Santa Monica, Calif., 1972).

9. J. S. Coleman, *et al.*, *Equality of Educational Opportunity* (Washington, D.C., 1966).

10. Horace Mann Bond, *The Education of the Negro in the American Social Order* (New York, 1934); Ambrose Caliver, *Education of Negro Leaders* (Washington, D.C., 1948); John Owen, "The Distribution of Educational Resources in Large American Cities," *Journal of Human Resources*, VII (Winter, 1972), 171–90.

11. See Samuel Bowles and Henry Levin, "The Determinants of Scholastic Achievement—A Critical Appraisal of Some Recent Evidence," *Journal of Human Resources*, III (Winter, 1968), 3–24.

12. For Chicago see Harold Baron, "Race and Status in School Spending: Chicago, 1961–1966," *Journal of Human Resources*, VI (Winter, 1971), 3–24, and for Washington, D.C., see Michelson, "For the Plaintiffs."

13. Owen, "Educational Resources."

14. Coleman, *et al.*, *Equality of Educational Opportunity*, Statistical Appendix; the reanalysis is found in Christopher Jencks, "The Coleman Report and the Conventional Wisdom," in Mostteller and Moynihan, *Educational Opportunity*.

15. Ruby Martin and Phyliss McClure, *Title I of ESEA: Is It Helping Poor Children?* (Washington, D.C., 1969).

16. John Pincus (ed.), *School Finance in Transition* (Cambridge, Mass., 1974).

17. Christopher Jencks and David Riesman, "The American Negro College," *Harvard Educational Review* (Winter, 1967), 3–60. An overall comparison of the black and white college experience is found in Institute for the Study of Educational Policy, *Equal Educational Opportunity for Blacks in U.S. Higher Education: An Assessment* (Washington, D.C., 1976). These comparisons ignore the cultural and symbolic importance of the black colleges.

18. A particularly gloomy picture is painted by Thomas Sowell, *Black Education: Myths and Tragedies* (New York, 1972), Ch. 10.

19. Much of this section is based on U.S. Commission on Civil Rights, *Equality of Educational Opportunity*. Brown v. Board of Education, 349 U.S. 294, at 300 (1955).

20. Reed Sarratt, *The Ordeal of Desegregation* (New York, 1966); U.S. Commission on Civil Rights, *Equality of Educational Opportunity*, 46. Even this figure does not reveal the degree of desegregation. In some states a school was considered to be desegregated if even one white student was assigned to a black school or vice-versa.

21. Coleman, *et al.*, *Equality of Educational Opportunity*, Statistical Appendix, 371. Also see the data in U.S. Commission on Civil Rights, *Racial Isolation*.

22. Armor and Schwarzbach, *White Flight*; Karl Taeuber, "Racial Segregation: The Persisting Dilemma," *Annals* (November, 1975), 87–96.

23. *Ibid.*

24. See Kan-Hua Young and Dean Jamison, "The Economic Benefits of Schooling and Compensatory Reading Education" (Princeton, N.J., 1974); Irwin Garfinkel, Robert Haveman, and David Betson, "Labor Market Discrimination and Black-White Differences in Economic Status" (Madison, Wis., 1977).

25. For example, between 1965 and 1975 the proportion of black families with female heads of household rose from about 24 percent to 35 percent, while for white families the change was from 9 percent to 10.5 percent. U.S. Department of Commerce, *The Social and Economic Status of the Black Population* (Washington, D.C., 1975), 107. The ratio of median income of black families to white families has actually fallen in the post-1970 period, while earnings of black individuals have risen over this period. Also, the relative incomes of black "husband-wife" families has risen over this period. *Ibid.*, 25, 32.

26. Alan Batchelder, "Decline in the Relative Income of Negro Man," *Quarterly Journal of Economics*, LXXVIII (November, 1964), 525–48; Dale Hiestand, *Economic Growth and Employment Opportunities for Minorities*

(New York, 1964); James Tobin, "On Improving the Economic Status of the Negro," in Talcott Parsons and Kenneth B. Clark (eds.), *The Negro American* (Boston, 1967), 451–71.

27. See James Smith and Finis Welch, *Race Differences in Earnings: A Survey and New Evidence* (Santa Monica, Calif., 1978), 25–26.

28. See the extensive discussions of these patterns in *ibid*; James Smith and Finis Welch, "Black-White Male Wage Ratios: 1960–70," *American Economic Review*, LXVII (June, 1977), 323–38; J. Haworth, J. Gwartney, and C. Haworth, "Earnings, Productivity, and Changes in Employment Discrimination During the 1960's," *American Economic Review*, LXV (March, 1975), 158–68; R. B. Freeman, "Black Economic Progress After 1964: Who Has Gained?" (Cambridge, Mass., 1977).

29. The seminal work on this subject is Gary Becker, *The Economics of Discrimination* (Chicago, 1971). See the recent challenges to human capital analysis by Mark Blaug, "The Empirical Status of Human Capital Theory: A Slightly Jaundiced Survey," *Journal of Economic Literature*, XIV (September, 1976), 827–55, and by S. Bowles and H. Gintis, "The Problem with Human Capital Theory—A Marxian Critique," *American Economic Review*, LXV (May, 1975), 74–82, and the defense by Finis Welch, "Human Capital Theory: Education, Discrimination, and Life Cycles," *American Economic Review*, LXV (May, 1975), 63–73.

30. Census data presented by Smith and Welch, *Race Differences in Earnings*, 16.

31. For theories of black-white discrimination, see Becker, *Economics of Discrimination*; Lester Thurow, *Poverty and Discrimination* (Washington, D.C., 1969), Ch. 7; Ray Marshall, "The Economics of Racial Discrimination: A Survey," *Journal of Economic Literature*, XII (September, 1974), 849–71; Stanley Masters, *Black-White Income Differentials* (New York, 1975), Ch. 1; Anthony Pascal (ed.), *Racial Discrimination in Economic Life* (Lexington, Mass., 1972); Michael Reich, "The Economics of Racism," in D. M. Gordon (ed.), *Problems in Political Economy: An Urban Perspective* (Lexington, Mass., 1977), 183–88.

32. For example, compare Richard Freeman, "Changes in the Labor Market for Black Americans, 1948–1972," *Brookings Papers on Economic Activity* (Washington, D.C., 1973), I, 67–120, and Freeman, "Black Economic Progress After 1964" with Smith and Welch, "Black-White Male Wage Ratios," and Smith and Welch, *Race Differences in Earnings*.

33. Smith and Welch, *Race Differences in Earnings*. These conclusions are largely extensions of interpretations made in earlier analyses by Welch, "Black-White Returns to Schooling."

34. This relationship is displayed in Smith and Welch, "Black-White Male Wage Ratios," Table 1, 324, and Smith and Welch, *Race Differences in Earnings*, 52.

35. Smith and Welch, *Race Differences in Earnings*, 11 and a comparison of Table A.1, 55 with Table A.2, 59.

36. *Ibid.* 47–50; also see Freeman, "Changes in Labor Market," and Richard Butler and James Heckman, "The Government's Impact on the Labor Market Status of Black Americans: A Critical Review," unpublished, 1977.

37. Robert Fogel and Stanley Engerman, *Time on the Cross: The Economics of American Negro Slavery* (Boston, 1974), 261; Becker, *Economics of Discrimination*, 149; Hiestand, *Economic Growth*, 51–55.

38. Smith and Welch, *Race Differences in Earnings*, Tables A.1, 55 and A.2, 59, 11.

39. Institute for the Study of Educational Policy, *Blacks in U.S. Higher Education*.

40. Gloria Hanoch, "Personal Earnings and Investing in Schooling" (Ph.D. dissertation, University of Chicago, 1965); O. D. Duncan "Discrimination against Negroes," *Annals*, CCCLXXI (May, 1967), 85–103; David L. Featherman and Robert Hauser, "Changes in the Socioeconomic Stratification of the Races," *American Journal of Sociology*, LXXXII (November, 1976), 621–51.

41. For example, see Alexander Bickel, *The Supreme Court and the Idea of Progress* (New York, 1970) particularly his assessment of *Brown*. Also see Nathan Glazer, *Affirmative Discrimination: Ethic Inequality and Public Policy* (New York, 1975), Ch. 3, and Kurland, "Equal Educational Opportunity," 60–61.

42. For more detail see John Hope Franklin, *From Slavery to Freedom: A History of American Negroes* (New York, 1956), and A. Meier and E. Rudwick, *From Plantation to Ghetto* (New York, 1976), Ch. 4–6.

43. This system is well-documented in Gunnar Myrdal, *An American Dilemma: The Negro Problem and Modern Democracy* (New York, 1944).

44. Barrington Moore, Jr., *Injustice: The Social Bases of Obedience and Revolt* (White Plains, N.Y., 1978), 459.

45. Doxey Wilkerson, "The Negro School Movement in Virginia: From 'Equalization' to 'Integration,' " *Journal of Negro Education*, XXIX (Winter, 1960), 17–29.

46. Richard Kluger, *Simple Justice* (New York, 1975), provides an excellent picture of the pre-*Brown* efforts.

47. Sarratt, *Ordeal of Desegregation*.

48. Martin Luther King, Jr., *Stride Toward Freedom: The Montgomery Story* (New York, 1958).

49. See Howard Zinn, "Nonviolent Direct Action in the South: The Albany Movement," in John Bracey, August Meier, and Elliott Rudwick (eds.), *The Afro-Americans: Selected Documents* (Boston, 1972), 680–99, and Bracey, *et al.* (eds.), *The Afro-Americans*, 709–18, for examples of the new tactics. See Lewis Killian and Charles Smith, "Negro Protest Leaders in a Southern Community," *Social Forces*, XXXVIII (March, 1960), 253–57, for an analysis of the changes in political strategy.

50. James Sundquist, *Politics and Policy: The Eisenhower, Kennedy, and Johnson Years* (Washington, D.C., 1968), 222.

51. August Meier and Elliot Rudwick, *CORE: A Study in the Civil Rights Movement, 1942–1968* (New York, 1973), Ch. 3.

52. Thomas Pettigrew, "Actual Gains and Psychological Losses: The Negro American Protest," in A. Meier and E. Rudwick (eds.), *The Making of Black America* (New York, 1969), 317–33, saw this as arising, in part, from expectations that were changing at a far more rapid rate than institutions.

53. Sundquist, *Politics and Policy*, 222–59.

54. *Ibid.* 238; Meier and Rudwick, CORE, Ch. 5.

55. Sundquist, *Politics and Policy*, 259–86; U.S. Commission on Civil Rights, *Twenty Years After Brown: Equal Opportunity in Housing* (Washington, D.C., 1975), 36–39.

56. Robert Haveman (ed.), *A Decade of Federal Antipoverty Programs* (New York, 1977).

57. Baron, "Race and Status in School Spending."

58. Phyllis A. Wallace, "A Decade of Policy Developments in Equal Opportunities in Employment and Housing," in Haveman (ed.), *Antipoverty Programs*, Ch. 8; Compendium of federal civil rights enforcement efforts in U.S. Commission on Civil Rights, *Federal Civil Rights Enforcement Effort* (Washington, D.C., 1970).

59. Myrdal, *An American Dilemma*, 77.

60. Andrew Greeley and Paul Sheatsley, "Attitudes Toward Racial Integration," *Scientific American*, CCXXV (December, 1971), 13.

61. *Ibid.*, 14; Orfield, *Must We Bus?*, 109.

62. Henry Levin reviews these programs in "A Decade of Policy Developments in Improving Education and Training for Low-Income Populations," in Haveman (ed.), *Antipoverty Programs*, Ch. 4.

63. Arthur Wise, *Rich School, Poor School* (Chicago, 1968); Kurland, *Equal Educational Opportunity*.

64. Kluger, *Simple Justice*, 945–46.

65. Bickel, *Supreme Court*; Kurland, *Equal Educational Opportunity*; Glazer, *Affirmative Discrimination*, Ch. 3.

66. The concept of "goal-free evaluations" has been developed by Michael Scriven; see Scriven, "Evaluation Perspective and Procedures," in W. J. Popham (ed.), *Evaluation in Education* (Berkeley, 1974), Ch. 1.

67. See U.S. Department of Commerce, *Status of the Black Population*, for set of general comparisons between the status of whites and blacks.

68. Certainly a major issue is whether a signal leap forward can be achieved within a reformist framework. The lack of success in improving the distribution of income in American society in light of both the high employment situation of the late sixties and the War on Poverty raises serious questions about the types of changes that are obtainable ultimately within a system of monopoly capitalism. On these issues see Reich, "Economics of Racism"; Andre Gorz, *Strategy for Labor* (Boston, 1968); Lester Thurow, *Generating Inequality* (New York, 1975); David Gordon, *Theories of Poverty and Underemployment*.

Notes to THE WHITE HOUSE AND BLACKAMERICA:
FROM EISENHOWER TO CARTER
*by William E. Leuchtenburg*

1. *Brown v. Board of Education of Topeka*, 347 U.S. 483 (1954).

2. James L. Sundquist, *Politics and Policy: The Eisenhower, Kennedy, and Johnson Years* (Washington, D.C., 1968), 224; Herbert S. Parmet, *Eisenhower and the American Crusades* (New York, 1972), 448–49.

3. Richard Kluger, *Simple Justice* (New York, 1977), 664–65; Arthur Lar-

son, *Eisenhower: The President Nobody Knew* (New York, 1968), 128.

4. Sherman Adams, *Firsthand Report* (New York, 1961), 331. Earl Warren has written that, at a White House dinner shortly before the *Brown* decision, Eisenhower said of opponents of integration: "All they are concerned about is to see that their sweet little girls are not required to sit in schools alongside some big overgrown Negroes." *New York Times*, March 15, 1977. For one justice's explanation of how the decision was arrived at, see Tom C. Clark oral history memoir, Lyndon B. Johnson Library, Austin, Texas, 33–34.

5. Parmet, *Eisenhower and the American Crusades*, 438.

6. Emmet Hughes, *The Ordeal of Power* (New York, 1963), 201. It should be noted that in 1956 the Democratic national convention also refused to endorse enforcement of the *Brown* decision. In an exultant letter to a Mississippi congressman, the governor of Mississippi boasted, "Harry Truman, Averill [*sic*] Harriman and Hubert Humphrey were politically liquidated." J. P. Coleman to Ross Collins, August 27, 1956, in Collins MSS, Library of Congress.

7. Benjamin Muse, *Ten Years of Prelude: The Story of Integration Since the Supreme Court's 1954 Decision* (New York, 1964). In a speech on the floor of the House, a Florida congressman declared, "The majority of the people, of both races, in the 8th Congressional District of Florida . . . view this decision as fraught with dangers comparable to the tragedies of World War I and II, and the emergence of the communist terror." "Newsletter from Congressman Billy Matthews," May 26, 1954, W. R. Matthews MSS, University of Florida, Gainesville, Box 229. See, too, Governor William B. Umstead to Kelly M. Alexander, June 24, 1954, in John Sanford Martin MSS, Duke University, Durham, N.C., Box 15. A retired Supreme Court justice wrote one of his former colleagues: "I was shocked at the attitude of the Va. Bar re your decision in the School Cases. Every one was saying it could not be enforced. I would have thought this to be expected in, say, Mississippi—but in Va. no." Owen J. Roberts to Felix Frankfurter, September 19, 1954, in Frankfurter MSS, Library of Congress, Box 97.

8. Parmet, *Eisenhower and the American Crusades*, 504–505; Everett Frederic Morrow, *Black Man in the White House* (New York, 1963), 218.

9. For early signs of progress in Arkansas, see J. William Fulbright to Raymond E. Baldwin, August 31, 1948, in Baldwin MSS, Connecticut State Library, Hartford, Box 41. Quote in Peter Lyon, *Eisenhower: Portrait of the Hero* (Boston, 1974), 747.

10. "Everybody now talks about the Federal troops being there to enforce integration. They are really there because the Governor of Arkansas used military force to prevent integration, and then refused to use the State Police authority to maintain order." Walter Lippmann to Irving Dilliard, October 11, 1957, in Lippmann MSS, Yale University, New Haven, Conn., Series III, Box 67.

11. Pittsburgh *Courier*, January 10, 1959, clipping, Drexel Sprecher MSS, John F. Kennedy Library, Waltham, Mass., Box 5. As late as 1965, when a group of historians marched with Martin Luther King, Jr., in Montgomery, we were startled to see the Confederate flag flying over the Alabama capitol.

12. J. W. Anderson, *Eisenhower, Brownell, and the Congress* (University,

Ala., 1964). "In the main the result has been a victory for the South when the substance of the bill as passed is compared with the provisions of the original bill and the 40-odd amendments which were proposed," a southern senator said of the 1960 legislation. "With our backs to the wall, the Southerners withstood the power of the Federal Government, the political pressure of those states appealing to the Negro vote, and the propaganda of the facilities available to the NAACP." "Statement by Senator Harry F. Byrd," mimeographed, Graham A. Barden MSS, Duke University, Durham, N.C., Box 202.

13. Neil R. McMillen, "Black Enfranchisement in Mississippi: Federal Enforcement and Black Protest in the 1960s." *Journal of Southern History*, XLIII (August, 1977), 355; Sundquist, *Politics and Policy*, 243; Allan Wolk, *The Presidency and Black Civil Rights: Eisenhower to Nixon* (Rutherford, N.J., 1971), 225n.

14. For a statement by a southern governor in opposition to discrimination against black customers, see "Remarks by Governor Leroy Collins," March 20, 1960, typescript, Collins MSS, University of South Florida, Tampa, Box 96.

15. "Analysis of 1960 Democratic Platform By Senator Strom Thurmond," mimeographed, in Howard W. Smith MSS, University of Virginia, Charlottesville, Box 204.

16. *Time*, October 28, 1957, p. 23; Roger Kahn, *The Boys of Summer* (New York, 1972), 362.

17. Transcript of radio-TV broadcast between Senators Kenneth Keating and Prescott Bush, September 10, 1961, Bush MSS, Connecticut State Library, Hartford, Box 5.

18. Ruth P. Morgan, *The President and Civil Rights: Policy-Making by Executive Order* (New York, 1970), 69–75.

19. James Hilty, *John F. Kennedy: An Idealist Without Illusions* (St. Louis, 1976), 10.

20. Note the language in Robert Kennedy's protest against the policy of a private Washington club in refusing to serve black guests: "The Metropolitan Club is not engaged in the war against communism but a great many of its members are. Large numbers of its members serve or have served in a national government that stands on the principle of equality and asserts that principle as its claim to respect on continents that are mostly dark and frequently bitter." Robert F. Kennedy to Board of Governors, Metropolitan Club, April 11, 1961, in Howard W. Smith MSS, Box 204. See, too, William J. vanden Heuvel, "Speech before the Students and Faculty of Hampden-Sidney College, Prince Edward County, Virginia," October 17, 1963, Edward N. Costikyan MSS, Columbia University, New York, N.Y. I am indebted to Costikyan for sending his papers to me before they were deposited at Columbia.

21. Robert F. Kennedy, Address at the Law Day Exercises of the University of Georgia Law School, May 6, 1961, mimeographed, Harry Byrd MSS, University of Virginia, Charlottesville, Box 270.

22. For the limits of the federal response to the freedom rides, see Pat Watters and Reese Cleghorn, *Climbing Jacob's Ladder* (New York, 1967), 57.

23. James Meredith, *Three Years in Mississippi* (Bloomington, Ind., 1966); John R. Junkin oral history memoir, Mississippi Department of Archives and History, Jackson.

24. Carl Brauer, *John F. Kennedy and the Second Reconstruction* (New York, 1977), 185.

25. Gerald H. Blessey oral history memoir, Mississippi Department of Archives and History. Some white students at Ole Miss, though, after seeing "the folly and potential disaster that rabid politics had brought on our state," resolved to turn Mississippi politics into more productive channels. Jesse L. White, Jr., oral history memoir, Mississippi Department of Archives and History, p. 10.

26. Robert F. Kennedy to Ross R. Barnett, March 8, 1963, Barnett MSS, Mississippi Department of Archives and History, Governors' Records, Vol. 1130.

27. Harry M. Ayers to Robert F. Kennedy, September 27, 1962, in Ayers MSS, University of Alabama, Tuscaloosa; Brauer, *John F. Kennedy and the Second Reconstruction*, 192; Frank E. Smith, *Congressman from Mississippi* (New York, 1964), 312. One protester against "this Mississippi military action" asked: "Is it not mental cruelty to James Meredith? For him, may it not lead to mental derangement?" Cornelia Dabney Tucker to Robert F. Kennedy, October 31, 1962, in Tucker MSS, University of South Carolina, Columbia, Box 2.

28. See especially the enlarged edition of James W. Silver, *Mississippi: The Closed Society* (New York, 1966).

29. Arthur M. Schlesinger, Jr., *A Thousand Days* (Boston, 1965), 971. Little more than a month before the president's death, Burke Marshall was still writing of Birmingham: "My estimate of the situation is that the whites do not have the sense or courage to take sufficient steps to give the local Negroes enough gains to enable them to oppose further demonstrations, and that accordingly the situation will get worse again." Burke Marshall, "Memorandum to Honorable Pierre Salinger, Re: Birmingham," October 9, 1963, in Burke Marshall MSS, John F. Kennedy Library, Box 1.

30. Muse, *Ten Years of Prelude*, 267.

31. *Public Papers of the Presidents of the United States: John F. Kennedy, 1963* (Washington, D.C., 1964), 469.

32. *Ibid.*, 483; *New York Times*, March 22, 1978. See, too, Charles E. Bennett to Sandra S. Garrett, August 6, 1963, in Bennett MSS, University of Florida, Gainesville, Box 31. "What is indisputably clear," wrote one observer, "is that by the time of his assassination in November 1963 President Kennedy had moved from a position of cautious and sparing use of his personal influence for civil rights to a posture of leadership that was bold and unreserved." Harold C. Fleming, "The Federal Executive and Civil Rights: 1961–1965," *Daedalus*, XCIV (Fall, 1965), 943.

33. Brauer, *John F. Kennedy and the Second Reconstruction*, 312–13.

34. Anne Moody, *Coming of Age in Mississippi* (New York, 1968), 319–20.

35. *Public Papers of the Presidents of the United States: Lyndon B. Johnson, 1963–64* (Washington, D.C., 1965), I, 9.

36. "Washington Report," December 18, 1963, John Stennis MSS, Mis-

sissippi State University, Starkville. For his role in getting the 1957 civil rights bill past the Senate Judiciary Committee headed by Eastland and the almost-united opposition of southern legislators, Senator Johnson had been denounced as one "willing to sacrifice the white people of the South," "a turncoat," and "a traitor to his own region." Augusta (Ga.) *Courier*, February 4, 1957, clipping, Earle C. Clements MSS, University of Kentucky, Lexington, Box 192. Years later, North Carolina's Senator Sam Ervin was still resentful of Johnson's role in bringing pressure on behalf of "civil rights bills, they were really civil-wrong bills, mostly." Samuel J. Ervin, Jr., oral history transcript, Richard B. Russell MSS, University of Georgia, Athens, p. 5.

37. *Public Papers of the Presidents of the United States: Lyndon B. Johnson, 1963–64*, I, 116.

38. Lyndon B. Johnson to Richard B. Russell, July 23, 1964, in Russell MSS, XV/EE Red Line File, Special Presidential File Correspondence.

39. In a comment on the Freedom Summer Project that he issued at the National Governors' Conference in Cleveland, Governor Paul B. Johnson of Mississippi warned against actions by "professional agitators" that "are designed to promote trouble that too often results in violence." Press release, June 9, 1964, mimeographed, Paul B. Johnson MSS, Mississippi Department of Archives and History, Governors' Records, Vol. 1138.

40. The award of the Nobel Prize "to a trouble-maker like Martin Luther King," said a Florida congressman, has "greatly cheapened if not completely destroyed the value of the award." A. Sydney Herlong, Jr., to Bonner L. Carter, November 10, 1964, in Herlong MSS, University of Florida, Gainesville.

41. *Public Papers of the Presidents: Lyndon B. Johnson, 1965* (2 vols., Washington, D.C., 1966), I, 132, 272. Johnson had been under fire during the previous year both for failing to send federal agents to Mississippi to protect registration workers and for refusing to accept fully the claims of the Mississippi Freedom Democratic party. For a critical, but judicious, treatment of these issues, see Steven F. Lawson and Mark I. Gelfand, "Consensus and Civil Rights: Lyndon B. Johnson and the Black Franchise," *Prologue* (Summer, 1976), 65–76.

42. *Public Papers of the President: Lyndon B. Johnson, 1965*, I, 287–91; Benjamin Muse, *The American Negro Revolution* (Bloomington, Ind., 1969), 169.

43. *Public Papers of the President: Lyndon B. Johnson, 1965*, I, 297; Lester A. Sobel (ed.), *Civil Rights, 1960–66* (New York, 1967), 301.

44. *Public Papers of the President: Lyndon B. Johnson, 1965*, II, 841.

45. Sobel, *Civil Rights, 1960–66*, 291.

46. Steven F. Lawson, *Black Ballots* (New York, 1976), Ch. 11; Andrew J. Biemiller to John Watts, December 5, 1969, in Watts MSS, University of Kentucky, Lexington, Box 85.

47. Wolk, *The Presidency and Black Civil Rights*, 233–34n; Agnew to Cody Fowler, June 3, 1971, in Fowler MSS, University of South Florida, Tampa. Steven F. Lawson graciously made the Fowler papers available to me when they were in his possession. The Agnew letter encloses a very lengthy document drafted in response to the demands of the Congressional

Black Caucus. Richard Nixon to Charles C. Diggs, Jr., May 18, 1971; John Hope Franklin interview by Sidney Hertzberg, Columbia Oral History Collection, Columbia University, New York, N.Y., p. 26.

48. Alexander v. Holmes County Board of Education, 369 U.S. 19 (1969); Carter v. West Feliciana Parish School Board, 396 U.S. 290 (1970); *Time,* January 19, 1970, p. 10. See, too, Rowland Evans, Jr., and Robert D. Novak, *Nixon in the White House* (New York, 1971), 151–56; Samuel Lubell, *The Hidden Crisis in American Politics* (New York, 1970); *Newsweek,* January 26, 1970, p. 21.

49. Charles S. Bullock, III, "Defiance of the Law: School Discrimination Before and After Desegregation," *Urban Education,* XI (October, 1976), 239. See, too, Elliot Zashin, "The Progress of Black Americans in Civil Rights: The Past Two Decades Assessed," *Daedalus,* CVII (Winter, 1978), 242–43.

50. In 1970 a Florida senator lamented, "While Southern members of Congress have steadfastly opposed the current disturbance in our public schools, we have not yet found a way to circumvent the rulings of the U.S. Supreme Court which are the root of the trouble." Spessard L. Holland to Roy R. Burnsed, March 31, 1970, in Holland MSS, University of Florida, Gainesville, Box 1008.

51. More than any other question, the issue of court-ordered busing made clear that racial politics no longer divided sharply on sectional lines. Some of the most bitter, and sometimes violent, resistance to busing came in northern states like Michigan. Moreover, it was not a northern legislator but the Speaker of the House of Representatives of Florida who wrote a constituent:

I realize that busing is inconvenient in many cases but I believe it is a necessary measure that must be taken if we are to provide equal educational opportunities to all of our children. This would not be necessary if the white community had not insisted on segregated housing and segregated public schools in past years. It also seems unreasonable to me that the white community insisted on busing black children miles from their communities in order to maintain segregated schools yet screams with outrage when the same is suggested for their children.

Richard A. Pettigrew to Mrs. Patricia K. Roberts, March 3, 1972, in Pettigrew MSS, University of Florida, Gainesville, Box 2. Similarly, Dick Gregory has commented, "All at once white folks is against busing! Every time I was on the highway when I was a kid, I didn't see nothing but buses full of white folks." Dick Gregory talk, February 1, 1972, typescript, Oral History Program, University of Missouri-St. Louis.

52. Allan P. Sindler, *Bakke, De Funis, and Minority Admissions* (New York, 1978).

53. McMillen, "Black Enfranchisement in Mississippi," 371.

54. Sar A. Levitan, William B. Johnston, and Robert Taggart, *Still a Dream: The Changing Status of Blacks Since 1960* (Cambridge, Mass., 1975); Charles V. Hamilton, "Blacks and the crisis in political participation," *Public Interest* (Winter, 1974), 188–210; Samuel Dubois Cook, "Southern

Politics Since 1954: A Note on Change and Continuity," in Ernest M. Lander, Jr., and Richard J. Calhoun, *Two Decades of Change: The South Since the Supreme Court Desegregation Decision* (Columbia, S.C., 1975), 12.

55. New London (Conn.) *Day*, September 5, 1978.

56. Kluger, *Simple Justice*, 774.

## Notes to WHITE ATTITUDES AND BLACK RIGHTS FROM *BROWN* TO *BAKKE* by Robert H. Wiebe*

* My thanks to James J. Sheehan for trying to untie the knots in a draft of this essay.

1. Charles A. and Mary R. Beard, *The American Spirit: A Study of the Idea of Civilization in the United States* (New York, 1942), 620–21.

2. *New York Times*, October 30, 1947.

3. Quoted in George Brown Tindall, *The Emergence of the New South* (Baton Rouge, La., 1967), 709.

4. Hodding Carter III, *The South Strikes Back* (Westport, Conn., 1959), 18–19, 28, 167, *passim*; Ralph E. Ellsworth and Sarah M. Harris, *The American Right Wing: A Report to the Fund for the Republic* (Washington, D.C., 1962), 23–24, 35. As one commentator noted, there was no "general repudiation of Senator McCarthy" or his cause after 1954. Retaining the same values, his followers merely "turned their attention elsewhere." G. D. Wiebe, "The Army-McCarthy Hearings and the Public Conscience," *Public Opinion Quarterly*, XXII (Winter, 1958–59), 493.

5. Neil R. McMillen, *The Citizens' Council: Organized Resistance to the Second Reconstruction, 1954–64* (Urbana, Ill., 1971), and Numan V. Bartley, *The Rise of Massive Resistance: Race and Politics in the South during the 1950s* (Baton Rouge, La., 1969), are basic sources in my understanding of the subject.

6. George H. Gallup, *The Gallup Poll: Public Opinion 1935–1971* (3 vols.; New York, 1972), II, 1332–33, 1401, 1487, 1517, III, 1616. Throughout the essay I have used polls to sketch the outlines of opinion, not analyze incremental differences or changes within it. Wherever possible, judgments rest on a repetition of comparable results in several surveys.

7. Lloyd A. Free and Hadley Cantril, *The Political Beliefs of Americans: A Study in Public Opinion* (New Brunswick, N.J., 1968), 121; Gallup, *Gallup Poll*, I, 748, II, 782–83, 810, 1402, III, 1598; Hazel Erskine, "The Polls: Negro Housing," *Public Opinion Quarterly*, XXXI (Fall, 1967), 488, 495. See also Paul B. Sheatsley, "White Attitudes toward the Negro," *Daedalus*, XCV (Winter, 1966), 217–38.

8. Martin Luther King, Jr., *Why We Can't Wait* (New York, 1963), 139–40, 14.

9. William Brink and Louis Harris, *The Negro Revolution in America* (New York, 1964), 142, 148–49.

10. Walter F. Murphy and Joseph Tanenhaus, "Public Opinion and the Supreme Court: The Goldwater Campaign," *Public Opinion Quarterly*, XXXII (Spring, 1968), 37.

11. William Brink and Louis Harris, *Black and White* (New York, 1967), 15.

12. Gallup, *Gallup Poll*, II, 1420, 1465; Brink and Harris, *Black and White*, 220; Murphy and Tanenhaus, "Public Opinion," 38; Hazel Erskine, "The Polls: Speed of Racial Integration," *Public Opinion Quarterly*, XXXII (Fall, 1968), 513–24.

13. Donald R. Matthews and James W. Prothro, *Negroes and the New Southern Politics* (New York, 1966), 436; Hazel Erskine, "The Polls: Demonstrations and Race Riots," *Public Opinion Quarterly*, XXXI (Winter, 1967–68), 655–64; Benjamin Muse, *The American Negro Revolution: From Nonviolence to Black Power 1963–1967* (Bloomington, Ind., 1968), 140.

14. Erskine, "Demonstrations and Race Riots," 672–73.

15. Brink and Harris, *Negro Revolution*, 144–45.

16. *New York Times*, October 13, 1947.

17. Brink and Harris, *Negro Revolution*, 148; Brink and Harris, *Black and White*, 127; Angus Campbell, *White Attitudes toward Black People* (Ann Arbor, Mich., 1971), 133; Erskine, "Negro Housing," 482–98.

18. Brink and Harris, *Negro Revolution*, 140. See also William Kornblum, *Blue Collar Community* (Chicago, 1974).

19. Brink and Harris, *Black and White*, 47.

20. Brink and Harris, *Negro Revolution*, 126, 130. According to a poll taken in 1971, 70 percent of America's blacks thought whites were sorry that slavery had been abolished. *The Harris Survey Yearbook of Public Opinion 1971* (New York, 1975), 328.

21. Hazel Erskine, "The Polls: Recent Opinion on Racial Problems," *Public Opinion Quarterly*, XXXII (Winter, 1968–69), 696–703; Erskine, "Demonstrations and Race Riots," 667, 674–75. See also Campbell, *White Attitudes*, 41–42.

22. Brink and Harris, *Black and White*, 109, 136. See also Melvin M. Tumin, *Desegregation: Resistance and Readiness* (Princeton, N.J., 1958), 195; Matthews and Prothro, *Negroes*, 343.

23. Hazel Erskine, "The Polls: Negro Employment," *Public Opinion Quarterly*, XXXII (Spring, 1968), 132–53.

24. Brink and Harris, *Black and White*, 134–36; Peter Binzen, *Whitetown, U. S. A.* (New York, 1970).

25. Matthews and Prothro, *Negroes*, 358.

26. Hazel Erskine, "The Polls: Causes of Crime," *Public Opinion Quarterly*, XXXVIII (Summer, 1974), 292. See also Hazel Erskine, "The Polls: Corruption in Government," *Public Opinion Quarterly*, XXXVII (Winter, 1973–74), 631.

27. Richard C. Cortner, *The Apportionment Cases* (Knoxville, Tenn., 1970), 148. See also Robert G. Dixon, Jr., *Democratic Representation: Reapportionment in Law and Politics* (New York, 1968), 408.

28. Cortner, *Apportionment*, 250.

29. Kevin P. Phillips, *The Emerging Republican Majority* (New Rochelle, N.Y., 1969), 39.

30. Campbell, *White Attitudes*, Ch. VII; Andrew M. Greeley and Paul B. Sheatsley, "Attitudes toward Racial Integration," *Scientific American*, CCXXV (December, 1971), 13–19; Gwen Bellisfield, "White Attitudes to-

ward Racial Integration and the Urban Riots of the 1960s," *Public Opinion Quarterly*, XXXVI (Winter, 1972–73), 579–84; Hazel Erskine, "The Polls: Interracial Socializing," *Public Opinion Quarterly*, XXXVII (Summer, 1973), 291; *Harris Yearbook 1971*, 350, 356, 360.

31. *Harris Yearbook 1971*, 55.

32. *Ibid.*, 327; *The Harris Survey Yearbook of Public Opinion 1970* (New York, 1971), 221; Campbell, *White Attitudes*, 130, 133.

33. *Harris Yearbook 1971*, 321; *The Harris Survey Yearbook of Public Opinion 1972* (New York, 1976), 283; Campbell, *White Attitudes*, 139; Erskine, "Negro Housing," 493; *Harris Yearbook 1970*, 223.

34. *Harris Yearbook 1970*, 223, 226–29; Campbell, *White Attitudes*, 133, 139; *Harris Yearbook 1972*, 283.

35. Polls on affirmative action are cited in *The Gallup Poll Index*, Report No. 151 (February, 1978), 8.

36. *Ibid.*, Report No. 127 (February, 1976), 10; Numan V. Bartley and Hugh D. Graham, *Southern Politics and the Second Reconstruction* (Baltimore, 1975), 189.

37. *New York Times*, April 2, 1978. Henry M. Levin helped me understand the implications of the statistics on family income.

38. Charles P. Roland, *The Improbable Era: The South since World War II* (Lexington, Ky., 1975), 176.

Notes to THE JURISPRUDENCE OF *BROWN* AND THE DILEMMAS OF LIBERALISM
*by Morton J. Horwitz*

1. 198 U. S. 45 (1905).

2. See e.g. the dissent of Justice Frankfurter in West Virginia v. Barnette, 319 U.S. 624 (1943) and his concurrence in Kovacs v. Cooper, 336 U.S. 77 (1949).

3. Rauol Berger, *Congress v. the Supreme Court* (1969).

4. Thomas Grey, "Do We Have An Unwritten Constitution?," *Stanford Law Review*, XXVII (1975), 703, Thomas Grey, "Origins of the Unwritten Constitution: Fundamental Law in American Revolutionary Thought," *Stanford Law Review*, XXX (1978), 843.

5. Edward Purcell, *The Crisis of Democratic Theory* (Lexington, 1974).

6. Regents of the University of California v. Bakke, 46 *U.S. L.W.* at 4903 (1978).

7. Owen Fiss, "Groups and the Equal Protection Clauses," *Philosophy and Public Affairs*, V (1976), 197.

8. 46 *U.S.L.W.* at 4903.

9. 16 *Wall.* 36, 71 (1873).

10. William Miller, "Proof of Racially Discriminatory Purpose Under the Equal Protection Clause," *Harvard Civil Rights, Civil Liberties Law Review*, XII (1977), 225.

# List of Contributors

*C. Eric Lincoln* is a professor of religion at Duke University. He has written numerous articles, book reviews, and edited several works on civil rights and black history. His major books include *The Black Church Since Frazier, The Blackamericans, My Face is Black*, and *The Black Muslims in America*.

*Vincent Harding* is director of the Institute of the Black World and recently a member of the oral history program at Duke University. Professor Harding has written on the civil rights movement in professional journals and is now working on a two-volume history of the black movement in the United States.

*Henry Levin* is a professor of education at Stanford University. In addition to serving on many governmental committees and agencies dealing with discrimination problems, he is also the author of *Workplace Democracy and Educational Planning, The Limits of Educational Reform*, and *Schools and Inequality*.

*William Leuchtenburg* is DeWitt Clinton Professor of History at Columbia University. An historian of twentieth-century America, he has written *The Perils of Prosperity, Franklin D. Roosevelt and the New Deal, The Great Age of Change, A Troubled Feast*, and *War and Social Change in Twentieth-Century America*.

231

*Robert Wiebe* is a professor of history at Northwestern University. In addition to articles and book reviews, he has written *The Search For Order, Businessmen and Reform,* and *The Segmented Society,* and coauthored *The Great Republic.*

*Morton Horwitz* is a professor of law at Harvard Law School. In addition to articles published in a variety of professional journals, he has written *The Transformation of American Law* which has been awarded the Thomas J. Wilson Prize by the Harvard University Press and the Bancroft Prize in American History.

*Lerone Bennett* is the senior editor of *Ebony* and a black history scholar. He has written a variety of articles and books ranging from *A History of the Negro in America* to *The Shaping of the Black American.*

# DATE DUE

| | | | |
|---|---|---|---|
| 12/18/87 | | | |
| FEB 0 3 1998 | | | |
| MAR 1 6 1998 | | | |
| MAR 3 1 1998 | | | |
| | | | |
| | | | |
| | | | |
| | | | |
| | | | |
| | | | |
| | | | |
| | | | |
| | | | |
| | | | |
| | | | |
| | | | |
| | | | |